CHICKEN SOUP FOR THE ENTREPRENEUR'S SOUL

CHICKEN SOUP FOR THE ENTREPRENEUR'S SOUL

Advice and Inspiration for Fulfilling Dreams

Jack Canfield
Mark Victor Hansen
Dahlynn McKowen
John P. Gardner Jr.
Elizabeth Gardner
Tom Hill
Kyle Wilson

Health Communications, Inc.
Deerfield Beach, Florida

www.hcibooks.com
www.chickensoup.com

We would like to acknowledge the following publishers and individuals for permission to reprint the following material. (Note: The stories that were written by Jack Canfield, Mark Victor Hansen, Dahlynn McKowen, John Gardner, Elizabeth Gardner, Tom Hill or Kyle Wilson are not included in this listing.)

Against All Odds. Reprinted by permission of David Anderson. ©2006 David Anderson.

Hats Off to Serendipity. Reprinted by permission of Sue Ellen Cooper. ©2005 Sue Ellen Cooper.

Chicken Stock. Reprinted by permission of Peter Vegso. ©2005 Peter Vegso.

To Be There for My Kids. Reprinted by permission of Cookie Lee. ©2005 Cookie Lee.

Project X. Reprinted by permission of Terri Duncan. ©2005 Terri Duncan.

(Continued on page 328)

Library of Congress Cataloging-in-Publication Data

Chicken soup for the entrepreneur's soul: advice and inspiration on fulfilling dreams / Jack Canfield . . . [et al.].
p. cm.
ISBN 0-7573-0261-0
1. Entrepreneurship—Anecdotes. 2. Businesspeople—Anecdotes. I. Canfield, Jack, 1944–

HB615.C536 2006
658.4'21—dc22 2006043513

ISBN 0-7573-0261-0

Publisher: Health Communications, Inc.
3201 S.W. 15th Street
Deerfield Beach, FL 33442-8190

R-08-06

Cover design by Larissa Hise Henoch
Inside book formatting by Dawn Von Strolley Grove

This book is dedicated to those who have taken risks to achieve their own dreams, and in finding success, have inspired others to do the same.

Contents

3. ESCAPING THE BOX

4. SUCCESSFUL PARTNERSHIPS

5. IT'S ALL RELATIVE

6. NEVER GIVE UP

The road goes ever on and on
Down from the door where it began.
Now far ahead the road has gone,
And I must follow, if I can,
Pursuing it with eager feet,
Until it joins some larger way
Where many paths and errands meet.
And whither then? I cannot say.

J. R. R. Tolkien

Acknowledgments

We wish to express our heartfelt gratitude to the following people who helped make this book possible:

Our families, who have been chicken soup for our souls!

Jack's family: Inga, Travis, Riley, Christopher, Oran and Kyle for all their love and support.

Mark's family: Patty, Elisabeth and Melanie Hansen, for once again sharing and lovingly supporting us in creating yet another book.

Dahlynn's family: Ken and kiddos Lahre, Shawn and Jason, for their help and patience. Another book is completed, and it is now time to celebrate!

Tom's family: Betty and children Terri Olsen, Marie Kernell, Terri Chier, Michelle Kelsay, Nina Zinn, Scott Hill and their families for their love and support. Terri Olsen for her dedication to this project in making it a success; Heather Bonham and Jim Nelson for their untiring work and writing.

John and Elizabeth's family: Burt, Wade, Bryant and Peden for being our inspiration. Betty and Dick Dickerson for their love and support. Dick and Katie Baker, Mary Haviland, Brandy Seiffert and Angel Tilton for their talent, support and effort in making this project possible.

Kyle's family: Heidi, Rebekah and Daniel for their consistent love and support. Also the entire JRI and YSS team for their incredible work and dedication.

Our publisher Peter Vegso, for his vision and commitment to bringing *Chicken Soup for the Soul* to the world.

Patty Aubery and Russ Kalmaski, for being there on every step of the journey, with love, laughter and endless creativity.

D'ette Corona for her amazing insight, valuable advice and true friendship.

Barbara LoMonaco, for nourishing us with truly wonderful stories and cartoons, and Dena Jacobson for being there to answer any questions along the way.

Patty Hansen, for her thorough and competent handling of the legal and licensing aspects of the *Chicken Soup for the Soul* books. You are magnificent at the challenge!

Veronica Romero, Teresa Esparza, Robin Yerian, Jesse Ianniello, Lauren Edelstein, Patti Clement, Laurie Hartman, Maegan Romanello, Cassidy Guyer, Noelle Champagne, Jody Emme, Debbie Lefever, Michelle Adams, Dee Dee Romanello, Shanna Vieyra and Gina Romanello who support Jack's and Mark's businesses with skill and love.

Ken McKowen for his superb editing of the final manuscript. Thank you!

Michele Matrisciani, Theresa Peluso, Andrea Gold, Allison Janse and Katheline St. Fort, our editors at Health Communications, Inc., for their devotion to excellence.

The sales, marketing and PR departments at Health Communications, Inc.—Terry Burke, Lori Golden, Kelly Maragni, Tom Galvin, Sean Geary, Patricia McConnell, Ariana Daner, Kim Weiss and Paola Fernandez-Rana—for doing such an incredible job supporting our books.

Tom Sand, Claude Choquette and Luc Jutras, who manage year after year to get our books translated into thirty-six languages around the world.

The art department at Health Communications, Inc., for their talent, creativity and unrelenting patience in producing book covers and inside designs that capture the essence of *Chicken Soup:* Larissa Hise Henoch, Lawna Patterson Oldfield, Andrea Perrine Brower, Kevin Stawieray, Anthony Clausi and Dawn Von Strolley Grove.

Doreen Hess and the customer-support center and shipping department at Health Communications, Inc. Without all of you, the place would come to a grinding halt!

All the *Chicken Soup for the Soul* coauthors, who make it such a joy to be part of this *Chicken Soup* family.

To those people who opened doors to some of the nation's top entrepreneurs: Aileen Van Noland, Debbie Lefever, Abbie Mouillesseaux, Kellie Randle, Kess Connelly, Pat Burns, Susan MacTavish Best and Ginger Hopkins. And to those freelance writers who helped pen stories: Terri Duncan, Julie Long, Gail Kulhavy, Gina Romanello, Ken McKowen and Banjo Bandolas.

Our panel of readers who helped with the grading of the first manuscript:

Theresa AuCoin, Alvin Brown, Bob Battye, Nick Beattie, Simon Bailey, Alan Sandlin, Barbie Gummin, Brent Dearing, Ginny Gilbert, Glenda Williamson, Jim Canfield, Jim Nissen, Leslie Skarra, Maria Fee, Rocky and Michelle Rowe, Mary Kay Sheets and Tammy Fadler, Debbie George, Danny Talbot, Jay Wood, David Eads, Barbara Stevenson, Vickie Rose, Jeffrey Omnidvt, Rock Jolly, Carol Worley, Jennifer Whitewing, Rodney and Thao Sommerville, Lorna Rasmussan, Jason Norris, Sandy Davis, Ben and Kathy McCrae, Karla Odom, Nancy Chaconas, David Green, Debbie Croxton and Marshall Odom.

And, most of all, everyone who submitted their heartfelt stories, poems, quotes and cartoons for possible inclusion in this book. While we were not able to use everything you sent, we know that each word came from a magical place within your soul.

Because of the size of this project, we may have left out

the names of some people who contributed along the way. If so, we are sorry, but please know that we really do appreciate you very much.

We are truly grateful and love you all!

Foreword

During the last decade, millions of women have begun to exercise, manage their weight and avoid disease because of Curves®. We are very proud of the contribution we've been able to make to the health of women, but we also know that we could not have done it alone. Our success is a reflection of the vital partnerships we have with ten thousand Curves' franchisees, people who are just as committed to helping women in their communities. Through these partnerships, women in over forty countries live longer, healthier lives.

We are proud for another reason. The blessing of Curves has provided an entrepreneurial opportunity for thousands of women who are now working for themselves, providing for their families and making a difference in their communities.

From the earliest days, we have always known and said that Curves is just an opportunity. Having a successful club requires talented, dedicated owners and managers who are willing to follow the Curves system, to do everything possible to build their businesses, and to help members achieve their goals. It can be hard work! We'll be the first to admit that the Curves opportunity is not a something-for-nothing, get-rich-quick deal. It's just an opportunity.

This is why our franchisees are such deserving partners in the entrepreneurial success that Curves represents. Thousands of women (and even men), have taken on this opportunity, have done the hard work, and have been greatly rewarded. We're proud of them and of their successes.

We live in a society where people are averse to risk and accustomed to security. An entrepreneur, however, willingly exchanges security for the chance of success. Risk is an unavoidable part of the equation. Entrepreneurism is not for the faint of heart. It requires optimism, faith, leadership, perseverance and a willingness to accept responsibility for one's own success.

As you read the stories in this book, think about the challenges that were met by the entrepreneurs featured. Think about the character that's required and the beauty of the human achievement. We hope that you would be proud to call yourself, Entrepreneur!

God Bless,

Gary and Diane

Share with Us

We would like to invite you to send us stories you would like to see published in future editions of *Chicken Soup for the Soul.*

We would also love to hear your reactions to the stories in this book. Please let us know what your favorite stories are and how they affected you.

Please submit your stories on our Web site:

www.chickensoup.com

Chicken Soup for the Soul
P.O. Box 30880
Santa Barbara, CA 93130
fax: 805-563-2945

We hope you enjoy reading this book as much as we enjoyed compiling, editing and writing it.

1

IN THEIR OWN WORDS

Don't quack like a duck, soar like an eagle.

Ken Blanchard

Against All Odds

Without a doubt, my life today is one of gratitude, and one of second chances.

Both of my parents are American Indians; my dad is a Choctaw Indian from Idabel, Oklahoma, and my mom is from the Lac Courte Oreilles Ojibwa reservation in Wisconsin. When they were young, both were victims of the Bureau of Indian Affairs' practice of taking American Indian children from their parents and sticking them in boarding schools for the purpose of mainstreaming them into the dominant society. While at the boarding school, my dad remembers being whipped by the teachers for speaking his Choctaw language.

Fortunately for me, my parents met at Haskell Institute for Indians in Lawrence, Kansas. My parents moved to Chicago and were married—being a good ol' Southern boy, naturally my dad would drive my mom down South every weekend until she learned how to cook Southern-style! And what a cook she turned out to be!

Growing up on the west side of Chicago, things were difficult for our young family. My parents were hard-working, blue-collar workers, but in order to make ends meet, we depended on government food subsidies. When I had friends over, my mom would make us snacks; when she went to the pantry, I was embarrassed by the silver and gold cans and white bags of food labeled "USDA" in big, bold letters. When I went to my friends' houses, their pantries had cans and jars with real company labels such as Campbell's Soup and Jiffy Peanut Butter. Many of my friends' parents owned small businesses. At a young age, I decided that one day I, too, would become a small-business owner, so I wouldn't have to rely on the government for help.

During the summer, the city would get really hot, with temperatures well over one hundred degrees for weeks at a time. Our little apartment became unbearable, so my mom took us kids to her reservation; we stayed in my grandmother's little four-room house, which had no running water or electricity. At night, I remember gazing into the heavens, thinking about the billions and billions of stars that sparkled in the northern sky. I wondered if my life would shine brilliantly like one of the bright stars above, or if my life would be like one of the billions of stars that just faded off into the vastness of space.

Determined to shine brilliantly, I followed my childhood dream of becoming a businessman. Starting at the age of eighteen, I owned several businesses, including a construction company, several resorts, a cabin furniture store, an Indian jewelry business and even a consulting business. While these first forays into the business world were successful at times, they were also challenging, and oftentimes failed. But I never gave up on my dreams, even when I thought the whole world was caving in on me.

There were times in my adult life when we were so broke that I dug through seat cushions looking for loose change to buy milk for our kids. There were agonizing times when I had to ask my wife for her jewelry, so I could take it to a pawnshop just to pay the rent. Banks shut down our checking accounts because we were badly overdrawn, followed by the raw embarrassment of having our neighbors watch as the repo man hauled off the family car.

Determined not to run away from my problems, but to accept these problems as opportunities for a new life, I decided to create the business of my dreams, one that would support my family, one that I would be proud to own. I went to numerous banks trying to raise money for my new enterprise, but not one would take a chance on me because I was a minority, I had no connections, I had no track record, I had no collateral and I had no one to co-sign a loan. Finally, a bank president in Chicago believed in me and gave me a ten-thousand-dollar loan on my signature alone. This loan eventually allowed me to follow my dream of one day creating a one-of-a-kind, award-winning barbeque restaurant.

My passion for barbeque began in Chicago as a kid. Every Friday, my parents would get out the cookie jar, and we would sit at the kitchen table and count the pennies, nickels, dimes and quarters they had collected during the week. Back then, I can remember how excited we were if we found a big silver dollar mixed in the coins! If we had enough money, we would go to my favorite restaurant—Eddie's Ribs next to the Logan Square train station on the north side of Chicago.

Walking through the door, I was always intrigued by the glass-enclosed smoker that was full of ribs smoldering over hickory wood. The pit master would test each slab of ribs with a big fork for tenderness, and once done, he then placed the slab on a big butcher block where he slathered the ribs with tasty barbeque sauce. I never believed anything could taste so heavenly.

In 1994, on the edge of the Lac Courte Oreilles reservation in the north woods of Hayward, Wisconsin, I opened the first Famous Dave's Barbeque Shack. Everyone thought I was nuts to build a barbeque restaurant in a northern town of only 1,800 people. They said I should go to Memphis where they really understood barbeque. But I never let them get me down. I stayed true to my dreams.

By the end of that first summer, Famous Dave's was serving nearly 6,000 people a week in a town of 1,800! People were driving hundreds of miles just to come and get some of my famous barbequed ribs. The amazing thing is that we never advertised—it was all word of mouth!

Today, we have thriving Famous Dave's Barbeque restaurants all over the United States, stretching coast-to-coast with many more in the works. In the quest to be the best, I have eaten in over ten thousand barbeque joints all over America. I have visited the big pits in Texas, the roadside smoke shacks in the Carolinas and the black-owned storefront BBQ joints in Chicago, Kansas City and Memphis, and I have personally cooked over a million pounds of ribs and made over a million gallons of sauce in the pursuit of perfecting the best ribs and the best sauce. With pride, I can report that both our ribs and sauce have been awarded "Best in America" at national cook-off competitions. But I'm more proud to say that my restaurants have provided jobs and opportunities to so many people all over the nation; that's worth more to me than any award.

Adversity has helped me become a stronger, wiser person, and getting sober after two decades of drinking has made my life even better. Today, I live my life in gratitude knowing that several times I should have been dead, but God had his protective hand over me. I believe that my success today isn't about Dave Anderson, but my higher purpose is about being able to make a positive difference in the lives of others who need a second chance, or sometimes even a first chance. I am here to serve.

David Anderson

EPILOGUE: *David W. Anderson is considered the nation's foremost Native American entrepreneur. Besides his restaurants, Anderson helped found three publicly traded companies, thus creating over twenty thousand new jobs. He was also selected by President George W. Bush to be the Assistant Secretary for the U.S. Department of Interior for Indian Affairs with a $2 billion budget, overseeing ten thousand employees. This position required a full Senate confirmation.*

Anderson has since stepped down from his government position to concentrate on philanthropic efforts and has given over $8 million back to his community. He also serves on many boards, including the National Board of Governors for the Boys and Girls Clubs of America.

Making a lifelong commitment to help at-risk Native American youth, Anderson created the LifeSkills Center for Leadership. Located in Minnesota, the center helps young people to believe in themselves and to dream big. The nonprofit has had such a profound impact helping Native American youth that Oprah Winfrey awarded Anderson her Angel Network Award in 2002.

To learn more about David Anderson, his restaurants and the LifeSkills Center, please visit the following Web sites: www.famousdaves.com *and* www.lifeskills-center.org.

Dahlynn McKowen

Hats Off to Serendipity!

I never knew her first name. She always wore the same outfit—a lavender blue dress covered in white polka dots and a red straw hat with a cluster of cherries pinned to the ribbon that encircled its crown. Her hair was pulled back in a bun, and her blue eyes sparkled with life. I can't remember the sound of her voice either, though we spoke to each other often.

It never crossed my mind to ask where she went when she was not with me; she must have had a home, and probably other friends. Like all small children, I thought I was the center of the universe and certainly thought I was the center of hers. She was very good about showing up when I needed companionship and always went along with my ideas.

Her name was Mrs. Silkins. Although she was an adult and I was a child, we were exactly the same size. She, of course, had the generously rounded curves of a middle-aged woman, while I had the skinny arms and legs of a gawky, rather sickly child. But none of these things mattered. We were the best of friends.

When I was around six years old, I discovered Mrs. Silkins had never existed. Sitting at the kitchen table and watching my mother chop vegetables, I casually said that it had been a while since I had seen Mrs. Silkins. Her head came up in surprise, her eyebrows raised. She said, "Don't you know that she was all in your head?" I sat, with my mouth agape, as my mother explained the concept of imaginary playmates. I suppose I must have known all along my beloved friend wasn't real, but I had fiercely believed in her. I was deeply saddened to hear the truth; since Mrs. Silkins had never existed, I knew that I would never see her again.

But I wasn't done with fantasy and make-believe and all the wonderful things associated with my vivid imagination. As a young adult, I discovered C. S. Lewis's fantastic allegories, beginning with *Out of the Silent Planet* and ending with *That Hideous Strength.* An idealized version of "what might be" was always more compelling to me than what actually was. And when I was truly grown up, I enjoyed the wonderful *Chronicles of Narnia* right along with my children.

I always sought out the whimsical, the beautiful and the fantastic throughout my life. After finishing college, I enrolled in art classes where I was drawn to illustration, particularly the type found in old children's books. In this genre, subjects were idealized and made more beautiful than in reality, the world was always sunny and safe, and dreams always came true. In the years following, as a greeting card illustrator and muralist, I enjoyed making "pretty pictures" and creating an idealized world—on walls, as well as on paper.

In the fall of 1997, I followed my instincts for the fanciful. I found a wonderfully bright red fedora in an Arizona thrift store. Though I don't remember thinking of Mrs. Silkins that day, it seems likely that, subconsciously at least, my warm memories of her red hat influenced me. I just had to have this hat—but secretly worrying what people would think if I wore it—and I recalled a poem entitled "Warning" by Jenny Joseph. The poem talked about the feelings of a mature woman, a woman who didn't care what she wore, what she did and what people would think of her for doing such outlandish things.

Determined to be that woman, I purchased the hat and proudly wore it out of the store. Sure, it didn't match what I was wearing, but I reveled in playing dress-up once again, but this time at age fifty-something!

Well, to make a long story short, I loved dressing up and playing make-believe again so much that I started giving fanciful and elaborate red hats and a copy of the poem to my fifty-something friends. Then one day, we decided to go to tea, wearing our red hats and donning royal purple clothes. We had an amazing time, and giggling like schoolgirls, we bestowed regal names to each of us, with me becoming the "Exalted Queen Mother."

Less than eight years later, I am the official Exalted Queen Mother of the Red Hat Society, a self-proclaimed "disorganization" with over forty thousand chapters in the United States and thirty-one countries worldwide. Its members—1 million strong—consciously choose to venture out in public wearing brightly colored, rather silly, purple outfits and red hats (or in the case of women under the age of fifty, lavender outfits and pink hats), rediscovering the joys of play and life. Certainly we acknowledge that we're growing older, and that isn't always fun, but we have chosen to emphasize the positive changes that aging brings.

I find it hard to see myself as an entrepreneur, but I guess the moniker is fitting; I saw the opportunity to pass along my love for the positive things in life, to follow my instincts and to remain true to my values. And I believe that the seed of the Red Hat Society was planted a long time ago; this notion was recently confirmed by Mr. John

Harney of Harney & Sons Tea, one of the licensees whose support sustains the Red Hat Society. In a recent talk about tea, he happened to mention that his company has begun using a new, improved fabric for fashioning tea bags—a mixture of silk and linen.

Would you believe that it is called "Silk-en"?

Sue Ellen Cooper
Exalted Queen Mother

EPILOGUE: *As the Red Hat Society continues to grow, its staff serves the membership from a home office, dubbed the "Hat-quarters," in Fullerton, California. The enterprise is supported by yearly chapter membership fees and by the sale of licensed, logo-bearing products, such as clothing, jewelry and housewares. It hosts international and regional conventions and cruises for its members and actively seeks venues and ideas to support its mission of fun and sisterhood for all women. Its Web site offers connections and information and is updated regularly with new ideas for having fun and making new friends.*

Sue Ellen Cooper has written two books about the Red Hat Society: The Red Hat Society: Fun and Friendship After Fifty *and* The Red Hat Society's Laugh Lines: Tales of Inspiration and Hattitude, *both published by Warner Books.* Designer Scrapbooks: The Red Hat Society Way *was recently published by Sterling, with a book about hats to follow. Red Hat Society romance novels (from Warner) will soon debut, and* Red Hat Society LifeStyle, *a bimonthly magazine, is available by subscription.*

For more information, please visit www.redhatsociety.com.

Dahlynn McKowen

off the mark.com
by Mark Parisi
IT'S A CEASE AND DESIST LETTER FROM BOOTH THREE...
RED HAT SOCIETY
offthemark.com

Chicken Stock

They always say that time changes things, but you actually have to change them yourself.

Andy Warhol

As an adult, I have many fond childhood memories of summers spent with my grandparents in rural Canada. One in particular was of a neighbor's farm. It made quite an impression on me as a kid. The owner was what folks called a "gentleman farmer" whose acreage was surrounded by crisp, white fencing. His home stood on a hill overlooking majestic horses, and well-fed cattle grazed contentedly in lush pastures. Although I had no idea what a gentleman farmer actually farmed, I decided that I wanted to be one someday.

I worked my way through college in a variety of jobs. Then, in 1970, I packed my bags and my newly acquired master's degree and headed out into the business world. Visions of white-fenced pastures occasionally popped into my head, but I was no longer an impressionable young boy. Hard work, and who knows how much divine luck, stood between the stately home of a successful businessman and me. At that moment, I was a guy sitting at the kitchen table scanning the want ads.

My search for gainful employment ended when I accepted a position with the Addiction Research Foundation, a huge provincial government agency in Toronto, Canada. Alcoholics who were homeless or had hit rock-bottom participated in clinical studies conducted by psychiatrists and scientists. The foundation chugged out tons of paperwork filled with statistics and correlations about the impact of addiction. Until then, I had never given much thought to those who were less fortunate than I am, and in that respect my new position was enlightening.

For their cooperation, the research subjects were given a place to live and access to counseling and rehabilitation. They were "employed" at a farm operation run by the foundation. One of my first assignments in my new position was to develop a more meaningful work program that would challenge and interest the men, as well as create a variety of tasks requiring different skills. The program also needed to keep the men busy and generate some revenue.

I decided on an antique refinishing business. At the time, it was popular with Torontonians to scour garage sales outside the city for discarded treasures. I was fond of antiques; I admired the craftsmanship and beauty and had an appreciation for the history of different periods. The patina of the wood belied not only character, but hinted at the mystery of memories absorbed over many years. What better way to combine my interests and my new challenges at work? I thought. We converted one of the old barns on the farm into a workshop, bought a few tools and started accumulating discards—furniture and people.

It didn't take long before the men were genuinely interested in their work. Each day they arrived at the barn and tackled their assigned tasks. Our next expansion was to begin building pine reproductions. We sectioned off part of the workshop and opened a retail shop. Sales were steady, and the program was a success! I had been taught in school to measure business success by profit-and-loss and marketing effectiveness, but how these men responded to their work surprised me and became an equally important lesson. Each restored piece of furniture became a metaphor for a life thrown away, a life that was now salvaged and returned to a desirable, useful, valuable state. The program was putting life back into their eyes, and they found a renewed sense of self-respect, thus reclaiming a productive place in society. They held jobs, learned and refined new skills, and found their misplaced honor once again.

I learned a lot from those men, knowing what they had been through and how they were turning their lives around. And they didn't do that alone; a staff of dedicated social workers cared deeply about these men, too. When I accepted that position with the Addiction Research Foundation, I certainly expected to apply what I had learned at the university and to acquire new knowledge and experience, but I never expected to include compassion, understanding and patience. And I certainly could not have imagined the impact this career opportunity would have on my future.

I spent another five years at the Addiction Research Foundation. During that time I married my wife, Anne, and we had our first baby, a girl. Life was good, but we were about to learn how fragile the good life could be. Our baby had a rare genetic disorder called Werdnig Hoffman disease and had only six months to live. Losing her was devastating. Shortly after, we decided to make some changes in our lives.

I enjoyed my work, but I often chafed at the serious culture, the endless bureaucracy and the tricky politics. One of my co-workers, Gary Seidler, had become a good friend, and we decided to become partners, move to the United States and start a publishing company. We chose south Florida, an unlikely place for a publisher of a trade tabloid newspaper specializing in the alcohol and drug field. The majority of writers and information related to the field were located in Washington, D.C., and this was 1976, before computers and high technology made information sharing seamless. We founded Health Communications and worked out of a small storefront for many years. In the 1980s, we started publishing self-help books for the professionals' clients, and when our first *New York Times* bestseller hit the list in 1983, we started being noticed by the New York publishing establishment.

My professional life was going well, but there was something missing for Anne and me in our personal lives. We wanted a family, and against everybody's advice, we had another child, a boy. The first time I saw my son, I knew instantly he had the same disorder our daughter had had. We lost him also.

I knew a few things by now. I knew the value of life. I knew how important love was and how much loss hurt. I knew it was just as important, if not more so, to address the human side of business, and I knew that the company I owned had to have a purpose other than making a profit. I wanted to wake up every day and be excited about coming to work. I wanted to know that the success I achieved was based on helping people reach their potential and live better lives. I wanted to honor those men who had taught me so much about compassion and resilience. I wanted to build a business that made a difference in people's lives—our customers, our employees, my community.

When we celebrated the tenth anniversary as a company, our list boasted two *New York Times* and dozens of national bestsellers from the experts in the addictions and self-help field. Health Communications played a significant role in developing the publishing genre of "recovery," and we had a positive impact on the lives of hundreds of thousands of people with our books, magazines and conferences.

Like business cycles do, ours turned. In the early 1990s, the recovery genre peaked, and we explored other niches to develop. Self-esteem was an area of interest, and we were introduced to an energetic young man named Jack Canfield who had developed a reputation as an expert in that field. We liked Jack's enthusiasm and his content, and we signed him to a book contract. As fate would have it, that manuscript never got delivered because Jack was focused on an oddly titled anthology called *Chicken Soup for the Soul* that he was developing with Mark Victor Hansen, one of the country's most sought-after motivational speakers.

Jack and Mark took their energy and enthusiasm to New York and pitched their idea to several publishers hoping to get a contract with an advance on *Chicken Soup*. Even though dozens of publishers declined, Jack and Mark never faltered. They were diligent about their efforts and undeterred in their beliefs that what the world needed was a little chicken soup. Still they received rejection after rejection. Finally, during a publishing industry trade show, they made one last push to get a deal, using the Health Communications booth as a base of operations. At show's end, Jack and Mark still had no takers.

As we packed up the booth, Jack asked if we would take a look at the proposal, give them some feedback and perhaps even be interested in publishing it. It wasn't the type of book suited to our publishing program, but we promised to do so, and I put the manuscript in my briefcase. While waiting for my flight home, I made use of the downtime and pulled out their proposal. By the time I read the story "Puppies for Sale," the lump in my throat turned to tears in my eyes, and we became committed to the title, to the authors and to the series. As they say, the rest is history.

Today, Anne and I have two wonderful, healthy daughters. Melinda has finished college and is a newlywed. Hayley starts her sophomore year at college this fall. They are beautiful, smart, compassionate women—just like their mother. The business Gary and I started nearly thirty years ago continues to thrive and has lived up to my expectations of what I wanted my company to be and exceeded my definition of success. And yes, I still remember that gentleman farmer—I'm working on that.

Peter Vegso

EPILOGUE: *The first* Chicken Soup for the Soul *book was published in 1993. The series continues to make publishing history, having released its 101st title in 2005. Millions of people worldwide have enjoyed* Chicken Soup for the Soul, *and millions of dollars from the sales of the series have been donated to charities associated with each book. The success of the series has also enabled Jack Canfield, Mark Victor Hansen, Gary Seidler and Peter Vegso to privately fund worthwhile causes that are close to their hearts and to reach for their dreams. Peter owns a 140-acre thoroughbred horse breeding and training facility in Ocala, Florida—complete with pristine, white-fenced pastures.*

Dahlynn McKowen

To Be There for My Kids

Mother is the heartbeat in the home; and without her, there seems to be no heart throb.

Leroy Brownlow

My mother and father emigrated from China to America in 1948. My brother and I were born soon after, making us both the first American-born members of our family. Upon coming to America, our parents worked extremely hard to make a living, and, as such, sacrifices were made to ensure a better life for all of us.

Our father worked seven days a week, and our mother would work all day. I remember waving good-bye to my mother every morning as she drove off to work, then I walked to school alone with a house key dangling on a chain around my neck. After school, I would come home to an empty house. When my mother finally came home, she had to clean and prepare dinner and didn't have time to help me with my homework or play with me. Looking back, I realize that this helped mold my independence and resourcefulness, because I had to figure out how to do things on my own. But at the time, I was resentful. In the mid-1950s, everyone else's mother stayed home and went to the PTA meetings and school field trips, and I didn't want to be different. I also remember having only one birthday party as a child; my parents were always too busy working. I vowed that when I became a parent I would do things differently.

Since making a living was always a struggle for my parents, education was very important to them. My father believed that you could use education to make your life better. He would always say, "People can take away your house or your possessions, but they can never take away what you have learned." I had high expectations of myself as well, so I worked all through high school and was able to put myself through college. I did my undergraduate work at University of California, Berkeley, and University of California, Davis, in business management and design, and then later went to Northwestern to get my MBA in marketing and finance.

I was determined to be successful and make my own money so that I could make my own choices. I went on to work as a marketing manager for major corporations, such as Johnson and Johnson, Hunt-Wesson and Revlon Cosmetics, then as a director of marketing for Mattel Toys. These jobs were very demanding, and I often wouldn't get home until midnight. While I enjoyed the success and challenge, I really wanted a family, and I didn't see how I could have children when I was working so many hours.

In between my hectic schedule, I decided to take a jewelry beading class for fun. I really enjoyed it and made jewelry just for myself. When I wore it, people asked about the jewelry and where I got it. They were surprised and impressed that I had made the pieces of artwork.

This interest intrigued me, so one day, I took a shoebox full of jewelry to work and began selling to colleagues during the off-hours. A woman asked if I would bring the jewelry to her home so some of her friends could see it, which I did, with great success! Afterward, I wanted to give her something for inviting me into her home and allowing me to sell to her friends, so I gave her some jewelry as a thank you gift. At the time, I didn't know there was such a thing as direct sales or party-plan businesses. I also didn't realize that I had just given my first "home show."

Once I saw that I could actually make money selling my jewelry, I decided to invest $300 to buy materials and really make a go of the business. Everyone discouraged me from doing so, including my husband, John, (who is now my biggest supporter)! They thought I was crazy to give up my great corporate job, saying it was a waste of my education to "hawk jewelry." But I had a vision and knew that I could make it work.

I recouped the initial $300 investment right away and sold over $8,000 worth of jewelry that first year. By trial and error, I developed a system on how to book shows and sell the jewelry. While still working at Mattel, I sold jewelry on the side for seven years and made over $86,000 that seventh year! This was the turning point; I had promised myself that if I was able to make half of my Mattel salary selling my jewelry, and was able to pay my mortgage, I would quit my job. I left the corporate world in April 1990.

During that time, John and I were trying to start a family. Five years had gone by, and I thought we might never be able to have kids. The summer after I left my job at Mattel, I learned I was pregnant with our son. In 1992, our daughter was born.

While raising our children, I continued to sell my jewelry and give home shows during the days and evenings, and also on the weekends, but I soon realized that there were only so many hours in the day. I thought, *The only way I can continue to grow my business is to teach other women how to sell my jewelry, too.* So in 1992, I started taking on other consultants.

My business has since grown into a multimillion-dollar corporation, and this success is a direct result of my vision, the hard work of my amazing corporate staff, as well as the dedication of 70,000 Cookie Lee consultants throughout the United States. And, most important, I stayed true to my original purpose, which was to provide a different life for my children, one that I could be a part of every day. I structured my career around what worked for my family, and as a result, the flexibility and profitability of selling my jewelry have also enabled our company's consultants to have the same opportunities for their families. For this, I am very proud and thankful.

Please excuse me, I must go. It's time to pick my kids up from school.

Cookie Lee

EPILOGUE: *According to jewelry magnate Cookie Lee—president and founder of Cookie Lee, Inc.—she made a conscious choice not to sacrifice spending time with her two children "for all the success and money in the world." Cookie Lee picks up her teenaged children every day from school and attends all of their events. And her business is also a family affair, as husband, John Lin, serves as the company's vice president.*

Cookie Lee, Inc., founded in 1992, has become one of the nation's largest jewelry direct sales companies by offering affordable, high-quality fashion jewelry sold by in-home jewelry consultants. Based in Tustin, California, Cookie Lee has annual sales of over $120 million and growing.

To learn more about Cookie Lee and her company, visit www.CookieLee.com.

Dahlynn McKowen

Some of the ladies wondered if Lisa was trying to manage too many home businesses at once.

Project X

I have always been driven to buck the system, to innovate, to take things beyond where they've been.

Sam Walton

It's no secret. Most people do not enjoy the experience of shopping for a used car. Though cars are a necessity in our society, few like the hassles and the haggling associated with making such a purchase. But we had a revolutionary idea that would forever change the used-car buying experience, and it was cloaked in secrecy and shrouded in mystery.

In 1991, I was senior vice president of Circuit City. Circuit City was on a mission to expand its investments into markets that offered future financial rewards combined with the best practices of a strong retail concept. This new market needed to be relatively untapped, with few if any major competitors. Though several options were explored, ultimately a select group of individuals including Richard Sharp, Circuit City's president and CEO at that time, decided that there was great potential in the used-car market. Thus began a secret operation that we referred to as "Project X."

The goal of Project X was to develop an industry-changing used-car retail concept, not just another run-of-the-mill car dealership. There were many doubters, but those of us intimately involved in the project possessed an unwavering belief that we could incorporate the characteristics of a big-box store into the used-car industry. This revolutionary idea would also involve the development of a high-tech computer system, an innovation that had never been applied to the automobile sales industry. In December 1991, a one-and-a-half-page proposal was presented to the Circuit City board for consideration, and the board approved spending up to $50 million testing the idea.

Our project was kept under wraps for two years. In the weeks and months that followed the acceptance of our proposal, we quietly recruited others, people who would become key players in the development of this unique concept. Those coming aboard were not always told outright exactly what the project entailed. Even after agreeing to be involved in the secretive endeavor, some, including computer programmer Richard Smith, thought we were joking. Why would Circuit City want to tarnish its image by associating itself with an industry perceived by many as replete with loud and obnoxious polyester-clad salesmen haggling over the price of a dressed-up jalopy? Our intention, however, was to radically alter that very image by forever changing the concept of used-car sales.

Our team surveyed thousands of consumers in order to determine what they liked and disliked about car shopping. Many were far more verbal about what they disliked than what they liked. Based upon their responses, it was obvious that buyers wanted to purchase a reasonably priced automobile in an environment that was hassle-free and haggle-free. In addition, they wanted to have at their disposal a large selection of makes and models. Guaranteed quality was also vitally important, as was shopping in a dealership that was customer friendly, with everything from on-site financing to a supervised children's play area.

Armed with this information and the invaluable input and assistance of automobile industry experts such as Mark O'Neil and Tom Folliard, the first CarMax superstore opened its doors on September 21, 1993, in Richmond, Virginia. In addition to giving customers what they wanted, we also provided consumers with sales associates who possessed the highest levels of personal honesty and professional integrity. Applicants went through a rigorous, multilayered hiring process, and only one in ten met our requirements and high standards for employment. Not only was our sales concept unique, so, too, were our associates. They were pioneers in the industry as well.

Now, more than a decade later, CarMax has grown from that one location to sixty-two used-car superstores, as well as seven new-car franchises. In the company's fiscal year 2005, CarMax sold over 253,000 used cars, more than anyone else in the United States. Though we had our ups and downs in the beginning, in 2002, CarMax became an independent company publicly traded under the symbol KMX, with earnings of more than $112 million. In addition, we are recognized as a Fortune 500 company, and in 2005 and 2006, CarMax was included in *Fortune*'s list of the "100 Best Companies to Work For."

The secret is out. Eliminating the hassles that come with buying a car and giving customers a fair deal makes the car buying experience much less painful. Selling used cars is like any other retail business, and our innovative idea has fundamentally changed the automobile retail business. Project X, now known as CarMax, cracked the code on how to make car buyers happy.

Austin Ligon
As told to Terri Duncan

EPILOGUE: *CarMax, whose home office is located in Richmond, Virginia, is now the largest used-car retailer in the United States and employs more than 11,000 associates. Austin Ligon serves as the company's president and CEO.*

CarMax's innovative business practices are what sets them apart from the industry and makes car shopping a hassle-free experience for their customers. Used-car superstore amenities include supervised play areas for children, and in addition to a wide, on-site selection of high-quality makes and models, there are more than 20,000 vehicles available online at www.carmax.com. *Customers are presented with written cash offers for their trade-ins, good for seven days regardless of whether or not they purchase a car from CarMax. Sales associates are knowledgeable, and because most are paid the same no matter which vehicles they sell, they do not pressure customers. Along with low prices, financing and no-haggle pricing policy, all vehicles are sold with five-day money-back guarantees as well as limited thirty-day warranties.*

It is safe to say that secretive Project X successfully turned the auto sales industry upside down—and it's obvious that Austin Ligon and his team love being on top!

Terri Duncan

The Accidental Entrepreneur

If you do build a great experience, customers tell each other about that. Word of mouth is very powerful.

Jeff Bezos

I'd like to tell you that I always planned to run my own business. I'd like to say that I knew at an early age that I would go to business school, make some great contacts and head out into the world with my business plan in pristine condition.

I'd like to tell you that, but it would not be true.

I'm what you would call an "accidental entrepreneur." Not only did I not plan to be an entrepreneur, I don't think I knew what the word meant when I was a young man. And I'm pretty sure that I didn't know how to spell it.

My college degree is in psychology. During my school years I drove a cab and tended bar (a requirement of my Irish-American heritage). A friend of mine was working at a home for troubled boys, and he would stop by the bar occasionally on his way home. The more he told me about the group home, the more interested I became. In short order, I began a fourteen-year career in social work at

St. John's Home for Boys in Queens, New York.

I never completed graduate school, but those fourteen years were equal to my earning an MBA, and a lot more. I learned so much about people—and even more about myself—than I would have ever imagined possible.

In my early days as a social worker, I was not good at all. I quickly became so frustrated that I approached Brother Tom, who ran the home, and told him I was leaving. He refused to let me quit and worked with me to develop a plan for my job.

I had to learn how to be more proactive, how to come to the boys with an agenda and goals. Just as important, I had to stop treating them like a group. You can't build a relationship with a group; you build relationships with people, with individuals.

Slowly I began to grow as a professional. But there was one kid I couldn't reach, Norman, one of the tougher kids in the home. No matter how hard I tried, there was little I could do to build a relationship with him.

One day I was planting some tomato plants on one side of the group home, a hint of the florist to come. Norman came walking by and began to make fun of me, the tomatoes and anything else he could think of. The same thing happened for several days in a row. I worked, and Norman stopped by to give me a hard time.

Slowly the conversations began to change. We moved, gradually, from talking about how dumb I was for trying to make these tomatoes grow, to what we could do to make them grow.

Every day, Norman stopped by to help me with those tomato plants. We began to talk about sports, girls, school and whatever was going on in Norman's life. The topics weren't important, but the conversations sure were.

I had learned how to truly make contact, how to build a relationship. This lesson, this philosophy, is one that I carry with me to this day at 1-800-FLOWERS. Establish a relationship first, then do business.

The relationship is the transaction. You can use technology (and we certainly do) to extend your reach and increase the number of your contacts, but you still have to build the relationship. Without the relationship, you have nothing.

Here are a few other "semi-commandments," as I called them in my book, *Stop and Sell the Roses* (Ballantine Books, 1998):

Waste your youth in higher pursuits. You don't have to live, breathe and eat business from age five to be successful. My fourteen years at the St. John's Home for Boys taught me a thousand lessons, including how to motivate others, set goals and manage crises. I wouldn't trade my time as a social worker for anything, and it certainly played (and continues to play) a key role in the success of 1-800-FLOWERS.

Don't go crazy about not getting an MBA. Although I wish I had attended the finest business schools in our country, I am living proof that other experiences can make you equally successful. Don't get me wrong—I certainly wish I had gone to the Harvard Business School or any of the top schools. But, given the choice, I'd rather live a case study than read one.

Don't try to know everything beforehand. If I had known everything about the flower business before I bought the first store, I never would have signed up. Sometimes you need to start down a road before you can see where it leads you. If you have a sense of entrepreneurship, take that first step.

Brand yourself. In an ever-changing world, the only constant you can control is YOU! Treat yourself like a brand, and remember consistency and credibility are your two greatest assets.

SOBs finish last. Given a choice, people will always

choose to do business with individuals and companies who value them.

Cheap is cheap. It is said that the smart entrepreneur goes where the labor is cheapest. Wrong. Go where the labor is smartest. Remember, you get what you pay for.

Trust those family ties. We have great associates at all levels of our company. Some have been with us for a very long time, others for just a year or two. In today's free-agent, deal-based world, though, only family is forever.

High margins aren't always important. Forget margins. Are you giving customers the goods and services that they want, when they want them? Satisfy those requirements, and the margins will take care of themselves.

Get personal. I have heard it said that people who star in their own commercials have fools for talent. Possibly, but I appear in our ads to let people know that I am a real florist and that this is a family business. It all comes back to relationships. If you can find a way to establish them, you are ahead of the game. If it just so happens that a commercial is the way to do it, then do it.

Remember: the wheel was already invented. I consider myself to be a creative plagiarist. Creativity really is the ability to learn from others and to apply those lessons to new situations. In almost everything new that you attempt, someone has already done it, sometimes successfully and sometimes not. Either way, there is a lesson to be learned.

* * *

One of my favorite things in life is to help things grow, from flowers to relationships to businesses. I hope that my story and words of encouragement will inspire you to grow.

Jim McCann

EPILOGUE: *Jim McCann—founder, chairman, CEO and television spokesperson of 1-800-FLOWERS—has built an international business from a single Manhattan flower shop. After acquiring the 1-800-FLOWERS telephone number in 1986, McCann focused on creating a reliable brand name and instilling a sense of trust and convenience in an industry that previously had no leader. Today, 1-800-FLOWERS is one of the world's leading gift retailers. And as his business grew, McCann pioneered its entry into other retail access channels, launching* 1-800-FLOWERS.COM *in 1995.*

You can learn more about Jim McCann by reading one of his many books, available at major bookstores, or by visiting www.1800flowers.com.

Dahlynn McKowen

Turning Tragedy into Triumph

People often ask me how, as a man, I became so committed to improving the quality of women's lives. It wasn't until age forty that I realized what had started me down the career path that was to become my passion in life.

One morning more than thirty-seven years ago, I was awakened by the passing school bus. I was thirteen years old, living at home with my two younger brothers and our mother, Doris Joy Heavin. She had just passed her fortieth birthday. She was a committed mother of five children and had wrestled with emotional and physical problems most of her life. Her doctors had placed her on an array of medications with little benefit.

As I awoke to the sound of the passing school bus, my brother Paul came in and told me that I'd better come quickly because Mother was sick. As I knelt beside her bed, I could feel the absence of warmth. I put my arms around her, first to feel for a sign of life, and then as a final embrace. I took my younger brothers, ages eight and nine, in my arms and gently told them that our mother was in heaven.

Her premature death was unnecessary. The high blood pressure that contributed to the blood clot that took her life was unnecessary. Rather than medicate the symptoms, she could have dealt with the cause of her high blood pressure. We now know that exercise and proper nutrition will almost always alleviate the causes of hypertension and most other chronic diseases.

Many years later, while teaching a fitness and weight-loss class to a group of about a hundred women, I realized I was subconsciously scanning the crowd for the face of my mother. I had what you would call an epiphany—it was then that I realized what had driven me all of my life and what my destiny was to be.

It is my desire that no little boy has to find his mother as I found mine.

Gary Heavin

EPILOGUE: *Gary Heavin and his wife, Diane, are the founders of Curves, the world's largest fitness franchise company. With more than 9,000 centers worldwide and over 4 million members, Curves is the fastest-growing franchise in history, according to* Entrepreneur *magazine. And through Curves franchises, the Heavins have created entrepreneurial opportunities for more than 30,000 people, 90 percent of whom are women.*

In 1976, Gary had completed three years toward a pre-med degree when he realized that he could help prevent the onslaught of deteriorating health and resultant illnesses by teaching proper fitness and nutrition/weight loss. He opened his first fitness center at age twenty.

Curves is a revolution in the fitness industry. Gary knew that the first step in promoting women's wellness is to get them into the gym; many feel uncomfortable exercising in the presence of men, which keeps them from joining traditional gyms. He also noticed women's social tendencies; even while exercising, they like to talk and benefit from each other's company.

With this in mind, Curves was designed to allow women to exercise in the comfort and camaraderie of a club designed exclusively for them. The Curves structure combines a thirty-minute circuit-training workout with fun and friendship mixed in, thus allowing a natural support system to fall into place.

With a degree in health and nutrition counseling, Gary is the author of two New York Times *bestselling books on exercise and nutrition. He was honored with the first ever "Visionary of the Year" award by the International Health, Racquet, and Sportsclub Association, and was named a 2004 Ernst & Young Entrepreneur of the Year, the first time in the history of the national competition that a health and fitness club operator had won this prestigious award. Currently, Gary is funding a $5 million study at Baylor University on the effects of exercise on women's bone density and metabolism.*

To learn more about Curves, please visit www.curves.com.

Dahlynn McKowen

2

DOLLARS AND SENSE

A business that makes nothing but money is a poor business.

Henry Ford

Cracking the Millionaire Code

None of us can change our yesterdays, but all of us can change our tomorrows.

Colin Powell

Have you ever had a million-dollar idea? Did you ever say to yourself, "Hey, that's a great idea," then let the idea fade away without acting on it, only to discover several months later that someone else had capitalized on your idea? Most of us have great ideas, yet we simply don't know what to do with them. *Ideas are the seeds of future fortunes.* Jack Canfield and I had just such an idea back in the early 1990s, and I'm glad we followed our hearts and our souls, or else the *Chicken Soup for the Soul* series never would have been born.

But wait! Sometimes a simple idea can even grow into billions! In the summer of 1990, on a train to London, Joanne Rowling did just that—a billion-dollar idea popped into her head. As she relates it, "All of a sudden the idea for Harry just appeared in my mind's eye. I can't tell you why or what triggered it. But I saw the idea of Harry and the wizard school very plainly. I suddenly had this basic idea of the boy who didn't know who he was, who didn't know he was a wizard until he got his invitation to wizard school. I have never been so excited by an idea."

As soon as she began to write, her life was thrown into turmoil by a series of events: the death of her forty-five-year-old mother from multiple sclerosis, her marriage to an abusive husband, a miscarriage, the birth of her first child, a divorce, being fired and trying to raise a child on government welfare. Four years after the initial Harry Potter "brainstorm," J. K. Rowling, as she now calls herself, decided to do what she was destined to do and wrote the book that would make her a billionaire and the richest woman in England.

Did you ever have an idea like that? Did you know what to do with it?

In May 1994—the same year that twenty-eight-year-old J. K. Rowling was toiling to finish the first *Harry Potter* book—a thirty-year-old researcher was sitting at his desk in a New York skyscraper. As he read reports about the growing Internet phenomenon, an idea struck him. "It was a wake-up call. I started thinking, *Okay, what kind of business opportunity might there be here?*" Fueled by this hunch, he quit his job, borrowed his parents' life savings, drove his wife to Seattle and then launched Amazon.com from their rented two-bedroom house. Five years later, Jeff Bezos was *Time* magazine's "Person of the Year" as well as a billionaire ten times over. Needless to say, billionaire Bezos has sold a lot of billionaire Rowling's books.

Think of how many success stories begin with a single, simple idea. Michael Dell started his company, Dell Computers, from his college dorm room. Twenty years later he was the world's youngest billionaire. Sam Walton opened the first Wal-Mart stores in Rogers, Arkansas, in 1962. Today, Wal-Marts crowd out the sun. This largest retailer in the world gives over $100 million in charitable contributions annually. All of this from a simple idea of "everyday low prices."

My longtime friend and business colleague Robert Allen and I share how to transform your million-dollar idea and make it a reality! Our latest book—*Cracking the Millionaire Code—Your Key to Enlightened Wealth* (Harmony Books, 2005)—reveals four important codes, all of which are essential to your success. In the spirit of entrepreneurship, here's a quick preview to open your idea floodgates and get you started on the path to enlightened success and wealth!

The Destiny Code. To crack the Destiny Code, you must discover your unique place in the universe. You arrived here on planet Earth encoded with divine DNA—a specific set of talents, gifts, opportunities, connections and sensitivities. We believe you have a destiny to fulfill. There is music in you, a song you are destined to sing, or instrument you are destined to play in the symphony of life. Some people discover their destiny quickly. Some people take decades to do so, and others never even look for it. When you tap into this pure vein of gold, you become who you were born to be.

The Prism Code. Destiny is the path you choose. Prism is the vehicle you navigate down that path. Prism is our description of the specific product or service that sets you apart—that displays your talents and gifts to the world. When you've discovered your prism, you don't earn a living, you earn a "loving." Your prism refracts your talent into a kaleidoscope of income stream.

Among the greatest crackers of the Prism Code is George Washington Carver, sometimes called the "inventor" of the peanut. Though Carver was born a Missouri slave, his research developed 325 products from peanuts, 108 applications for sweet potatoes, 75 products derived from pecans and over 500 dyes and pigments from 28 different plants.

The Angel Code. You can't do it alone. You need a team. Fortunately, there are people who were destined to be on your team. They'll help you fulfill your destiny, and you'll help them fulfill theirs. They bring the missing pieces of the puzzle; your picture is not complete without them. How do you find them? How will they be attracted to you? How will you know you can trust them? This is all part of cracking the Angel Code.

This code is explained in further detail in our book; in a nutshell, the way to crack the Angel Code is to form myriad "circles" that will offer you endless resources, resources that are both visible and invisible. Once you crack this code, you'll feel as if these resources are heaven-sent!

The Star Code. Cracking the Star Code is the process of discovering and serving a very special group of customers—treating them like the stars they are. Of all the codes to crack, this is one of the easiest to envision and the hardest one to regularly implement. The success rate of start-up businesses would soar if each new entrepreneur would simply focus on cracking this one code.

* * *

Codes are everywhere. ZIP codes. Gate codes. Area codes. Bar codes. PIN codes. Pass codes. Secret codes. Postal codes. Country codes. Morse code. Membership codes. Security codes. Color codes. Genetic codes. Entry codes. Exit codes. You can't live without codes!

This is my gift to you, my friend. The four key wealth codes—Destiny, Prism, Angel and Star. Crack them carefully, then behold a higher power within yourself and create a greater future for our world.

Mark Victor Hansen

[EDITORS' NOTE: *Besides being a cofounder of the* Chicken Soup for the Soul *series, Mark Victor Hansen is also an enthusiastic crusader of what's possible and is driven to make the world a better place! A worldwide public speaker for over three decades, Hansen focuses solely on helping organizations and people from all walks of life, reshaping their personal vision of what's possible and how to recognize opportunities and turn them into actions. To invite Hansen to speak to your organization, or to learn more about* Cracking the Millionaire Code: Your Key to Enlightened Wealth, *please visit* www.markvictorhansen.com *or call 949-764-2640.*]

Uncertain Certainty

As the reporter left, I sat there with my head in my hands wishing I hadn't opened my big mouth. Here I was, just twenty-six years old, telling an old hometown reporter that I was going to build the most successful real estate company in his state in just five years, *from scratch*.

It really hadn't occurred to me that the most respected and successful real estate company in Indiana had been around for over a hundred years. I had just moved to Indianapolis for the opportunity to build my own company, and I didn't know a soul. I was young, cocky and ready to claim my stake even though I didn't know the difference between a profit and loss statement and an accounts receivable statement. I had never balanced a checkbook, let alone built and run my own company. In any case, it was November 1986, and that's what came out in the paper the next week because of the lack of control between my brain and my mouth.

When I got a bit ahead of myself in the past, I just put my head down and started selling. Selling was easy for me, but building and running a company was a whole other animal. At the time the article came out, my RE/MAX of Indiana headquarters consisted of one executive office in a shared office suite setup, with a shared secretary who answered the phone for over a dozen or so different businesses.

Up until that time, I was a fairly successful real estate agent in Toronto, Canada. I had moved to Indiana to try my hand at building something for myself, something that, if I did it right, would provide me with a bright future and, I hoped, a chance to become a millionaire. I so desperately wanted to become one that I had written about it in my goals five years earlier when I was just twenty-one years old. Although I only went to grade eleven, wonderful mentors had told me that I had more within me than school could ever do for me. For whatever reason, I decided to believe them, rather than the insecure feelings I felt about myself.

So, with my insecure head held high and the RE/MAX concept as my ally, I started to set up appointments with managers and owners of every real estate company in the state. I started with the big boys first, the guys who were numbers one and two in the state, doing billions in sales with over a thousand people in their sales forces.

The first meetings were disastrous—they politely laughed and escorted me out of their offices. Their attitude was, "Why do we need you? We already have in place what you are trying to build from scratch." The answer? They couldn't see past their own success to the future and hence were closed-minded from the get-go.

After about four months of daily prospecting and sharing my vision and my story, I got a call from one of the top managers in the state. After our first meeting I knew I was onto possibly the first and biggest deal of my very young career. After several months of discussions, we snagged one of the biggest fish in the pond and were on our way. Within a month's time, another unhappy manager called from the number-two company and expressed interest as well. It wasn't long before he and another group purchased the franchisee rights to several more areas. This allowed us to gain credibility and traction.

At the end of the first year, we had nearly one hundred salespeople at our awards banquet. We were off to the races!

No matter where I turned, everyone thought that we were going to go bankrupt within short order. That made sense because I later found out that two other people prior to me had owned the RE/MAX region of Indiana, and both had failed! Regardless, in this case my ignorance proved to be a great strength, as I didn't really care what had happened in the past. I was prepared to forge ahead and build my company. For me it was simply a matter of sharing with enough people the vision of a better future for themselves and then exceeding their expectations month in and month out.

The next challenge for me was to learn how to run a business and to understand all the moving parts. At first it was overwhelming, especially because I didn't know what I didn't know. For a while it seemed as if I had bought myself a job that was strangling me. Not only did I have to sell, I had to deliver all the promises I made, take care of legal duties and make sure finances were in order. That was just the beginning. What it takes to build and run a hundred-person operation is vastly different than a thousand-person operation.

To help me deal with the growth and education I needed, I formed a mastermind group made up of some very successful regional owners in the RE/MAX organization. These individuals helped me shave years off my learning curve and saved me hundreds of thousands of dollars in mistakes. From them, I learned a very valuable lesson: specialized knowledge is worth its weight in gold.

Just six years later, we hit the billion-dollar sales mark. It took those other companies over twenty-five years to get to where persistence, planning and a great attitude helped my company get to in just six years. Today we are grateful to do over $4.5 billion a year in sales and have over 1,600 salespeople.

From those early days of not knowing what to do, today I feel comfortable on stage teaching business owners how to build their companies while living an extraordinary life. It all boils down to three things: finding what you love to do, becoming excellent at it, then telling the whole world about it.

John Assaraf

EPILOGUE: *Over the last two decades, John Assaraf has built four multimillion-dollar companies: RE/MAX of Indiana, Bamboo.com, The Street Kid Company and currently OneCoach. Not bad for a kid whose teenage years were turbulent at best.*

Besides the tremendous success realized through his RE/MAX company, Assaraf was instrumental in making Bamboo.com the world's leading provider of imaging infrastructure for the Internet. He then wrote The Street Kid's Guide to Having It All *(Longstreet Press, 2003), which topped many bestseller lists, including Barnes & Noble, the* New York Times *and the* Wall Street Journal. *He also has been featured on ABC, CBS, CNN and NBC, as well as hundreds of radio shows and in print media.*

In January 2005, Assaraf cofounded OneCoach, a next-generation business community that helps business owners and self-employed professionals increase revenues, profits and values while living extraordinary lives.

To learn more about Assaraf, please visit his Web Site www.OneCoach.com.

Dahlynn McKowen

A Recipe for Success

In the summer of 1980, I was thirty-five years old and had been out of the workforce for eight years as a stay-at-home mom to our two daughters. But come that September, both girls would be in school, thus allowing me to return to work full-time. My husband, Jay, had a career as vice president of operations at Lien Chemical Company, and I wanted to do my share, especially with the cost of two college tuitions looming. I didn't start out wanting to set the world on fire, I just wanted to find something to supplement our family income, earning extra money we could sock away for our daughters' educations and their futures.

But heading back into the workforce had its advantages and disadvantages. While I would be earning money for our future, I didn't want to miss our daughters' school functions such as being room mother or chaperoning field trips. I wanted to bake cookies with the girls after school and take them to the library. I needed to find a job that allowed me to do all these things, and possibly more. With Jay's help, I decided to start my own business, drawing on my years as a former home economist and teacher. I decided to sell high-quality kitchen tools at home parties.

But my home parties (a.k.a. direct-selling parties) would be different. They would be informative and fun. I would incorporate a cooking demonstration into each party and let the guests try the tools by helping out with the demonstration. I needed a name for my new business, and after a brainstorming session with some friends, we came up with "The Pampered Chef."

At the beginning, I was on a mission: I wanted the business to make a difference in people's lives. I knew that the best way to fulfill my mission was by drawing families together, and what better way than through shared conversation and collective laughter during mealtime? It is where we live between bites.

I talk about the launch of my business and the ultimate success of The Pampered Chef in my 2005 book *The Pampered Chef: The Story of One of America's Most Beloved Companies* (Doubleday). One section of my book offers eleven tips for start-up entrepreneurs, five of which I would like to share with you:

Follow your passion. I loved working in the kitchen, and I loved teaching. With my business, I was able to combine these two passions. When I was in college, I was able to get through difficult math and science courses because I knew I had to in order to graduate with a home economics degree. The same is true in business. There are some chores that you as an entrepreneur must endure. If you are passionate enough about the other facets of the business, you will put up with what you don't particularly enjoy. If you find something you love, I assure you that your work will be considerably easier.

I believe that one of the key elements to success in business, and in life, is having a passion for what you do. My passion for my work plays a vital role during difficult times; it fortifies my resilience and ability to overcome obstacles, supports my dedication to remain true to my original vision and fuels my determination to succeed.

Be the best you can be. I have always had a single goal: to be the best I can be at what I do. So should you. For the vast majority of us, this isn't such a difficult task because most work isn't rocket science. Martin Luther King Jr. put it eloquently when he said, "If a man is called a street cleaner, he should sweep the streets as Michelangelo painted or Beethoven composed music or Shakespeare wrote poetry. He should sweep streets so well that all the hosts in heaven and earth will pause to say, 'Here lived a great street sweeper who did his job well.'"

Watch your overhead. With a bankroll of only $3,000 to start my business, I didn't have any choice; I had to watch my overhead. It taught me discipline, which I have been mindful of throughout my business career. Of course, even with a small bankroll, with credit the temptation to overspend is always present. Simply put, don't do it! Establish a budget and stick to it. I kept my overhead down. For several years I worked out of my house until it was bursting at the seams. It's easy to spend money; anyone can do it. It's more difficult not to spend. Oftentimes, start-up entrepreneurs who get off to a good start find that success goes to their heads. They want to let the world know they've done well; they want to impress people, they overspend. In a matter of time, high overhead takes such a heavy toll that the entrepreneur is unable to withstand even a short downturn in business. Don't let this happen to you.

Go with your instincts. In the beginning, I operated on sheer instinct. Yes, Jay, my husband, was there for me to bounce ideas off, but in the end, if we didn't agree, I made the final decision. Over the years I have found my intuition and instincts about my business are seldom wrong. If I have to work too hard to sell myself on an idea, it's probably not a good idea. Unless Jay strongly objected and convinced me of a flaw in my judgment, I stuck with my intuition. Jay respected my intuition even when it didn't make good business sense to him. Was my intuition always right? Of course not! No entrepreneur is ever 100 percent right. If you're always right, then you're not taking enough risks. Fortunately, my batting average was high enough that I learned to trust my intuition.

It's only a business. There were times when I was stressed and overwhelmed with work, and Jay would say to me, "It's only a business."

"But Jay . . . ," I'd start to say, and he'd interrupt, "Doris, this is still only a portion of your entire life. Don't get so hung up with it. Don't take yourself so seriously."

What wonderful advice. This is not to say that I always appreciated hearing it. When I got wrapped up in the business, it was hard to take a breather and unwind. Fortunately that's what I eventually learned to do. Thinking that it was only a business put things in perspective. My family was my number-one priority. They are the reason I started the business. Sure, on rare occasions I become so focused on a pressing problem that I momentarily put the business before my family. But it happens rarely, and whenever I catch myself falling into that trap, I say to myself, "Doris, it's only a business!" That phrase is a reminder to keep priorities in order.

* * *

Maintaining a balance between work and family is one of our company's missions, one that is appreciated and enjoyed by the nearly 70,000 Pampered Chef consultants. All entrepreneurs in their own right, I am proud to have helped them start their own businesses, proud to have them be the first impression to the 12 million customers who attend home parties each year. And the party is definitely not over yet!

Doris Christopher

EPILOGUE: *Doris Christopher is the founder and chairman of The Pampered Chef, Ltd., the premier direct seller of kitchen tools in the world. In twenty-six years, Christopher has taken a home-based business and has grown it into a multimillion-dollar company, with over 1 million home shows given annually throughout the world. In 2002, the company was acquired by Berkshire Hathaway.*

Christopher continues to lead her company into the future, creating start-up business opportunities for new consultants, and pampering the rest of us along the way! To learn more, visit www.pamperedchef.com.

Dahlynn McKowen

Better Than a Lemonade Stand

Shoot for the moon. Even if you miss, you'll land among the stars.

Les Brown

My experience as an entrepreneur began when I was eight years old, living in Michigan with my family. I saw a G.I. Joe toy advertised on television and became convinced I had to have it. My mother decided this would be a good time for a financial lesson. "You can have it if you use your own money," she said. I didn't much care for that, so I asked my father. He considered buying it for me, until he talked it over with my mother and learned what she already had told me.

So I was stuck. *How could I earn the money I needed?* I thought. Then I had an idea—I'll make the money with an all-American lemonade stand! I became excited, thinking about the hordes of money I could earn! In search of venture capital, I cracked open my piggy bank and took out my life savings: a whopping $5.30. I went to the supermarket and bought as many lemons and as much sugar and juice concentrate as I could afford. I just knew, come that weekend, my stand would be a super-stand!

I even thought of advertising and laid out a plan for signage. On Saturday, in the early-morning darkness, I posted signs everywhere with arrows pointing the way to my house. My entire neighborhood would know where my lemonade stand was located. I returned by seven o'clock, just as the sun was peeking over the horizon. Confidently, I pictured how the cars would line up around the block while waiting for lemonade. I was sure there was going to be a traffic jam, and I made plans on how to serve all my customers as quickly as possible. I lugged jug after jug of lemonade to the table at the end of our long driveway, ready for action.

At eight-thirty, the first car drove by, and I was sure this was going to be the beginning of the rush of customers. I stood on my lawn chair, waving my poster enthusiastically. The car slowed down, and I caught the eye of the woman who was at the wheel. She smiled at me, gave me a "thumbs-up" and kept going. *That's all right,* I told myself. *That's just the first car. That's not a problem.*

An hour later, a second car approached. *This one definitely looks like a lemonade customer,* I told myself. But he, too, passed by. All the driver gave me was a friendly "go-get-'em" honk. Still confident, I told myself it was early in the day, and I had plenty of lemonade and plenty of time. This was going to be a great day. Eleven cars went by. They all slowed down, and the drivers all smiled at me. Most of them waved, which was very encouraging, but nobody stopped to open their wallets. By four that afternoon, I had not sold one glass of lemonade.

Thirty minutes later, my parents walked down the driveway and bought two lemonades. They paid me a dollar. Sipping on her cool lemonade, my mother asked, "How have sales been today?"

"Well, I didn't earn enough for the toy," I said.

"How close did you get?"

"Not too close," I said, knowing I needed twenty dollars. "I'll probably need another Saturday."

"Well, tell me, how close did you get?" she asked again.

"Well, Mom, I made one dollar."

Silence. My mother looked stunned.

"Does that include the dollar we just gave you?"

"Yes. But I had so much fun!"

More silence, then, "Fun? You didn't make any money, and you just lost your savings. Fun?" she asked, puzzled.

"Yeah. I found something I really like to do. I took an idea and turned it into a business. It was the most fun I've ever had. I have a new goal: I'm going to be the CEO of my own big company . . . when I'm still a kid."

The look on my mother's face said it all: That was a fairly ambitious declaration for an eight-year-old boy who had just lost his life savings. Later, I realized that the biggest problem with my lemonade stand wasn't my product, it was my timing. Michigan in March was not the best time to be selling ice-cold lemonade, as forty-degree temperatures don't exactly encourage lemonade sales!

My second venture, an early-morning service carrying newspapers from the bottom of driveways up to customers' front doors, was much more profitable than my first. As a kid, I learned to take the money I made from one business and start another. I came to realize that my love of entrepreneurial adventures would stay with me forever.

The lemonade-stand experience did inspire me to run a big business someday. Now, twenty-two years after that cold spring morning, and many successful businesses in between, I am retired at the age of thirty. And I still drink lemonade.

Daryl Bernstein

EPILOGUE: *At the age of eight, Daryl Bernstein established his infamous lemonade stand. At twelve, he launched a mailorder company on his kitchen table. At fifteen, Bernstein wrote the best-seller* Better Than a Lemonade Stand: Small Business Ideas for Kids *(Beyond Words Publishing, 1992). The book, which prompted the* Wall Street Journal *to call Bernstein a "kid whiz," has helped thousands of kids around the world start their own profitable small businesses, with little or no start-up costs.*

But Bernstein didn't stop there. At sixteen, he was named a "Global Leader for Tomorrow" by the World Economic Forum. At age twenty, Bernstein wrote the celebrated book The Venture Adventure: Strategies for Thriving in the Jungle of Entrepreneurship *(Beyond Words Publishing, 1996). By the age of twenty-three, he had grown Global Video, his kitchen-table venture, into the largest producer and distributor of educational videos in the United States, with over 100 employees and 30 million catalogs mailed annually. Then, at the ripe old age of twenty-four, Bernstein sold his business to a NASDAQ-listed company and began his first retirement.*

Bernstein has been featured on CNN, National Public Radio, the BBC, and Radio 3 Hong Kong, as well as in the New York Times *and hundreds of other publications around the world. He currently speaks to corporate and academic audiences, acts as an advisor to fast-growing businesses, manages his investments and lives on the beach in Santa Barbara, California.*

For more information, visit www.darylbernstein.com.

Dahlynn McKowen

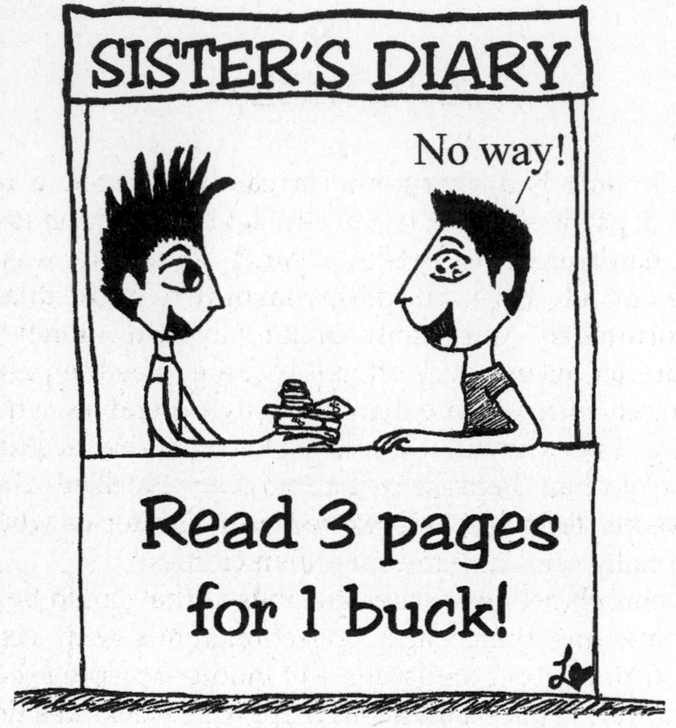

And guess what, dude, my parents paid me $50!

Life's a Hobby

McClellan's had everything: a candy counter, a toiletries department, sheets, towels, toys, lingerie, housewares, hardware, even pets! And Mr. T. Texas Tyler was in charge of it all—his store was my favorite five-and-dime.

Unfortunately, our family didn't have the money to shop at McClellan's very often. My father was the pastor of a church with no more than thirty-five attendees, which meant a tiny salary that stretched to meet the mealtime needs of six kids. Because we had no car, we walked wherever we needed to go, and relatives from California would occasionally send us hand-me-down clothes.

The church people were as gracious as they could be by supplementing the meager collection funds with vegetables, fruit or other foodstuffs. My mother accepted them all with warm appreciation, but there were weeks at a time without meat on our supper table. An extra fifty cents or even a quarter that could be spent at McClellan's was far beyond our reality.

I attended Altus High School in Altus, Oklahoma, but I didn't feel comfortable in the swirl of students my age who had new clothes and money for snacks. I was usually the kid washing dishes in the cafeteria to earn a lunch pass. Then, when enrolling for my junior year in 1958, I saw something on the class list that changed my life forever: "D.E."—distributive education, more commonly known today as "work-study."

I quickly learned that D.E. was a special program where students could work part-time for the businesses in town. We were allowed to leave during the school day, received credit for the work/class and also earned money along the way. Of course I immediately applied to work at McClellan's, and I was accepted!

On the first day of school, I left at ten-thirty and walked the mile to McClellan's, as excited as I'd ever been in my entire young life. Mr. Tyler greeted me, then got me started by teaching me to sweep the floors with the yarn broom and a concoction of sawdust and light oil. When that was done, Mr. Tyler sent me to the stockroom and showed me how to check in the new merchandise.

That evening, after I walked the mile back to our house across the tracks, I excitedly told my mother about my day and that I had a real job. I'd worked alongside her and my brothers and sisters in the cotton fields for years to earn money for our family, but this job at the five-and-dime was a whole new experience.

I quickly fell into the rhythm of working forty or more hours a week. My schooling was suffering, but retail was such a joyous contrast to the rest of my life that I couldn't cut back. I studied everything Mr. Tyler did and realized a lot of his work related to being a great organizer. The more I watched, the more I became convinced I could be a store manager—I could be just as successful, too! This epiphany became my goal.

Mr. Tyler taught me many things, from how to display merchandise attractively to trimming the front windows. He'd even take me down to the corner drugstore sometimes just to talk about the business and pass along his wisdom. I began to see that the sky was the limit in retail. You could open more stores, expand existing stores—there was no end. From the very beginning, I loved the work, and that's an important point: to succeed in retail, you have to love it.

About this same time, I splurged every so often on a pretty, young part-timer in the stationery department by taking her across the street to the drugstore for a five-cent Coke. Today, that young clerk is my wife, Barbara, the love of my life. I also splurged on my first big purchase, a 1951 Ford that set me back about $200. But when I noticed Barbara's current boyfriend drove a convertible, I decided to upgrade to a yellow 1953 Ford convertible to compete for her attention. My car turned out to be the lemon its color indicated, but I did get her attention!

After I put in time with the Air Force Reserve at Sheppard Air Force Base in Wichita Falls, Texas, I returned to my job at McClellan's and married Barbara—I was nineteen and she was seventeen. A year later, I began working for another five-and-dime chain called TG&Y, which was expanding much faster—the Wal-Mart of the era. At age twenty-one, I applied for and received a manager slot in a new store in Oklahoma City. I had four thousand square feet and six employees, and it was my chance to show what I could do.

Many promotions and two sons—Mart and Steve—came along as I learned the dynamics of retail management. Then, in 1970, Barbara and I started our own business; I saw potential that TG&Y was not capturing. Our family-centered store included a large and very popular pet department; there were many types of birds, and rows and rows of saltwater and freshwater fish. I brought in truckloads of ten-gallon fish tanks and put them on sale at incredibly low prices, even lower than wholesale. My theory was that once someone buys a fish tank, they have to put stuff in it—fish, gravel, the pump and all the other paraphernalia—and they'd buy it all from our store!

Recognizing that these retail concepts worked in the pet department, I wondered if the same thing could happen in our crafts department, but I lacked start-up money. A friend and I borrowed $600 from the bank, bought a frame chopper and began making miniature picture frames on our kitchen table for wholesaling. Barbara and the boys actually glued more frames than I did, so I paid the little guys seven cents per frame.

Two years later, we branched out to a retail store specifically dedicated to arts and crafts, opening the first Hobby Lobby store near the Oklahoma state capitol building. It was only 300 square feet of arts and crafts. Jump forward over thirty years, and today I'm the chairman of eight different affiliated companies as well as the CEO of Hobby Lobby! We're still family owned, but now, when my wife, the kids and I decide to make a business move, we don't have to ask Wall Street about it!

David Green
As told to Gail Kulhavy

EPILOGUE: *With the opening of a new store about every two weeks, David Green is one of the most prolific retailing giants in the country. His modest beginnings in the 1970s have grown into almost 400 stores in twenty-eight states, with sales in the billions.*

The largest privately owned arts and crafts retailer in the world, Hobby Lobby's headquarters is located in a 2.6-million-square-foot manufacturing, distribution and office complex in Oklahoma City. Affiliated companies include Hemispheres, Bearing Fruit Communications, HL Realty, Crafts Etc! and Mardel, a popular Christian office and educational supply chain found in six states.

A past Ernst & Young national retail/consumer Entrepreneur of the Year award recipient, Green is also dedicated to myriad ministry projects. Cites Green, "We believe that it is by God's grace and provision that Hobby Lobby has endured. He has been faithful in the past; we trust him for our future."

To learn more about Green and Hobby Lobby, please visit www.hobbylobby.com.

Gail Kulhavy

Reasoning for the Seasonings

A man's reach should exceed his grasp, or what's a heaven for?

Robert Browning

I've always felt that my soul has been carved out of the snow and rock of the Colorado mountains. Nature is my passion—it's a part of me, and always has been, even when the nature I loved so much had a propensity to take my breath away, literally.

I grew up in the beautiful Colorado Rockies. As a child, I suffered from severe asthma and was always on the sickly side. One day, while gasping for a breath during a particularly cruel attack, I made a lifelong commitment to fight my asthma and to get healthy. There were too many things on this earth I wanted to do, and one of those included climbing to the top of the Rockies' 14,000-foot majestic peaks.

Because I had such a love for the outdoors, on days when my asthma was under control, I would hike the mountains, enjoying the flowers and wild berries. During my childhood years, I made money by picking wild berries for ladies making jelly. Then in the late 1960s, the decade of free thinking and healthier choices, I became a health food fanatic on a mission. Determined to significantly change people's eating and drinking habits, I felt that if I could create the best-tasting tea in the world that was also super-healthful, I could bring better health to millions of people.

By the grace of God and lucky timing, I started Celestial Seasonings at the birth of the modern natural foods movement. Before 1970, natural food stores did not exist. If people watched their diets at all, the extent of their healthy intentions was purchasing vitamins. In the early 1970s, however, millions of young people demanded healthful, natural and unpolluted food. Contrarily, the scientific trend in North American food corporations' product offerings reflected the belief that you could have better health through the standardization of test-tube food. That set the stage for the birth of an alternative "back to the earth" food revolution by America's youth.

In the fall of 1971, I left Boulder on my first real sales trip to the East Coast. I was twenty-one, idealistic, enthusiastic, broke and ready to change the world by becoming a part of the natural foods movement. I went peddling my first branded tea—"Mo's 24 Herb Tea"—and had a Tupperware container of Red Zinger tea to show people. One of the turning points in the history of Celestial occurred on that trip. While in Connecticut, I met a CEO of one of the largest food corporations in the world. We had a heated debate about natural foods fresh from the farm versus chemically produced, scientifically engineered food. This gentleman actually believed that people would be better off if all foods were sanitized, standardized and produced in stainless-steel vats rather than raised on farms. I, on the other hand, touted the health benefits of my teas, natural foods, exercise and overall good living.

After nearly an hour of what became a very tense conversation, the CEO said, "Why don't you give up your silly natural food tea company and get a real job? Come work for me." I left that discussion on fire, ready to take on the big boys. I just knew in my heart that the natural foods movement would rise up and provide healthy products, no matter how difficult the challenge would become. And difficult was the one word that described many years of poverty and growth experienced by Celestial Seasonings.

The initial capital investment for Celestial was $500, provided by my early partner John Hay. From there, finding the money to grow became our greatest challenge over our first ten years of existence. During the lean years when we barely had enough cash to make payroll, I would think of that CEO telling me to give up this silly company and get a real job. He was just the inspiration I needed to stay the course. I was determined to make a difference.

Many people have asked if I'm surprised how large Celestial Seasonings eventually became. My answer surprises most folks. From day one I thought Celestial would reach at least $100 million in sales within ten years. What shocked me was how hard it was to get there—it took thirty years to hit that number.

As I look back at our success, what I see is passion, dedication, hard work and the joy of achievement that permeated our entire company. I've since retired, but about once a month, somebody comes up to me and says, "I know one of your first partners." I respond by asking who they are referring to, and they proceed to give me a name of someone I may or may not remember. The person they were talking about might have been working on a tea bag production line or packing trucks in the warehouse, but that individual was so involved that he felt he had been a partner. I love those stories.

Truth is, Celestial has been about the thousands of people on a mission to make a difference. Celestial Seasonings was not about Mo Siegel any more than the river is about the riverbank.

Mo Siegel

EPILOGUE: *Mo Siegel did what he set out to do—create a healthful, natural tea for the masses. Over thirty years later, Celestial Seasonings continues to be America's number-one specialty tea company and one of the most popular tea companies in the world.*

Siegel retired from the company in 2002, setting his sites on conquering a life aspiration—climbing the fifty-five mountains in Colorado that are over 14,000 feet high. In the summer of 2005, he completed all of these very complicated, exhilarating and daring mountain climbs with just one close call, but other than that, hardly a scratch!

This bold mountain climber now spends his time investing money, sitting on the board of directors of five for-profit companies and two nonprofit organizations, raising the last of his two teenagers (he has five children), loving his wife, Jennifer, being "Grandpa" to four grandchildren, doing nonprofit work, hiking with his dogs, skiing, traveling, reading and spending time with friends.

Siegel is also an author, having penned with Nancy Burke Herbs for Health and Happiness: All You Need to Know *(Time-Life, 2000). He also authored, along with his wife, Jennifer, (who, Siegel admits, did most of the work), the title* Celestial Seasonings: Cooking with Tea *(Park Lane Press, 1996).*

To learn more about Mo Siegel and Celestial Seasonings, please visit www.CelestialSeasonings.com.

Dahlynn McKowen

Let's Talk Business, Woman-to-Woman

I started my business, "eWomenNetwork," from scratch, alone in my home office, but I didn't do this entirely by myself. I did it by learning, listening, interacting and engaging with other dynamic women.

The very nature of my company means I am always meeting new, fabulously wonderful women. And I have learned something from these women that I want to share with you: how to become a successful woman entrepreneur and realize your dreams, both in business and in life.

With these lessons in mind, I have created ten ingredients that, when combined, will help you achieve your life's dreams:

#1—Live your vision. The first ingredient to running any successful business is to have a vision. It's not enough to be competent at what you do; in Corporate America, it's the pyramid, and the more you climb the ladder of success, the more the pyramid narrows. The same is true if you own your own business, except that those who rise to the top of the pyramid are those who are successful against their competitors in the marketplace. Everyone is smart, everyone works hard, and everyone is focused on delivering their product or service to the customer in a better, cheaper, faster, more meaningful way.

Look for transformational opportunities—evaluate, evaluate, evaluate. Create your vision, hold on to it, measure it and make sure you have the fuel you need to continue going after your dream, building your business and overcoming the many challenges you'll face along the way. Vision is paramount to your success.

#2—Overcome obstacles. Another ingredient in building a wildly successful company is the ability to overcome obstacles. No matter what business you're in, you're going to encounter impossible-to-foresee barriers, and you're undoubtedly going to make mistakes.

When I started eWomenNetwork, the original business plan was based on an online networking organization. While conducting focus groups, women said they were too busy to attend yet another meeting. What they wanted was a way to connect with other women at a time that worked for them best, around their home and work schedules. Online networking appeared to be the answer to their needs.

Thus, I launched my company purely as an online networking organization. But then I discovered that some of our members wanted to meet in person. It was then I realized I had asked the wrong question to the focus groups; my original question was, "Would you attend another meeting?"

So I created face-to-face networking opportunities, calling them "events" instead of meetings. I completely reengineered and expanded the company's business model to not only include the high-tech ability to connect via the Web site, but also to connect via "high-touch, personal networking."

This shift to incorporate both online and personal networking opportunities for our members created success I could never have anticipated. I definitely learned from my mistake!

#3—Inspire others. The third ingredient is an ability to inspire others. It's all about pioneering and getting other people to join you, climb on board with you, and follow you to your destination. It's about helping them picture that destination, what that service or product is going to be and how it's going to better their lives. This is such an important skill, something that you can learn to do. You can have the best product in the world or be the tops in a revolutionary service, but if you can't inspire others to see what you see, it's going to be lonely. In the end, you will falter. None of us makes it alone.

#4—Develop your "A-Team." When you're starting your business, you sometimes wear all the hats—product development, accounting, human resource specialist, marketing, sales and so on. You'll find that you're so busy working in the business that you're not working on the business.

You must end your "nobody can do it like I can" thinking. Instead, surround yourself with people who can outsmart you. To grow your business, you must build an A-Team—people with focused experience and expertise in particular aspects of running a business. By creating your own A-Team, you'll have time to focus on your vision, grow the business and inspire new customers. Now that's the sign of a really successful entrepreneur.

#5—Trust your intuition. Throughout the entire development of your company, your convictions will be tested, and it's important that you challenge the data. You'll need to look, listen and investigate. But most of all, you will need to use your power of intuition and trust your gut instincts.

You must be willing to stand alone in the end. You must be willing to go to the edge and eventually jump, knowing that you will build your wings on the way down. Being an entrepreneur is not about living in a safe place;

entrepreneurs know that life is about getting comfortable with the discomfort of living on the edge. This is the journey and the process of owning, running and growing a business.

#6—Above all, maintain integrity. As an entrepreneur, you can know everything and still fail the test. Yes, you have all the answers, but without integrity, chances are you will fail that test, and your company will fail as well.

We're all tempted to take the easy way out, to not be honest with employees and others, to promise what we know we can't deliver. Each of us has an opportunity every day to make decisions that tell others who we are. The impact these decisions have on trust and our relationships can't be overestimated. Always take the high road and do the right thing. Don't let anyone's logic talk you out of this. That way you can look back without regret, no matter what happens.

#7—Eliminate negativity. As women, particularly as business owners, we must think about with whom we spend our time. Who is it that's supportive and giving us energy? Who is it that's draining and taking it away? Many of the people who love you and want the best for you also want you to play it safe, but unfortunately being an entrepreneur is not always about playing it safe.

Toxic people are the people who prevent you from going after your dreams. They're the people who look at the glass half-empty versus half-full. They zap you of your energy without ever adding to your energy cup. Know when to wish them well and move on without burning bridges.

#8—Connect to capital early on. Develop a solid relationship with your banker. While the bank's drive-thru lanes are effective from the perspective that they provide convenience and expediency, this is not a relationship with a bank. I'm talking about a relationship with a woman banker. In fact, if you don't have the banker's name and her phone number programmed into your cell phone, then you don't have a relationship with a banker.

The best time to build a relationship with a banker is when you need nothing. The worse time to start a relationship with a banker is when you need a loan. I occasionally make the daily deposits, and while I'm there, I'll drop off an article or sales brochure with my banker; it's important to keep your banker updated on your company's doings and progress.

Your banker is instrumental to your growth. Even if you started your business with no outside capital, there will be times over your business career that you'll need capital assistance, whether it's a line of credit or an SBA loan. You'll find it to be a much more productive and successful experience if you have an established relationship with your banker well in advance.

#9—Find ways to support your positive attitude. Your smile is an ingredient that will attract others to you. Your attitude is more important than your degrees and diplomas, your awards and accomplishments, your circumstances and successes.

When I was starting eWomenNetwork, I was scared. Cash flow was extremely tight between making payroll and paying the lease, and I was stressed and stretched. But I knew my employees wanted to be part of a winning team; they wanted to hold on to that vision that I painted when I hired them; they didn't want to hear me come in and talk about my woes.

There are going to be many stressful days, days when you'll feel incredibly disappointed and discontent. I still have days like this, just like anyone else, and do you know what I do? I change my attitude, which instantly makes me feel better. I pretend that I'm going onstage for the day. I walk out the door and get in my car, saying, "It's show time!" And at the end of the day, I say, "That's a wrap." I take a fabulous bath with a few candles, eat some decadent chocolates, then call it a day, in a much, much better mood than when I started the day.

#10—Develop and expand your network. The final important ingredient in this recipe for success is to continue developing and expanding your network.

When I walk into a room and see one hundred people, I know that I am speaking to thousands. I'm not just being introduced to the people in that room; by my connecting and establishing relationships with these one hundred people, I'm actually being introduced to their vast networks.

I firmly believe that behind every successful woman is a huge network, one that she has built by meeting new people. The way I build my network is this: When I meet someone new, I smile and use my five favorite words, "How can I help you?" I then accept their business card, and on the back I write what it is that they are looking for or what their biggest challenge is. I do my best to follow up, expecting nothing in return but a simple thank-you.

This is just one way I network, and it has helped me expand my business and life. It's about giving without expectation of anything in return, even though what I do get in return is possibly a new business contact, networking opportunity and even a new friend.

* * *

Wherever you go, go with excitement, understanding that the enthusiasm you create as a female entrepreneur will be contagious. Start an epidemic. And I do hope we have an opportunity to connect. It would be an honor to have you as part of my network.

Sandra Yancey

EPILOGUE: *Sandra Yancey is the founder and CEO of eWomenNetwork, Inc. Her company is the fastest-growing membership-based women's business network in North America, and eWomenNetwork.com is the number-one online resource for connecting and promoting women and their businesses worldwide.*

Founded in 2000, eWomenNetwork is headquartered in Dallas, Texas. Under Yancey's leadership, eWomenNetwork has pioneered a whole new way for women to promote themselves and achieve their business objectives. One of the underlying principles of eWomenNetwork is "It takes teamwork to make the dream work!"

The organization boasts a database of over 500,000 female business owners and executives and conducts nearly two thousand events for professional women in cities across North America annually. The eWomenNetwork.com Web site receives over two hundred thousand hits daily, making it the most visited businesswomen's Web site in the United States and Canada, with the largest photographic profile directory of women business owners in the world.

Yancey also hosts the "eWomenNetwork Radio Show" on WBAP News/Talk 820, the highest rated and most listened-to station in Texas, and the largest ABC radio affiliate in the United States. An author as well, Yancey penned the bestselling Relationship Networking: The Art of Turning Contacts into Connections *(eWomenPublishingNetwork, 2006). Additionally, her eWomenNetwork Foundation has awarded hundreds of thousands of dollars in cash grants, in-kind donations and support to women's nonprofit organizations and scholarships for emerging female leaders of tomorrow.*

To learn more about Sandra Yancey and her company, please visit www.eWomenNetwork.com.

Dahlynn McKowen

"Your sermon was fine, but you're supposed to end with 'Amen'—not 'dot com'."

Fields of Dreams

There is nothing in a caterpillar that tells you it's going to be a butterfly.

Richard Buckminster Fuller

Had we started farming with the goal of becoming the largest grower of organic produce in the world, we probably would have been daunted into inaction. But Earthbound Farm didn't start as a grand plan. It was more like a succession of choices that added up to an impact much larger than we could have ever imagined.

When we began in 1984, we were just two New York City kids fresh out of college who wanted a back-to-the-land break before beginning "real jobs" and making our mark. We wanted to get away from elevators and taxi cabs and be absorbed in a world of crickets chirping at twilight and the smell of musty earth beneath a wide-open sky. So we moved to a small raspberry farm tucked in the fertile hills of California's Carmel Valley and planned to support ourselves by selling berries by the roadside.

Since we knew next to nothing about farming, we welcomed a crash course in growing raspberries from the previous farmer. He showed us how to add synthetic fertilizers to the drip lines and spray fungicides. But something just didn't feel right to us about putting chemicals on the berries we were going to eat. Amid a sea of naysayers, at a time when organic was virtually unheard of, we found a copy of *Rodale's Encyclopedia of Organic Gardening* and set about growing our raspberries . . . organically.

We were altogether seduced by the land. Our driveway was lined with almond, apricot and plum trees, and fig and apple trees dotted the property. We rose at dawn with the roosters and tended the farm until the sun dipped into dusk. We picked grapes from the vines and stomped them into wine, and enjoyed simple meals created from the bounty around us.

As content as we were, we discovered that we couldn't survive on raspberries alone. We began growing organic baby lettuces and specialty greens and selling them to adventurous local chefs. Our one-year hiatus turned into two, while rows of pristine produce crowded out any thought of "real jobs." We'd thoroughly settled into the gentle rhythms of farm life when, out of the blue, our bread-and-butter client left the area, and we were left with a field of rapidly maturing baby lettuces and nobody to buy them.

After the initial shock had worn off, we were able to see the challenge as big opportunities. Because we were so busy in the fields all day, we had gotten into the practice of washing and drying a week's worth of baby greens and storing them in Ziploc bags. Having the convenience of fresh salad every day helped us stay away from junk food when we didn't have time or energy to cook. It worked so well for us that we had been toying with the idea of marketing the concept, and now we had our chance. We started harvesting, washing and bagging organic baby greens, and set off to try our luck at local specialty stores.

But it was the 1980s, when globes of iceberg dominated the produce section, specialty greens were all but unknown outside of high-end restaurants, and there were no packaged salads at all. We struck a deal with some skeptical grocers; if no one bought our salads, they didn't have to pay us. But the bags did sell . . . and sell and sell and sell. Before we knew it, our living room had become a packing factory, and organic bagged salads had become our career. Unbeknownst to us, Earthbound Farm had become the first company in America to successfully market bagged salads.

By 1992, we were running a $3 million business out of our 800-square-foot house. It was time to move. We constructed a packing facility on a thirty-two-acre farm we had bought in nearby Watsonville. We thought it would last us forever, but it turned out to be more of a launching pad than a resting place. An unexpected contract with a club store chain in 1993 meant that we would need much more acreage and a larger packing facility to keep up. In a very short period of time we went from being a niche supplier of specialty produce to serving large retail outlets across the country.

Between the fact that the chain didn't want "organic" on our label (initially they were only interested in the gourmet and convenience aspects of our bagged salads) and the fact that organic cropland was hard to come by, it would have been easy at that point to shrug our shoulders and say, "Well, guess we'll just forget the organic part." But we didn't. Those years on the raspberry farm and having a family of our own (our daughter was born in 1990 and our son in 1992), had heightened our passion for growing organically, providing the healthiest food possible for both people and the planet. "Organic" may not yet have taken hold in mainstream America, but we had already become wholeheartedly devoted to giving people an organic choice.

To keep up with the explosive demand, we needed more land and serious farming expertise. We gained them both by partnering first with Mission Ranches in 1995 and Tanimura & Antle four years later, both multigeneration family-run farms in the Salinas Valley. In the decade following that first partnership, Earthbound Farm grew from 800 organic acres to over 25,000. During 2005 alone, the land we farmed organically kept more than 267,000 pounds of toxic pesticides and 8,432,000 pounds of synthetic fertilizers out of the environment and preserved nearly 1,383,000 gallons of petroleum.

We may have started with the humble aspirations of selling a day's crop of raspberries from a rickety table by the roadside, but the choices we made day after day and year after year to trust our intuition and stay true to our values helped us achieve something we never dreamed possible. Millions of people now enjoy the convenience of organic salads, fruits and vegetables, and the earth is a healthier place because of the company we started over twenty years ago. But the journey isn't over yet. Each day we become ever more passionate about bringing Earthbound Farm's mission to fruition: to bring the benefits of organic food to as many people as possible and serve as a catalyst for positive change.

Drew and Myra Goodman

EPILOGUE: *Drew and Myra Goodman started farming in their backyard without an ambitious agenda, but Earthbound Farm's success wound up proving that organic farming was viable on a large scale and could actually feed the world—which was considered a fairytale notion by many at the time. The company is credited with popularizing "spring mix" on the American salad plate as they led the way in prewashed, packaged salad.*

Earthbound Farm is now the largest grower of organic produce in the world, and the Goodmans still lead the thriving business, whose farm-fresh organic salads, fruits and vegetables are available in three-quarters of the supermarkets in the United States, as well as in Canada, Mexico and even Taiwan.

Maintaining a strong connection to its roots, the company still operates a roadside farm stand in Carmel Valley, California, just down the road from the location of the original farm. To learn more about Earthbound Farm, visit www.ebfarm.com.

Dahlynn McKowen

3

ESCAPING THE BOX

Aerodynamically the bumblebee shouldn't be able to fly, but the bumblebee doesn't know that so it goes on flying anyway.

Mary Kay Ash

The Shackmeisters

Hello! My name is Tommy. And yes, I admit, I'm a "Shackmeister" at the Shack Up Inn, Mississippi's oldest B&B (bed and beer), located at Hopson Plantation just outside Clarksdale, Mississippi. Clarksdale is a town internationally known as the birthplace of the Mississippi Delta Blues, the music that spawned rock 'n' roll in everything you hear on the radio today.

I've been asked to share with you the incredible story of the Shack Up Inn's ascent to the top of the cotton field hospitality industry; there is no doubt in my mind that the Hiltons and Hyatts of this world will read and reread this story to glean ideas to help them enter this almost-untapped market.

So as to not disappoint you all, I guess I better pony up some "corporate history" and introduce my fellow Shackmeisters, because Lord knows, I personally can't take the credit for this entrepreneurial chaos and success!

It all started with James Butler, a.k.a. Jimmy D. As owner of Hopson Plantation, Jimmy D decorated his twelve-acre property, complete with the original commissary that over the decades he had filled with an unbelievable collection of artifacts found in the Mississippi Delta. It was here that the Hopson music scene first took root and still lives today. Coined "de master of multitasking," Jimmy D also has a long history in local and worldwide politics, but just between us, this is actually a front for his position as a CIA (Clarksdale-Is-Awesome) operative.

Enter our next Shackmeister, Bill Talbot, whom we call "Mr. Bill." Legend has it that Mr. Bill bought an old four-bay tractor shed from Jimmy D in 1996, then renovated it as his home, using all salvaged materials. Total renovation costs came to $38.62. (Note: This shed would later become the lobby of the Shack Up Inn.) Hailing from the fine isle city of faraway Dublin, Mr. Bill won a whooping total of $26 at the Isle of Capri slot machines and invested it all in offshore banking! Now wealthy and firmly entrenched in full-blown retirement, Mr. Bill is often seen mowing the grass at our fine establishment, in a Forrest Gump–like fashion, completely content with his successes and the turf he tends.

Then in 1997 here I come, Shackmeister #3 (a.k.a. Tommynation), a songwriter from Nashville with a recent hit and a few extra dollars. At the invitation of Jimmy D and Mr. Bill, I moved an old sharecropper's shack to Hopson Plantation and renovated it into a songwriter's retreat. I brought a sense of culture to our business team; as the winner of the No-Bell-Piece prize for my bestselling *Success Is a Six Pack Away* series, I've recently started negotiations with Bob Vila to do a weekly series called "This Old Shack," which will air on CAS (Cadillacs, Airstreams and Shacks), the plantation's own cable channel.

Right from the start it was obvious that a 300-square-foot shack was the perfect size for twenty or so party people, but not quite large enough for two songwriters of the same gender to share. So a second shack was moved in, and the name "Shack Up Inn" became formalized in our ingrained and Southern vernacular.

So there we were, just three guys hanging out and having fun in the old cotton field when tourists found their way out to Hopson and saw our "shackdom" in the making. Then wouldn't you know it, these tourists offered us money—*real money*—to stay in our shack! Who'da thunk it!

Of course we were suddenly faced with the usual problems of starting a hospitality empire: Who's going to clean the toilets and change the sheets during the lunch hour? Who's going to wash the sheets for that matter? Who's going to pick up the Moon Pies? (For you Yankees out there, a Moon Pie is a wonderfully sweet Southern delicacy.) Oh my goodness, the logistics were overwhelming—I'm sure the Hiltons and Hyatts faced similar dilemmas when starting out.

The three of us forged ahead the best we could, and then out of the blue, a third shack became available; all we had to do was move it to the property and fix it up. But we had a little problem; we had spent all of our capital on twelve-pack architecture and six-pack construction renovating the first two shacks! But we weren't going to let a little thing like poverty stand in the way of our somewhat blurred vision of an international shackopoly.

Enter Jim Field, a.k.a. Jeem Blue, a Colorado architect who believed in our sketchy and somewhat unfocused business plan to turn the shacks into a name as well known as the Ritz. Jeem, as you may well ascertain from his name alone, is descended from French nobility, yet his roots run deep in the Mississippi Delta soil. Our fourth Shackmeister, Jeem is, by necessity, a jet-setting, globe-trotting adventurer but is most at home on the porches of the beloved shacks where he unwinds and lives the "good life," much as Hugh Hefner does in Hollywood.

With the influx of Jeem's additional funds, we had three shacks up and running and were going through Moon Pies like crazy! Then we were confronted with something that completely blindsided us; we were offered three *additional* shacks to add to our collection. Can you believe it? How were we going to pay for them? The banking community had yet to see how our unique mixture of shacks and flooded fields would be something people would pay money to see, let alone stay in overnight.

And this brings us to our last Shackmeister, Guy Malvezzi, a.k.a. AK47/Gyrator Man, the all-knowing head of a worldwide shoe conglomerate. Gyrator Man brought keen marketing skills to the shack table. With an ever-present finger on the pulse of the American and worldwide public, he is now brokering a deal that could lead to an upscale international hotel/restaurant chain to be called "McShack Up Inn." With yet another infusion of mind-boggling dollars from our newest partner, we purchased and renovated the three shacks, bringing our total to a six-pack of shacks!

Truly entrepreneurs in spirit and vision, all five of us Shackmeisters have two things in common, the first being an overpowering affection and equally misinformed view of the hospitality industry, and second, possessing an overwhelming appreciation for the Delta Blues! The five of us, cypress prophets all, forged a common mission upon creating the Shack Up Inn to bring the blues home to the cradle and rock our guests in the process! We have six front porches tailor-made for playin' the blues, and there's a piano or guitar or both in every shack, with many of the instruments donated by our guests and left out for everyone to enjoy.

Thanks to a write-up by the *Atlanta Journal Constitution,* the international press soon caught wind of us and, yes sir, business was booming! And those local bankers who turned us down for a loan were now more than glad to help us; we bought the cotton gin on the property that belonged to Jimmy D and his family, but had long ago ceased as a gin. We added five rounded grain "bin rooms" (guest rooms) and created the "Cotton Gin Inn." We're adding five more "bins" to the gin and will soon start transforming the rest of the building into our lobby and gift shop.

It's been a wild and wonderful ride. All this craziness started from the vantage point of fun and music, but took on a life of its own. Mind you, we had to evolve the business and grow with it, too. Along the way we've met some extremely interesting people from around the world, heard some great music and have made new and long-lasting friends.

Now when I go through the shacks and read the guest books, it amazes me that people have such profound experiences here, experiences that they have found no place else. We don't offer hotel rooms where they lay their heads for one night and move on. At the Shack Up Inn, our guests stay in honest-to-God shacks, with an old Coke machine as a refrigerator, memorabilia from decades of Southern culture, orphaned furniture adopted from the side of the road and one of the largest collections of funeral fans in three counties! Guests create their own special memories and develop a keen understanding of the cultural heritage aspects of the Mississippi Delta and a completely unique form of Southern hospitality.

So when you think Sunset Strip or Madison Avenue, think Hilton or Hyatt. But when you think gravel roads, cotton fields and Moon Pies, think of the Shack Up Inn. We have no listed phone number and no signage, so if you want to find us, you've really got to want to find us. This was Gyrator Man's marketing plan. So far it's working.

We hope to see you soon. Your Moon Pie is waiting!

Tommy Polk

[EDITORS' NOTE: T*he ultimate destination for blues and cultural lovers, the Shack Up Inn is definitely a one-of-a-kind tourist destination. To learn more, a trip to their Web site is not to be missed:* www.shackupinn.com. *Guaranteed you'll be ready to pack your bags and head to Mississippi after your on-line visit!*]

Ripples

The best way to predict the future is to invent it.

Alan Kay

Life's an adventure.

If a psychic with a crystal ball had sat me down when I graduated from high school in 1970 and told me, "First you are going to be a scientist. Then you are going to be an attorney, and then you are going to be a publicist," I'd have laughed my silly head off. That was the year I dropped out of college, hopped on a ten-speed bicycle, went cross-country through Canada and then hitchhiked around the country for a year.

I ended up going back to school, where after six years I got one degree, and then two years later another, and then landed a job working for the federal government as a hydrologist in the wilds of central Idaho.

And that's how I found the world of publicity.

I wrote my first news release after getting sick on a little tiny microscopic bug called *Giardia lamblia.* I did some original research with federal funds and discovered that due to inadequate water treatment, there was a small-scale epidemic of *Giardia* going on in the western United States. To publicize the finding and help people deal with the situation, I wrote an article and sent out my very first news release. The first four words of that news release were, *"Don't drink the water!"*

Here's what happened next.

The local newspaper in Salmon, Idaho (circulation 2,700) published the article. I was interviewed by the Associated Press. That made a splash as the article was published in newspapers across the country, drawing attention to the disease and the risks of drinking wild-land water. They christened it "backpacker's disease," and it became pretty widespread knowledge that drinking out of streams and creeks was a risky thing to do.

It took ten years, but the U.S. government eventually passed regulations requiring upgrades to noncommunity water supply systems, and people drinking water from water systems in small towns all over America are now protected at a much higher level. And a couple of other things happened.

Woody Allen wrote a play. The title of it was *Don't Drink the Water.*

A popular light beer company did a commercial that had two very good-looking Hispanic college students talking to one another, and one says to the other, *"You can drink the light beer in America, but don't drink the water."*

And I experienced the exhilarating feeling that comes from sending out a news release that causes ripples in human consciousness and shares knowledge with people from coast to coast.

It was the quest for this feeling that motivated me to create a news service to help people get their words out. I coined the business "Imediafax." I would write news releases, and then I would send them out to custom-targeted media lists. Voila. People get publicity.

It's a remarkable business. You get to work with some of the most creative and brilliant people in the world. It goes way beyond the fact that you can make money. It's all about what happens when you give ideas to others.

I learned that I'm just here to help showcase and share their creative efforts and the fruits of their labor. That's my role in life. There's pleasure in getting to share so many good things in a way that can benefit so many others. In fact, the real satisfaction comes in seeing what happens. Some of the releases result in significant publicity in major media or noteworthy publicity on a national scale. Many of these are of broad general interest while others are industry-specific. Some publicity results in significant financial gain. Sometimes what a client seeks is public knowledge and political action.

My business took several years to create, day-by-day, word-by-word, release-by-release. It's amazing to think that this business captures the best of the collaborative efforts of hundreds, if not thousands, of people. But it does.

And to this day, whenever I send out a news release for a client, I still get that feeling of throwing rocks in the pond and watching the ripples flow.

Paul J. Krupin

EPILOGUE: *Paul J. Krupin is president of Direct Contact PR (formerly IMEDIAFAX: The Internet Media Fax Service). A custom, publicity service, Direct Contact PR sends out over a million news releases each year on behalf of hundreds of inventors, authors and publishing companies. Although he is experienced and works in numerous areas, Krupin's work is most highly regarded in the independent publishing industry, and his expertise and book publicity achievements have been written about in dozens of books.*

A retired federal government scientist and once-upon-a-time attorney, Krupin has been described as a longtime PR guru who has developed sure-fire, proven strategies for getting publicity. He works with individuals, companies and organizations, helping them write effective news releases and copy, then assists in selecting the desired deployment tactic to reach the right media. Krupin also offers a highly personal set of copywriting, consulting and custom-targeted news release distribution services.

Krupin is an author in his own right, with over twenty-five books to his credit, including the book Trash Proof News Releases *(Direct Contact Publishing, 2001). His Web site contains numerous articles and a free download of this book.*

To learn more about Krupin and his company, call 800-457-8746 or visit www.DirectContactPR.com.

Dahlynn McKowen

off the mark.com
by Mark Parisi
I DON'T CARE WHAT ANYONE ELSE SAYS... I DO MY BEST THINKING INSIDE THE BOX...
LITT
www.offthemark.com
ATLANTIC FEATURE ©1998 MARK PARISI
MarkParisi@aol.com
MARK PARISI

It Started with a Sparkle

It takes a lot of courage to show your dreams to someone else.

Erma Bombeck

My parents have always told me that when I was born, I opened my eyes and they sparkled like blue diamonds.

My childhood was filled with colorful, creative days. I spent endless hours transforming lumps of colorful clay into wondrous, creative pieces of jewelry. My bedroom was my first boutique, and my parents were my first customers. I dreamed that someday I would make and sell beautiful, sparkly things to people all over!

I never lost the desire to design unique and wonderful pieces of jewelry and became obsessed with developing innovative techniques. As a teenager, I made tiny collage pins with pictures and bits of fabric and lace. My love of collage inspired me to create an entire collection of brooches from old watch parts, vintage costume jewelry and interesting found objects.

In the early 1990s, I had the opportunity to travel to Europe and work as a fashion model. I spent the daytime hours traveling to castings and bookings, but when the sun went down, I whiled away the hours making jewelry. I often went treasure hunting, scouring Parisian flea markets and antique shops in search of beads and crystals to transform into new treasures. I mixed them with my own hand-sculpted crosses designed from polymer clay and wore the finished pieces to fashion shoots. There I was, amid such beautiful people and beautiful things, but it was my jewelry that often garnered the attention! Many times, the stylists, makeup artists, designers and photographers bought my designs and then asked for more!

When I returned to the States, I made the decision to change careers. I had grown weary of starving myself in order to stay "model thin" and did not feel creatively fulfilled. I began working behind the scenes as a makeup artist and discovered that I was much happier behind the camera than in front of it! I also fell head over heels in love! Alfonso was handsome and goofy, and we laughed about the same corny stuff. He was also an artist, and we liked the same music. I had found my creative match.

While I was passionate about Alfonso, I also remained passionate about designing jewelry. I chose to devote more time to my sculptural jewelry process and created a small work studio in a tiny apartment. Visions of beautiful, sparkly things not only danced in my head, but on it; when I was unable to find the clips that I envisioned to wear in my new short haircut, I simply decided to make my own. I made micro-clips that were designed to be worn in clusters, crystal butterflies and delightful insect silhouettes. I created "anywhere" clips adorned with flowers that could be clipped anywhere from a purse to a ponytail. There were even glittering crystal headbands fashioned from wire and crystal beads. I was so inspired that I stayed up night after night coming up with new ideas. I often wore my designs as I left in the mornings, but frequently returned unadorned. Girls sometimes stopped me as I sauntered along, inquiring about my creations and purchasing them on the spot.

It was Alfonso who suggested that I take my jewelry to some hip boutiques. He was certain that my designs would be a big hit with the trendier crowd who frequented those retail establishments. I was reluctant to do so. *Who would want to buy my quirky designs?* I thought. Nevertheless, Alfonso was not deterred. He created beautiful boxes to showcase my collection, and off he went. When he returned, he had a stack of orders and our little company, Tarina Tarantino Designs, was born.

In August 1998, a high-profile magazine did a feature story on Tarina Tarantino Designs. Soon after, we moved the company out of that tiny, cramped apartment and into a small studio space in West Hollywood. We hired a half-dozen employees and worked many long hours to meet the demand for our collections. Actresses, entertainers and people who simply wanted to feel like movie stars were wearing my wonderful, whimsical creations!

In October 1999, Alfonso and I married after a three-year engagement. This was our opportunity to celebrate everything that we had accomplished as a couple and as business partners. Everything from the cake to the tables to the wedding party was decorated with our designs. It was a beautiful day, and there were sparkling crystals everywhere you looked!

Alfonso and I now have two sparkling daughters, Chloe and Olivia. We have moved the business twice to accommodate our growth and recently opened a gorgeous retail shop on Melrose Avenue in Los Angeles. The creation of Tarina Tarantino Designs has been an amazing journey. Sometimes, I have to pinch myself just to be certain that all of this is real. How fortunate I am to be living the dreams I had when I was just a little girl with sparkling blue eyes!

Tarina Tarantino
As told to Terri Duncan

EPILOGUE: *Tarina Tarantino Designs recently marked its ten-year anniversary. The designer's whimsical collections feature jewelry, hair accessories and belt buckles beautifully crafted from Swarovski crystals, Lucite, wood and semiprecious stones.*

Tarina serves as the company's vice president and designer, and her husband, Alfonso, is president and creative director. In addition to the Tarina Tarantino shop on Melrose Avenue in Los Angeles, California, there is also a boutique in Milan, Italy. For more information or to purchase items from Tarina's numerous collections, visit www.tarinatarantino.com.

Terri Duncan

Monster Ideas

Don't let anybody tell you how long you should take a shower, because you can change the world in a thirty-minute shower.

There's something about the hot water flowing over your head that makes what I call the "good part" and the "absent part" of your brain talk to each other. This is immediately apparent when you break out into song, even though you know you're one of the world's worst singers. It also means that when you stand there with the soap in your hands (maybe a bad visual, but go with me here), you begin to try to reinvent the soap. You think, *I can put this clear soap together with this cream soap . . . I can make a better soap than what's out there today!* Then you think about the packaging, then you look over and you say to yourself, *The shampoo doesn't have very good packaging.* The next thing you know, you imagine walking down the grocery store aisle, reinventing cereal boxes and soups. In your mind, you've become a grocery tycoon overnight while standing in the shower.

From that point, you dream up a cool business idea. Your mind very quickly goes to rapid development—you have a product and you have customers! You turn off the shower and step one foot out onto the bath mat, then suddenly, you can't remember anything you were just thinking about. It's almost as if the window closed and whatever genius you created in the shower can never be duplicated, because you can't open that session back up. Many times you can't even remember what you were trying to figure out in the first place.

Some of you are skeptical, so I have a test for you: Have you ever been halfway through your shower and you ask yourself, *Did I wash my hair?* If you're like me, you bring your fingers up to hair and rub to see if your hair is squeaky clean. Unsure, you dump some more shampoo on your hand and do the process over again, even though if you think about the amount of effort it takes to wash your hair, there's absolutely no way you should forget whether you washed your hair or not.

This is an active example that your mind, body and spirit are all moving into your subconscious where you not only invent new things, but you solve problems and potentially create opportunities or big ideas. My point is that you have to pay attention to your subconscious. Learn to focus on your idea and maintain that idea long enough so when you "get out of the shower," you're able to capture your idea on a nearby pad of paper.

I have another test for you. Do you ever head home from work when, all of a sudden, you realize you're in your driveway? You remember leaving your office, maybe you remember getting into your car, but you completely lost a thirty-five-minute commute. This is another example of learning to pay attention to your subconscious. I suggest keeping a pad of paper in your car, also—here again, immediately write down your daydreaming and thinking so you don't lose it.

For me, another example of listening to my subconscious occurs when I'm reading nonfiction; I find my mind aggressively solving problems in the background while reading an inspirational story. When I'm reading that book, I write ideas—for example, solving business problems—right in the gutter of the book. After making my notation, I turn the page down. As soon as I've finished with the book, I go back and copy the ideas I have written down.

And the last place my subconscious is working overtime is when I'm sleeping. And yes, I do keep yet another pad of paper next to my bed, ready to catch my dreams and ideas. This leads me to a small, but important, life story:

Going back to Monster.com's humble beginnings, which began in 1994, I had an ad agency, Adion, which specialized in human resource communications, specifically recruiting and retaining of talent. Our success was built around the concept of creating "big ideas" for our clients. The idea was to come up with a big idea (many times with our client), and everything else was just the support to get that big idea done. One day, a client said, "No more big ideas. I want a monster idea." Hence, the beginning of our "monster" concept was born.

I've always loved technology, anything that would make our business more efficient. When the monster idea was requested by our client, I was just learning about bulletin board systems—BBSs—a precursor to the World Wide Web as we know it today.

I actually had a dream about a monster idea, a BBS (bulletin board) for jobs. I woke up at 4:30 in the morning, and with a combination of these concepts, my dream was that I created a monster bulletin board, calling it the "Monster Board." Paying attention to my subconscious, I went to a coffee shop and wrote down much of the interface and the concepts that are still used at Monster today. But by April 1994, we recognized it wasn't going to be a BBS that we were going to build—it was going to be a "mosaic site" (now known as a Web site).

After we had been in business about four months, and business was really a relative term in this instance, we were selling just a few job postings for twenty-five dollars each. Business got to the point that we needed to do something dramatic, so we sent out a press release to about a thousand different media outlets. The response was tremendous. This extra marketing effort was the turning point and the real beginning of our Monster brand.

People always ask me about the name "Monster." I think it's probably the single most important decision made in the life of this company, because by calling ourselves "Monster," people can remember it. This was key. The idea that the word "Monster" equals jobs or careers is something that's evolved over time. But the fact that when you sit down at your PC and you can't think about where to go, and into your mind pops, *Hey, I'm going to go check out Monster.* This one-word trigger is probably the single most important driver of Monster's success.

The next real big event in the company's history was in 1995. I entered into an agreement to sell Monster to TMP Worldwide, a Yellow Pages and recruitment company. Andy McKelvey, founder and CEO of TMP, and I came up with the concept of bringing my ad agency into the TMP fold and creating a new division with the Monster Board as the centerpiece. The new division was called "TMP Interactive."

The next big moment for Monster—kind of a defining moment—was when we decided in January 1999 to rename the division "Monster.com" and to advertise on the Super Bowl. Our "When I Grow Up" commercial, which was not that popular during the game, ended up being one of the most popular commercials of the entire year.

Monster.com is now in twenty-five countries, and millions upon millions of job seekers use the site. There are over a million job postings and over 300,000 employers. Through the years, Monster.com has become the largest and the most popular job search and career management site on the Internet.

If I can leave you with one good piece of entrepreneurial advice, it's this: listen to your subconscious, learn to capture its power, and maybe, just maybe, you'll be the one to come up with the world's next monster idea!

Jeff Taylor

EPILOGUE: *As founder of Monster.com, Jeff Taylor is now focusing his efforts on helping millions of baby boomers via his next big idea—"Eons."*

It is predicted that upwards of 77 million baby boomers will retire from their official occupations over the next few years, leaving their world open to new possibilities and second careers. Recognizing this emerging demographic, Taylor created Eons, a Web business targeted at the fifty- to one-hundred-plus age group. A combination of megatrends and the perfect storm, Eons is a new revolution of the baby boomer generation and the Internet, all converging around a big idea.

"My idea was to create a challenge-brand that puts Eons in the center of activity and excitement, to challenge and help people live to be one hundred, or to die trying," shared Taylor.

To learn more about Taylor and Eons, please visit www.Eons.com.

Dahlynn McKowen

Look Mom, No Hands!

"No one's going to pull you up by your bootstraps. You'd better figure out what you're going to do with the rest of your life."

These words, spoken to me by my husband, Ron, in 1993 after two years into my hand disability, triggered the turning point in my battle with my hands. But when he offered his advice, it was hard to imagine any kind of future, let alone trying to put on a pair of boots without thumbs or hands to help!

At age thirty-six, I had developed de Quervain's disease. de Quervain's disease is a debilitating hand malady (not really a disease, but the medical profession refers to it as such) that can be triggered by many things, such as a hand injury due to a serious fall. But in the majority of cases, it's akin to carpal tunnel syndrome or repetitive hand injury and mainly affects the thumbs. Symptoms include burning pain, numbness, tingling and loss of grip strength. I had all of these symptoms; losing the use of both my hands and thumbs shook me to my very core and completely changed every aspect of my life.

It was in 1991, while I was working as a supervising accountant for a software company, that the de Quervain's disease set in. Back then, there was little or no protection for workers who could no longer type on their computers due to tendonitis and carpal tunnel, let alone de Quervain's disease. Due to my excruciating pain, I asked my staff to do more data entry work; I was terminated by the company for not being a "team player." In retrospect, losing that job was the best thing that could have happened to me. My doctor agreed, and he immediately put me on disability.

I had been working steadily since the age of fourteen (after-school jobs during my youth, full-time work upon graduation) and to be told that I could no longer work made me both giddy and scared. I was giddy because I knew my hands would have a chance to rest and, I hoped to heal, but I was also scared because I had always worked and was accustomed to a certain level of income, as well as a personal sense of accomplishment by earning my keep.

I took the doctor's advice and spent two years on disability, attempting to heal my hands through surgery, medication and physical therapy. The surgery was not successful and, in fact, made my right hand worse. One of the few good things I can say about my two years off was that I attended nearly eighty San Francisco Giants baseball games. (I'm a big fan of my local team!)

In 1993, that fateful year when Ron told me to pull myself up by my bootstraps, a neighbor shared that he had seen a computer speech recognition demonstration at a trade show—the software was called DragonDictate (today it's called NaturallySpeaking). He thought I could possibly use this new technology to get back to work. Speech recognition software transforms the spoken word into the written word using a PC. It's a very complex, behind-the-scenes technology, and not intuitive to use the first time.

With a little detective work, I tracked down the software

company who created Dragon—formally ScanSoft but now known as Nuance—and learned as much as I could about the product. I was very surprised by what I learned, but equally disappointed to find out that there were no companies dedicated to teaching this very intricate and complicated software system. It was then that I formulated a plan to once again become a productive member of society.

Back in those days, speech recognition software only worked in DOS and required a $5,000 computer on which to run it. It was "discrete speech," meaning that you had to put a pause in between each and every word. But as soon as I saw the technology, I knew I had to start a speech recognition training company to teach others like me to use this very elaborate software; I wanted to be the first in the industry to do so.

I was pretty sure my workers' compensation company would want to lock me up in the funny farm if I told them I wanted to launch a speech recognition training company, so I thought of a slightly different plan to get me going in the right direction: I proposed starting my own accounting business instead. After all, I had been in the accounting field for nearly twenty years and also had a small bookkeeping business on the side, so my request wouldn't be so strange.

Even though the workers' compensation people were skeptical at first, they approved my back-to-work plan. I built a custom computer with enough memory to handle the Dragon software, then taught myself how to use the software. After figuring out the nuances of Dragon and creating a custom training program and manual, I launched my company in October 1993. I did not let the workers' comp company down; I started that accounting business, and it was very successful. After six months, the workers' compensation company deemed me to be "rehabilitated" and cut me loose from their program.

I immediately closed my accounting business and concentrated on my original plan. With a wing and a prayer and no money down, I leased office space in San Mateo, California. I founded the company, calling it Zephyr-TEC. I am often asked how I came up with the name for the company. I wasn't sure what to call my new business, and my husband suggested that folks name their businesses after their kids. Well, we had no children, just our cat named Zephyr. "Zephyr" is the Greek word for a gentle west wind. So, I decided to call the company Zephyr-TEC, with TEC standing for "Training, Evaluation and Consulting." Zephyr-TEC became the first company of its kind in the nation, solely dedicated to training injured people how to use a computer by voice so they can keep working.

Starting small, I hired the company's first two employees in 1994 (and one of them, Page Filson, is still with the company today). This was the mid-1990s, when computers were just starting to be used by nearly everyone in the workplace on a daily basis, so I was firmly established in the speech recognition industry when the epidemic of carpal tunnel and repetitive hand injuries hit Corporate America in the late 1990s.

Things have come a long way since 1993, for the technology, my company and me. The technology is light-years ahead of where it was when I started, and continuing development ensures it will meet the needs of tomorrow's workers. My company has returned thousands of people to their computer jobs, helping to minimize the impact of these devastating hand and arm injuries on their lives.

Personally, my life has become much richer as I see those with far worse disabilities than mine making their way back to work with the help of our company's training programs. I continue to use speech recognition to this day and cannot imagine my life without it. So thanks for the sage advice and helping me with my bootstraps, Ron. I couldn't have done this without you!

Renee Griffith

EPILOGUE: *With its headquarters based in California, Zephyr-TEC is the largest dedicated training company for computer speech recognition software in the country. With several offices throughout the United States, the company offers its training programs in every corner of the nation via its eLearnSpeech™, which consists of live, one-on-one online training. And training in speech recognition isn't just for those with disabilities, as many clients are those who would rather talk to their computers than type.*

As CEO and founder, Renee Griffith's deep sense of commitment in helping others is evident by the people who work for her, many of whom had hand injuries when they joined the company. With the many awards bestowed upon her company, Griffith continues to be a well-regarded leader in this very technical industry. To learn more about Griffith and her company, visit www.Zephyr-TEC.com.

On a personal note, in 2002, I lost the use of my dominant hand and thumb, and have only limited use of my wrist, arm and shoulder due to a very serious fall. Griffith and the Zephyr-TEC staff trained me in Dragon NaturallySpeaking; the majority of this book was written using this speech recognition software.

Renee—if it wasn't for you and Zephyr-TEC, I wouldn't have been able to coauthor this book, or maintain my livelihood as a freelance writer and author. Thanks for helping me with my bootstraps!

Dahlynn McKowen

Mother Knows Best

When Al Gore invented the Internet, I'm sure eBay was what he had in mind.

I, unfortunately, stumbled into selling on eBay only to shut my mother up about this eBay "hokeypokey" nonsense. She insisted that selling on eBay would be good for my storefront furniture and pool table business. So there I was at 1:30 A.M. in October 2001, staring at my computer screen with just eleven minutes and thirty-six seconds remaining in my first-ever auction. My $1,950 pool table had a high bid of $165. I figured I'd just lost a bundle—but at least I would prove to my dear mother that eBay may work for garage sale junk, not for a "real" business such as mine.

Depressed, I continued staring at my computer screen. I hit the F5 key to refresh the screen and there was finally another bid—wow, $170. I hit F5 two minutes later and, holy cow, it was now $400, enough to cover the shipping costs! With four minutes remaining, I began witnessing the magic of eBay every time I tapped F5; $1,200, then $1,825, then $2,000, then $2,175! When the auction time expired, I tapped F5 one more time. Final bid: $2,250—more than I would have sold it for in my store!

It had become clear to me, not to mention many economic experts, that the eBay juggernaut was, and continues, on a very successful path. Between the first and second quarters of 2003, eBay increased its earnings by 92 percent. Meg Whitman, eBay's CEO, missed her prediction that the company would be doing $3 billion in sales by 2005; they exceeded their target more than a year early! In 2003 there were 80 million members on eBay, and by the end of 2004 there were over 115 million registered members. I am not alone in sincerely believing that the greatest success stories on eBay have yet to be written.

When I started selling on eBay there were a few good how-to books, but no proven models for success. So I built my own model that at one point yielded my eBay online stores close to a million dollars a month in real, tangible sales. This didn't happen as easily as you may think. I had gained my share of experience in sales long before Pierre Omidyar founded eBay.

My first real job was selling kitchen knives for a direct-sales company during my senior year at Tulane University in New Orleans. Because my friends couldn't afford knives, I sold them to my professors, then to their friends, and finally to most of the New Orleans Saints football team. That first year I had become the number-one sales rep in a company with 30,000 sales reps. I decided to skip law school and joined the company as a manager. Ten years and thousands of paring knives later, I left to work for an Internet start-up.

In March 2000, after two years of long hours and little pay building our Internet company, just as bankers were lined up and our IPO was ready, the dot-com bubble burst. Our company crashed, taking with it my hundreds of thousands of shares of stock options. At age thirty-three, I found myself out of work and $80,000 in debt. I needed a job quick.

I listened to motivational tapes about running a home-based business; exciting, but most of their "opportunities" were unrealistic. While I liked the idea of a home-based business, I settled on the reality of a small retail furniture and pool table store. I have never been a nine-to-five type of person, but I needed a steady income.

As I mentioned earlier, my first foray into the world of eBay was offering one of my overstock pool tables simply to satisfy my mother. That first success did not cause me to jump in with both feet. Initially, what I thought I had found was a neat sales channel for unloading extra inventory.

As I slowly began offering more items for auction, I ran into some unforeseen problems. Throughout January 2002, most of my auctions were getting shut down. After working with some of eBay's legal and policy folks, I corrected the problems and no more of my auctions were shut down. A couple of months later, I found myself at eBay's corporate headquarters as one of the specially selected sellers who periodically are invited to provide management with suggestions for improvement. What I saw and learned while at their San Jose "Ivy League" campus made me realize that eBay was a very big deal. The following week I closed my furniture store. I had just become one of the 175,000 people who were using eBay as their full-time source of income. I was riding eBay full steam ahead.

On eBay, the entrepreneurial spirit of the American Dream became the reality of a worldwide opportunity. Here, I had instant access to 115 million potential customers (and counting) without spending a dime on advertising. They hadn't taught me that in business school. And because eBay wasn't a business school subject, no successful eBay business models existed. To the benefit of small-business owners like me who possess the drive, energy and a bit of business know-how, eBay turned the traditional business model upside down, allowing us to compete successfully against the big guys.

What I learned in my eBay crash course provided me with a business model that allowed me to become extremely successful, yet most of what I learned is really basic business strategies:

- If you want to succeed, you begin by setting realistic goals. You then make the decisions and implement the actions that will advance you toward those goals.
- Competition forces you to be more competitive. Success means staying ahead of the curve, changing strategies as your competition catches up.
- You must venture into the unknown; that alone will yield great benefits and rewards. Very few people are truly innovative, and very few possess the courage to try new things.
- Accept responsibility for the outcome of things over which you have control. Mistakes are inevitable, and you will make your share. The key is to learn from them and move on.

My final advice to you? Make a beeline for your computer and go into business for yourself. The framework is there, compliments of eBay. Use it to make your dreams your reality!

Adam Ginsberg
As told to Ken McKowen

EPILOGUE: *Adam Ginsberg discovered eBay in 2001, and just a year after he started selling his wares, eBay named him their number-one new seller (quite a feat, considering there are over 600,000 sellers on the site at any given moment). Ginsberg spent three years as an eBay "Titanium Powerseller" and personally sold over $20 million online during that time.*

An expert in home-based businesses, Ginsberg strives to help others generate income on eBay. "My commitment is to teach others how to maximize their potential on eBay and online auctions—whether it's to earn extra cash or to have a full-time business that you can operate from home," shared Ginsberg. He established Ginsberg Consulting, designed to provide educational seminars, home-study programs, software and related materials available for purchase, all of which help accelerate the eBay sales learning process.

In 2005, Ginsberg released How to Buy, Sell and Profit on eBay *(HarperCollins), a book full of expert tips and personal secrets on how to succeed using the nation's top Internet selling site. He is also a much-sought-after speaker and media expert.*

To learn more about Adam Ginsberg, please visit www.adamginsberg.com.

Ken McKowen

Reprinted with permission of Mark Parisi and Off The Mark ©2004.

The Cave Collector

If we could sell our experiences for what they cost us, we'd all be millionaires.

Abigail Van Buren

I had been given yet another new nickname, the "Mother Lode Mole." This moniker was bestowed upon me by a San Francisco Bay Area television reporter during a feature story about my cavern business, based in the foothills of the great Sierra Nevada. As a cave collector, I was used to it. Another television reporter shared with viewers that I had the "pale look of a shut-in." Honestly, it doesn't bother me one bit. I love living my life underground, exploring Mother Nature's magnificent caves and sharing it all with the public.

Recently, again in front of television cameras, I tried to explain my collection of four public show caves and a gold mine by saying, "It's better than collecting stamps." With apologies to all philatelists, for me, being a "cave entrepreneur" is the perfect marriage of hobby and career.

I find that many life-altering events result from small actions and chance meetings, and my life is no exception.

When I was just fifteen years old, I was in the school library when a book, *The Darkness Beneath the Earth,* caught my eye. My life forever changed when I reached for that book, for it revealed the fascinating, mysterious world of cavern exploration. I was hooked.

I was seventeen years old the first summer I worked in Kings Canyon National Park, located in the southern Sierra Nevada. During the summers of 1956 and 1957, while selling groceries and pumping gas at Cedar Grove Village, I was irresistibly drawn to nearby Boyden Cavern, a public show cave, and Church Cave, which was wild, untamed and closed to the public. I became acquainted with one of the guides who worked at Boyden Cavern, and he and I struck out to explore the whole Boyden/ Church cave system. After that, all of my free time was spent in the exciting pursuit of exploring these wonderful caves. Spelunking late into the night and sometimes into the early morning hours, I became an accomplished explorer of the dark and mysterious world I had so avidly read about.

After years in the United States Air Force, and later in the computer/semiconductor business, I still spent much of my leisure time exploring caves. One weekend in 1972, I sat at a Boyden Cavern picnic bench enjoying a cool beer and resting after a long caving trip. The owner of the business, who was having a bad day, came out and stood looking at the Kings River rushing by. He spewed, "I hate tourists, this canyon and the cave! For two bits I'd sell the whole thing!" I picked up a quarter that was on the table and tossed it to him. He looked at it and then at me and said, "Well, we could talk about it." I knew I had to buy it, even though it would require me to quit my safe nine-to-five job, sell everything I owned, including a house with a swimming pool and an airplane. And I had to convince my wife she would enjoy life in the mountains with an uncertain income. I did so without reservation. I knew it was absolutely the right thing to do.

My introduction to self-employment was an amazing educational experience. I took over the operation of Boyden Cavern during the Fourth of July weekend, the busiest time of the summer season. I had to quickly learn how to juggle the work of keeping generator equipment and everything else running (no power company there), and serving the throngs of happy holiday visitors. At the end of the day, I reflected on the fact that I just spent an entire day showing my beautiful cavern to appreciative visitors, and I also got to take a box of cash home and count it! Work. Take home money. Have a good time. I was going to like being an entrepreneur.

Successfully running a seasonal cave business gave me the confidence to add to the collection, first with Moaning Cavern in 1977, then California Cavern in 1980, and Black Chasm Cavern in 2000, all of which are located in the Sierra Nevada foothills. Not being content with running just cavern tours, I leased Sutter Gold Mine in 2001, a modern mine that had recently been closed, with the mining equipment still inside. This addition allowed me to show visitors the difference between nature's amazing limestone creations filled with arrays of stalactites and other crystalline formations, and the underground labyrinth of the gold mine, which was created by heavy equipment and human sweat.

During the early years, I took particular notice of the extreme curiosity of our daily visitors: "Where does that go?" or "What about other passages in the cave?" or "Has all of this cave been explored?" were common questions they asked about the off-limit sections of the tours. That's when I realized there were a lot of inexperienced, would-be adventurers who would love to go exploring the mysterious passages and chambers of my caves, testing their ability to conquer fears of darkness and tight places.

In 1980, with the purchase of California Cavern, my entrepreneurial skills kicked in when I developed the world's first regularly scheduled "wild cave" exploration trips for the general public. The endeavor was so successful that I added another wild cave trip at Moaning Cavern, this time including a very attention-getting 165-foot rope descent. "The Rappel" was the first such true mountaineering-style rope descent ever offered to novice visitors. This rappel was not anything like an amusement park ride; it was real, just like rappels that cavers and mountaineers do, utilizing the same equipment and techniques. I trusted that with outstanding, well-trained personnel and equipment this type of activity could be made available to anyone looking for a truly authentic adventure. I was right. It also attracted an avalanche of television and news reports that resulted in even more visitors to the caverns.

I take great pleasure in offering the public a range of adventures. Thousands of visitors enjoy fascinating walks on lighted trails, crawling through tight passages filled with mud, rafting across deep underground lakes and hanging from the rappel while experiencing the incredible beauty of my underground world. I enjoy watching ordinary people do extraordinary things, things they didn't think they could do.

My love of being a cave collector has taken me around the world. Besides exploring other caves, I am a sought-after speaker and consultant on cave management and development. I am a director and past president of the National Caves Association and first vice president of the International Show Caves Association. I formed Sierra Nevada Recreation Corporation in 1977 and have been active in both the environmental and historical preservation of my five properties, one of which is designated a National Natural Landmark, and another a California State Historical Landmark. I take extreme pride in what I do, but more important, I thoroughly enjoy what I do! And all it took was one book to change the course of my life. I hope the same for you.

Stephen Fairchild

[EDITORS' NOTE: *To learn more about Stephen Fairchild and his five underground adventure caves, please visit* www.caverntours.com *or call 209-736-2708, toll-free 866-762-2837.*]

4

SUCCESSFUL PARTNERSHIPS

Two heads are better than one.

Polish proverb

Two Guys, Three Buckets

If I have a thousand ideas and only one turns out to be good, I am satisfied.

Alfred Nobel

Picture the first day of business for 1-800-DENTIST: two guys sitting on upside-down, five-gallon plastic buckets, waiting for the phone, which was on a third upside-down bucket, to ring. Quite the image for what would become the nation's largest dentist referral service, huh?

Back in those days, there was no money to waste on furniture, as my partner Gary Saint Denis and I had marshaled about $10,000 in start-up capital from very trusting relatives. It was early 1986, and we had spent the last six months driving all over Los Angeles trying to convince dentists to join our new patient matching service. We talked to hundreds of them. Finally, by June, we had managed to wrangle eighteen members.

I had been a junior copywriter at an advertising agency, and Gary a stockbroker, before we started 1-800-DENTIST. We had an idea, a phone number and no money, only a desire to work for ourselves and still eat lunch out every day. Looking back, having no cash was a huge advantage. Throwing money at a problem is seldom the best answer and often prevents you from making the key discoveries that only come from constraints. And this theory even applied to our office space; we had no private offices for the first three years. A little claustrophobic at times, our forced closeness helped us refine every aspect of our operation. But we did eat lunch out every day, giving us the opportunity to quietly analyze the business, and also flirt with the waitresses!

So how did we manage with no money? Simple. In order to fund the growth of the business, when a dentist would join the service, we would have them pay us the first and last month's membership, like an apartment lease. This gave us the cash flow to buy increased advertising each month, so that we could afford to keep adding more dentists. It was like a perpetual-motion machine.

In the first years of the business, when Gary and I would drive around the Los Angeles area meeting with dentists, we would occasionally pass roofers working on top of a building. Gary would say to me, "At least we're not working with hot tar." That became our mantra through the tough times, when we didn't know if we were going to make it. It kept us optimistic, remembering that we were lucky to be entrepreneurs in America, taking our shot.

One of the most important aspects to launching our business was to create a company where we wanted to go to work every day. As such, as our company grew, we made it a point to create a casual, friendly, open environment for our employees, and have always related very personally with them. The remarkable thing was that this design, which was more of a personal goal, turned out to be one of the cornerstones of our business model. Today, 1-800-DENTIST is a twenty-four-hour, seven-day-a-week operation; thousands of calls from throughout the country are received each day at our Los Angeles center and are answered by actual people, not machines. But mind you, it's not a boiler-room environment of a large call center; the cubicles have lots of space (and real chairs, now!), and the operators enjoy great views from the windows and also music, which is played throughout the building. We also pay for their parking and health benefits, host games for extra cash bonuses, have monthly dress-up days, have a massage therapist on staff and much, much more!

We definitely encourage an open, fun and warm atmosphere among the staff, and this attitude is reflected to our customers when they call. We found that when people are looking for a dentist, they often have tremendous apprehension about the process, operating somewhere between fearful and terrified. The fact is, it can be hard to choose a dentist, because in most cases there's no way of assessing their clinical skills prior to a visit. But most people put off a trip to the dentist because they're expecting an unpleasant experience. So when they call 1-800-DENTIST and hear a friendly and compassionate voice, it puts them at ease and makes them more comfortable with the dentists we recommend. When we started our company, we had some inkling about the importance of hiring and retaining well-trained and friendly call center operators, but the ripple effect of their job happiness and how they greet and help our customers rewarded us tenfold. Matter of fact, I can proudly state that this is the essence of our success.

No one can tell you what will succeed when you start your business. You have to follow your passion and trust your gut. Most people, including the general manager at my former ad agency, told us at the beginning that 1-800-DENTIST was a dumb idea. Proving them wrong became a great motivator. A few years ago I was meeting with a venture capitalist to raise money for a separate business project, and to give him background, I described how the 1-800-DENTIST business worked. He mistakenly thought I was pitching him on starting what was already my existing business. He exclaimed, "That would never work!" I explained that it was already a booming multimillion-dollar business, and then ended the meeting, thanking him for letting me know so quickly how useless he would be as an advisor.

To this day, I try never to discourage someone from starting a business, even if I think the design is flawed or the idea goofy. You can waste years trying to figure out the perfect execution of your business idea and raise enough capital to absorb every shock. You'll be wrong. Get started. Take action. Run lean. Have fun.

Back to that very first day, with us two guys sitting on those buckets. By 6:00 P.M., the phone had rung fifty times. *Hey,* we thought, *what we told the dentists would happen might actually come true. Should we buy chairs?* Nah, let's get a couple more buckets.

Fred Joyal

EPILOGUE: *Fred Joyal is the CEO and cofounder of 1-800-DENTIST, a branch of parent company "Futuredontics." As the largest dental referral service in the nation, over 2.5 million people contact 1-800-DENTIST each year to find a screened member dentist.*

Joyal is also the on-air spokesperson for 1-800-DENTIST, having appeared in over forty television commercials, print and video news releases. His boy-next-door looks, charming smile and soothing delivery of the company's message has shepherded many a dentist-weary soul to call 1-800-DENTIST and make an appointment.

To learn more about Fred Joyal and 1-800-DENTIST, please visit www.1800dentist.com.

Dahlynn McKowen

The Taste of Success

Enthusiasm is the yeast that raises the dough.

Paul J. Meyer

It was the summer of 1965. The music of the Beatles and the Beach Boys could be heard from the speakers of newly minted Mustangs and T-Birds. Lyndon Johnson was in the White House, and the New York World's Fair was offering a hope-filled but commercialized glance into the future.

It was that very future I was concerned about. I graduated from high school at age seventeen and had dreams of becoming a doctor. The problem was that I couldn't afford my dream; my job at the local hardware store paid minimum wage, a mere $1.25 an hour. For me, a college education seemed as far-flung as the prospect of a man walking on the moon.

It was a typically hot and humid day at my family's home in Bridgeport, Connecticut, when the phone rang. Dr. Peter Buck, a family friend, called to announce that he had changed jobs and was moving his family to Armonk, New York, only forty miles away. It was time for celebration, indeed, for it had been almost a year since we had seen Dr. Buck and his family.

Plans were quickly made for a reunion. It was on that fateful Sunday afternoon in July 1965, during a barbeque at the Bucks' new home, that Dr. Buck and I would forge a business relationship that would forever change the landscape of the fast-food industry.

The more I thought about college, the more I wondered about how I could find the money. As we pulled into the Bucks' driveway, it occurred to me that perhaps I could ask Dr. Buck for some advice. *Maybe he would loan me the money,* I thought to myself. After all, Dr. Buck had known me for half my life. Knowing my parents couldn't afford to pay for college, and once he heard how badly I wanted to go to college, there was a good chance that he would offer to help. So I asked him.

"I think you should open a submarine sandwich shop," was his response.

What? What an odd thing to say to a seventeen-year-old kid, I thought. But before I could respond or express my surprise, I heard myself say, "How does it work?"

Dr. Buck explained the submarine sandwich business. He said that all one had to do was to rent a small store, build a counter, buy some food and open for business. Customers would come in, put money on the counter and then I would have enough to pay for college. To Dr. Buck, it was just as simple as that, and if I was willing to do it, he was willing to be my partner.

As my family was preparing to return home later that day, Dr. Buck pulled out his checkbook and wrote me a check for one thousand dollars, his investment in our new venture.

On the drive back home, little did I know that if I succeeded in opening a submarine sandwich shop, I would accomplish more than funding my college education. Success would mean adventure and excitement on a nonstop roller-coaster ride that would eventually be called SUBWAY restaurants. Success also meant hard work and perseverance that eventually would lead to financial independence and everything that comes with it, not just for me, but also for thousands of other people associated with the SUBWAY brand around the world.

Fred DeLuca

EPILOGUE: *Fred DeLuca was born in Brooklyn, New York, in 1947 to Carmela and Salvatore DeLuca. For the first several years of his life, they lived in the humble, low-rent, basement apartment of a two-family house—something newlyweds could afford. When he was five, the DeLuca family moved to the Bronx to a new development, which everyone called "the projects." "It was public housing, and for us, it was a step up," says DeLuca.*

Carmela and Salvatore were a hard-working couple who instilled in Fred the value of an education. His mother not only told him how important it was to go to school, she also gave him the confidence to believe that he could graduate from high school, and college, too. "When we began SUBWAY in 1965, I had no money, no collateral and no business savvy. I was simply a seventeen-year-old kid who needed to find a way to pay for his college education," reflects DeLuca.

Recently, the SUBWAY restaurant chain celebrated its fortieth anniversary and has achieved many milestones. It is the world's largest submarine sandwich chain, with more than 25,000 restaurants in eighty-three countries. In fact, the SUBWAY® chain operates more locations in the United States, Canada and Australia than McDonald's does.

Numerous awards and accolades have been bestowed upon Fred DeLuca, the SUBWAY chain and its thousands of franchisees. The SUBWAY chain has earned a reputation for offering a healthier alternative to traditionally fatty fast food, and its name and products have been featured in countless newspaper and magazine articles, and on television and radio news programs.

DeLuca is proud of the hard work and accomplishments of the many members of the SUBWAY family. "It is our mission to provide the tools and knowledge to empower entrepreneurs to successfully compete in the QSR (quick service restaurant) industry worldwide. We take pride in serving each other, our customers and our communities, and we know that our success depends on the initiatives we take individually and on our ability to work as a team."

It has indeed been a roller-coaster ride for Fred DeLuca. He travels extensively to meet with SUBWAY franchisees around the world and went to Washington, D.C., to help launch the SUBWAY F.R.E.S.H. Steps Childhood Obesity Prevention initiative, a multimillion-dollar public awareness advertising campaign that highlights the importance of taking steps to make healthier choices and lead active lives. Most recently, DeLuca was inducted into the International Franchise Association's Hall of Fame and was honored with an invitation to carry the Olympic Torch while it traveled through Brooklyn, New York, the city of his birth. Not bad for a seventeen-year-old kid from "the projects!"

Dahlynn McKowen

READER/CUSTOMER CARE SURVEY

CFCG

We care about your opinions! Please take a moment to fill out our online Reader Survey at **http://survey.hcibooks.com**. As a **"THANK YOU"** you will receive a **VALUABLE INSTANT COUPON** towards future book purchases as well as a **SPECIAL GIFT** available only online! Or, you may mail this card back to us and we will send you a copy of our exciting catalog with your valuable coupon inside.

First Name ________ MI. ________ Last Name ________

Address ________ City ________

State ________ Zip ________ Email ________

1. Gender
❒ Female ❒ Male

2. Age
❒ 8 or younger
❒ 9-12 ❒ 13-16
❒ 17-20 ❒ 21-30
❒ 31+

3. Did you receive this book as a gift?
❒ Yes ❒ No

4. Annual Household Income
❒ under $25,000
❒ $25,000 - $34,999
❒ $35,000 - $49,999
❒ $50,000 - $74,999
❒ over $75,000

5. What are the ages of the children living in your house?
❒ 0 - 14 ❒ 15+

6. Marital Status
❒ Single ❒ Married
❒ Divorced ❒ Widowed

7. How did you find out about the book?
(please choose one)
❒ Recommendation
❒ Store Display
❒ Online
❒ Catalog/Mailing
❒ Interview/Review

8. Where do you usually buy books?
(please choose one)
❒ Bookstore
❒ Online
❒ Book Club/Mail Order
❒ Price Club (Sam's Club, Costco's, etc.)
❒ Retail Store (Target, Wal-Mart, etc.)

9. What subject do you enjoy reading about the most?
(please choose one)
❒ Parenting/Family
❒ Relationships
❒ Recovery/Addictions
❒ Health/Nutrition
❒ Christianity
❒ Spirituality/Inspiration
❒ Business Self-help
❒ Women's Issues
❒ Sports

10. What attracts you most to a book?
(please choose one)
❒ Title
❒ Cover Design
❒ Author
❒ Content

TAPE IN MIDDLE; DO NOT STAPLE

NO POSTAGE
NECESSARY
IF MAILED
IN THE
UNITED STATES

BUSINESS REPLY MAIL

FIRST-CLASS MAIL PERMIT NO 45 DEERFIELD BEACH, FL

POSTAGE WILL BE PAID BY ADDRESSEE

Chicken Soup for the Entrepreneur's Soul
3201 SW 15th Street
Deerfield Beach, FL 33442-9875

FOLD HERE

Comments

Do you have your own Chicken Soup story
that you would like to send us?
Please submit at: **www.chickensoup.com**

Beer Goggles

"Beer goggles" is an old slang term referring to how much better things (usually members of the opposite sex) look after a couple of brews. You might say that Gambrinus, the patron saint of beer, strapped a healthy pair of goggles on us when we embarked on our journey to take Realbeer.com from a mere vision to a success.

I met my future business partner and cofounder of Realbeer.com, Pat Hagerman, online. You could call it the first business-related Internet blind date in history. But I'm jumping ahead; let me explain how it happened.

Among the first people I'd shown my Realbeer.com idea to were the owners of the Riverside Brewing Company, located in Riverside, California. I shared my plan with this father-and-son team and boasted Realbeer.com would be the online community and publication for promoting import and specialty beers. Unsure of me and this crazy Internet idea, they asked another member of the family, an engineer who sometimes used the Internet (this was back in 1994, so even this limited use qualified him as an expert), to check out my Web site. That man was Pat Hagerman.

After checking out the site, Pat realized that I was real and became intrigued by my idea. A beer enthusiast himself, he understood the potential of what I was trying to do. He immediately e-mailed me, asking if I was looking for investment. I sensed a shared passion for both beer and the Internet and suggested we meet in person to discuss the idea—over beers, of course. Two meetings at the San Francisco pub, Connecticut Yankee, and three cocktail napkins later, we had our business plan and made a commitment to create a company together. Our heads were spinning with the sheer audacity of what we'd decided to do.

Years of successfully growing ad agencies had prepared me for my role as an entrepreneur. Pat was young, single and liked the excitement that building a company from the ground up offered. We quit well-paying jobs to embark on the American Dream of building our own business and being our own bosses. The beer goggles were working perfectly, and our future looked bright.

As we dove into building Realbeer.com, Pat and I found our personalities, skills and backgrounds were ideally complementary. We were yin and yang with operations and creative talents. Like a lot of entrepreneurial stories, ours was characterized by a combination of luck, good timing and a healthy dose of blissful ignorance about what could and couldn't be done. And we both knew that bringing an idea to life in a new medium was going to take more than a shared passion and hard work—it was going to take evangelism, literally.

Back in the mid-1990s, you couldn't just send out a pamphlet about the Web and expect anyone to take you seriously. So Pat set up operations on our home front in San Francisco while my better half, Darci, and I hitched up an Avion trailer and hit the road to "appleseed" the business. We'd never pulled, much less lived in, a travel trailer before, and as we headed toward I-5 and Southern California, Darci and I looked at each other and burst out laughing for about a mile and a half. It was incredible and incredulous. What were we thinking? Yet we were committed to our path. We were on the road and doing it, and we didn't look back.

While Pat dealt with the trials and tribulations of building the bricks-and-mortar side of the company, Darci and I bivouacked in some of America's most remote corners, singing the praises of craft beer, the possibilities of the Internet, and sharing our vision of Realbeer.com. Along the way, brewers and beer media opened their doors, homes and, fortunately, checkbooks to participate in the online community we were struggling to establish.

When Darci and I finally returned to San Francisco at the end of our travels in June 1997, we had some great momentum behind us. Over 500 breweries, brewpubs and beverage marketers had been exposed firsthand to our story and the opportunities our publication offered. As those companies established an online presence—and all of them did—they reached out to Realbeer.com to access the beer-enthusiast community we'd built and nurtured. Companies began contacting us for advertising and/or Web site development without ever having met us in person. Many only knew us through word of mouth and the goodwill we'd established with the industry. It wasn't long before our little company's growth became exponential, and we had more work than we could handle.

Along the way, we discovered others who enjoyed their own view of the future through beer goggles, from members of our online community to angels and mentors throughout the beer industry. Jim Koch, founder of Boston Beer Company, brewer of Sam Adams, hired us, and also shared a wealth of free business advice. Pete Slosberg, creator of Pete's Wicked Ale, pored over our business plan for us. Dan Gordon of Gordon Biersch, brewer extraordinaire and closet tech-geek, introduced us to investment contacts in nearby Silicon Valley. Jack

Joyce, formerly of Nike and CEO of Rogue Ales in Oregon, shared war stories that rammed home important business lessons at strategic times. Tom Daldorf, a craft-beer legend and publisher of *The Celebrator Beer News,* introduced us to the industry and lent credentials to our claim of community before we'd earned them. Countless others invested their contacts, content and advice with us because we had shared their stories with our ever-growing online congregation.

Today, with over 400,000 unique visitors per month and thousands of pages of content, Realbeer.com is the largest publication of its kind in the world. Our community's continued success is a testament to the strength of our company's amplified passion and that of our audience of craft beer enthusiasts. It's like the ultimate Homer Simpson success story: take a dream . . . add beer . . . anything is possible.

Mark Silva
As told to Banjo Bandolas

EPILOGUE: *The slogan for* Realbeer.com is *"What part of beer don't you understand?" All you need to do is visit the site to learn everything you absolutely want to know about beer, from raw ingredient formulation to current beer industry news to how to choose the right beer glass.*

Silva and Hagerman's site also features a strong community bulletin board, where beer enthusiasts and novices alike can share information and learn more about the craft of making and enjoying beer.

To learn more about this company, please visit www.realbeer.com.

Dahlynn McKowen

Built from Scratch

There's nothing wrong with being fired.

Ted Turner

You want a formula for success? Take two Jews who have just been fired, add an Irishman who just walked away from a bankruptcy and an Italian running a no-name investment banking firm. Add—then subtract—Ross Perot. Lease space from a shrinking discount chain, fill a space the size of a football field full of hardware (and a few hundred empty boxes), and you've got a company.

At least that's the way we did it.

* * *

The creation of The Home Depot began with two words in the spring of 1978:

"You're fired!"

Twenty years ago, we were two out-of-work executives. Our situation was not a lot different than millions of others who were shown the door. We had little in the way of capital and faced some daunting personal and legal challenges as we tried to get our careers back on track.

In our early years, we lived on the edge, with no balance sheet and a lack of financing. It took great romancing to establish the vendor base necessary to open and maintain the broad product selection for which we quickly became known. We were always pushing boundaries beyond where our industry's conventional wisdom suggested we could go.

And it paid off: In just twenty years, our company, The Home Depot, has multiplied exponentially from four stores in Atlanta to 775 stores, 160,000 associates and $30 billion in sales. Almost all of our growth has come from internal expansion and very little through acquisition. How did we and our associates do it?

Building The Home Depot was a tough, uphill battle from the day we started in a Los Angeles coffee shop shortly after we were fired. No one believed we could do it, and very few people trusted our judgment. Or they trusted our judgment, but just didn't think the whole concept of a home improvement warehouse with the lowest prices, best selection and best service was going to work. They certainly didn't realize that what we were planning would turn out to be a revolution in the retail business.

While we want to tell the story of The Home Depot because it's a great entrepreneurial tale, our larger goal is to convey what we learned along the way about customers, associates, competitors, growing a business, building a brand, and many other topics everyone in business needs to know.

We're two regular guys from similar modest personal backgrounds and religious orientation who were given a strong drive to succeed by our respective parents. The values that form the core of The Home Depot's business philosophy are bigger than one person. They developed from our families as well as from key business experiences in the early days of our careers.

But we're not a company that's just about numbers. The numbers are important as a measure of our success. But we've attained them because of a culture that is agile and flexible enough to change directions as quickly as events demand it. When something isn't working in our stores, we don't keep doing it the wrong the way simply because the rules say to do it that way. Instead, we do it the right way and change the rules. We do things because they're the right things to do for our customer.

A set of eight values has been our bedrock for the past twenty years. Although they were not put in writing until 1995, these values—the basis for the way we run the company—enabled us to explode across the North American landscape and will be the vehicle for reaching our ambitious goals in the international marketplace.

We're only as good as people—especially the men and women working in our stores every day. If the front line isn't absolutely committed to the cause, we can't win. That's why we believe a sure way of growing this company is to clearly state our values and instill them in our associates. Values are beliefs that do not change over time; they guide our decisions and actions. They are the principles, beliefs and standards of our company. We call this process of enculturation "breeding orange."

In summary, we care about the customer and we care about each other. Our values are not platitudes that are dead on arrival on a lobby wall plaque, but are the spine that shapes the way we do business. These are The Home Depot's core values, although they are so universal that they should apply to every company:

- **Excellent customer service**. Doing whatever it takes to build customer loyalty.
- **Taking care of our people.** The most important reason for the The Home Depot's success.

- **Developing entrepreneurial spirit.** We think of our organizational structure as an inverted pyramid: Stores and customers are at the top and senior management is on the bottom.
- **Respect for all people.** Talent and good people are everywhere, and we can't afford to overlook any source of good people.
- **Building strong relationships with associates, customers, vendors and communities.**
- **Doing the right thing, not just doing things right.**
- **Giving back to our communities as an integral part of doing business.**
- **Shareholder return.** Investors in The Home Depot will benefit from the money they've given us to grow our business.

Bernie Marcus and Arthur Blank

EPILOGUE: *This story was taken from the book* Built from Scratch—How a Couple of Regular Guys Grew The Home Depot from Nothing to $30 Billion *(Random House), which was penned by Bernie Marcus and Arthur Blank in 1999. Since this book's release, The Home Depot has grown to 2,051 stores, 355,000 associates and $81.5 billion in sales. To learn more about The Home Depot, visit* www.homedepot.com.

Dahlynn McKowen

Reprinted with permission of Mark Parisi and Off the Mark ©1996.

From Underdog to Top Dog

In 1997, at the age of fifty-two, the rug was pulled out from underneath me. I was facing a divorce after twenty-seven years of marriage, had huge debt and no means of income. I was beyond depressed. To top it off, I broke both my legs! My divorce attorney jokingly gave me what turned out to be a life-changing piece of advice: "Carol, you need to either get a therapist or a dog." I chose the dog.

In the next couple of weeks, I started looking through the classifieds for the perfect pup and soon answered an ad for a four-month-old bulldog. When I arrived at the kennel, I found myself face-to-face with the saddest-looking puppy you can imagine—the mirror image of what I felt in my heart. We were both underdogs looking for a big dose of unconditional love. I wrapped my new best friend in a blanket, took her home and named her Zelda. The name appealed to me because it started with the letter "Z," and I was hoping that what felt like the end might be the beginning.

With Zelda in my life, I started to heal and feel happy, yet I desperately needed to find a solution for my debt and lack of income. I had four credit cards and was living off my credit limit; time and money were running out.

Fortunately, a friend who knew of my financial plight told me about an annual Christmas card contest that a local pet store was sponsoring. The winner would receive forty pounds of free dog food every month for a year. With the Christmas theme in mind, I borrowed a Santa hat from a neighbor, filled the bathtub with bubble bath and lowered Zelda into the tub. With the hat on her head and a beard made from the bubbles, Zelda was the perfect Santa imposter. I snapped the photo and sent it off to the store with the one-liner: "For Christmas I got a dog for my husband . . . good trade, huh?" Six weeks later, I received the news that Zelda and I had won the contest. I remember asking Zelda how many ways she knew to fix dog chow!

No closer to solving my financial problems, I began to take stock of my personal strengths to find a solution. I had worked many years in advertising as a creative director, writing one-liners and designing ads for corporate clients. *Maybe I could write and design a greeting card line around Zelda, using my personal experiences surviving tough times for creative inspiration,* I thought. A couple of years earlier I had written a book, *Bumper Sticker Wisdom*. It hadn't sold many copies, but I'd learned a lot about the publishing industry. Perhaps I could also feature Zelda and the one-liners in a book? My mind was bursting with ideas! Looking back, I realize our lives are like jigsaw puzzles without the picture on the box; we collect pieces that fit together, but it takes a while to see what picture will be revealed.

Next, I wrote a business plan outlining how to launch Zelda. I aimed high; my goal was to eventually license Zelda cards with Hallmark. I researched the greeting card industry. It was important to come up with something no one else in the industry had done before. I saw two areas where Zelda would be different. First, no one had taken an individual living dog, given it a name and designed an entire greeting card line around it. Second, no one had designed a line of cards around familiar and unfamiliar wisdoms, phrases like, "If you can't take the heat, get out of the kitchen" or my line, "Life is tough . . . wear a helmet." Combining those two aspects, I came up with "Zelda Wisdom" as the name for my company.

However, I knew I couldn't do it alone. I needed the best professional people I could find to help me launch Zelda Wisdom. Shane Young is a genius photographer. Sandi Serling is a public relations wiz. I had worked with both of them in my advertising career; we respected each other and loved working together. I couldn't pay them, so I convinced them to be my partners. Who could say "no" to a face like Zelda's?

We started with a small budget of less than $40,000—the credit line that remained on my charge cards. I bought twenty-four costumes right after Halloween at reduced prices. Shane and I photographed around the clock, and luckily Zelda loved being the center of attention. She also, we discovered, loved caramel ice cream bars as a reward for her time in front of the camera. We convinced a printer to produce the twenty-four card images and three poster images and give us ninety days to sell them and pay the bill.

The gift stores in Oregon and Washington were our test market, and in order to reach them, we needed publicity. With her many contacts in the media world, Sandi landed Zelda in local newspapers and on television stations. Storeowners started calling to order Zelda Wisdom cards and posters. The results were extraordinary. People not only found the cards humorous ("Go braless . . . it pulls the wrinkles down"), but the wisdom was something they could relate to ("I get enough exercise just pushing my luck"). The stores kept ordering more. Our product was flying off the shelves.

Within a few months, we knew it was time to take the giant leap. We rented a booth at the National Stationery Show in New York City. More than fifteen hundred small greeting card companies like Zelda Wisdom would be at the show, and we were hoping to be picked up and licensed by one of the larger card companies. To that end, we sent a press kit and invitation to a top licensing agency. We had heard the firm sometimes represented small "underdog" companies with "top dog" potential. I remembered the advice a friend once told me: "If you don't ask, you're guaranteed not to get an answer."

At the stationery show, I used my advertising background to help us get noticed. We placed a full-page ad in the show's catalog—unheard of for a small card company like ours. The page was white with only Zelda's logo (Zelda dressed in a bee costume) and the one-liner, "Why BEE normal?" On a video monitor in our booth, we ran clips of Zelda appearing on various TV shows. Everyone stopped to watch this funny bulldog running around in her bikini while sporting red, lip-shaped sunglasses! When the executives from the licensing agency stopped by, they had to fight their way to our booth! Here was a bulldog that was making people think, laugh and want more. Zelda was the hit of the National Stationery Show!

We signed a contract with the licensing group, and they brought us licensees for Zelda Wisdom cards, books, calendars and stationery. Soon there were contracts for Zelda Wisdom giftware and apparel. Russ Berrie, Inc., is now producing an entire line of stuffed Zeldas.

Today, we have reached our goal, and Zelda Wisdom cards are being produced and distributed worldwide by Hallmark. In 2005, Zelda cards were Hallmark's number-one selling mass greeting card line. There is even a *Dear Zelda* column on our Web site where Zelda gives some tough but tender advice to her fans. My biggest reward, however, is hearing from those who are touched by Zelda's philosophy and who recognize there is a Zelda in all of us. One of my favorite cards is Zelda dressed as an angel with the line, "They sent me, the other angels were busy." Zelda was my angel, and now I share her with people around the world.

Zelda and I started out as underdogs, but we are proof that you don't have to be thin, rich, young or wrinkle-free to become successful. You just have to be you, and never, never, never give up.

Carol Gardner
As told to Julie Long

EPILOGUE: *Carol and Zelda have finished their seventh book, titled* Zelda's Moments with Mom: Memories a Mother Never Forgets *(Andrews McMeel, 2006). Zelda is the spokesdog for the Delta Society Pet Partners* (www.deltasociety.org), *an international organization promoting service and therapy dogs. Zelda is a certified therapy dog, and she and Carol work with children who have learning disabilities. Carol also gives inspirational and motivational talks to organizations around the world. Her speech, "How to Go from Underdog to Top Dog (Without Barking Up the Wrong Tree)," has received rave reviews. For more information on Zelda Wisdom, Inc., visit* www.zeldawisdom.com.

Julie Long

Closer Than a Brother

The disappointment was so thick that you could cut it with a knife. After twenty years in the convenience store and grocery business, with the dream of some day owning his own grocery store in his hometown of Holdenville, Oklahoma, Wilburn Smith was devastated. He had worked his way up to a $30,000 manager's salary at the very store he wanted to buy, on the promise that he could purchase it from the owner when he retired. But when this fateful day came in 1980, the owner sold it to someone else.

Wilburn's lifelong dream was crushed in one instant. His cousin, Mike Smith, whether out of kindness or because he saw hidden potential, asked Wilburn if he would be interested in selling the legal services of Pre-Paid Legal, a new company marketing legal plans. Mike was one of the first salesmen I ever hired at Pre-Paid Legal, my struggling company that was only eight years old at the time.

Salespeople were paid a commission on their sales, which meant Wilburn would have to make presentations to people face-to-face if he wanted to make money. After a week of training and completing twenty-five individual sales on his own, Wilburn was ready to start offering the service to groups, which offered the potential to make even more money. The only problem was that Wilburn was scared of public speaking.

Realizing this fact, Mike took Wilburn with him to give a team presentation to the Oklahoma City Fire Department. The first day went fine as presentations were done together and Wilburn could hide his nervousness. The next day, however, Mike was unexpectedly called away, and Wilburn was suddenly on his own. Scared to death, Wilburn drove around the station for thirty minutes and then sat in his parked car for another thirty minutes. Finally mustering up enough courage, Wilburn walked inside and gave his presentation. Much to his relief, the presentation wasn't as bad as he expected, and by the end of the week he had signed up nearly fifty firefighters! Wilburn's income his first year was only $25,000, but he knuckled down and performed even better the following year, doubling his income.

Around that time, John Hail, a longtime trusted friend who had played a significant part in saving our company from bankruptcy just a few years earlier, called me to say he had a great marketing idea that would be a huge boost to our company. As I listened, he outlined why Pre-Paid Legal should migrate its current commission-based marketing program into a multilevel marketing approach. I would have laughed in his face and walked away if he had been any other person, but I trusted John and knew he wouldn't offer a crazy idea like this if he didn't truly believe in it.

Hesitant to get into the multilevel marketing game, I agreed to let John give it a try on the condition that he start the venture at least 500 miles away from our company's headquarters in Ada, Oklahoma. I didn't want to be embarrassed if it flopped. Within the year, however, John's marketing group doubled our revenues. He certainly had my attention! I then gave John permission to present the opportunity to our full-time sales force.

When John made the initial presentation, there was skepticism among the group, but one person was convinced that it was just what the company needed: Wilburn Smith. He saw the potential immediately and enthusiastically supported John's proposal. Upon instituting the new concept, company sales went from $2 million to $42 million in four short years, and revenues haven't been that low since.

Under this new sales system, Wilburn's commissions began to climb dramatically. The company was so successful in writing new business that we found ourselves on the brink of disaster, as we had run out of money paying advance commissions. Compensation was similar to that of the insurance industry—we paid commissions three years in advance, so as the sales exploded, so did our need for cash. Now I was faced with two terrible options: stop paying advance commissions or go bankrupt.

We suspended the commissions until we could generate enough revenue to pay them again, and the fallout was that we lost most of our sales force, but not Wilburn! He hung in there, working harder than ever. He believed in me, in the service and in the company. I truly believe that if it weren't for Wilburn, Pre-Paid Legal would not exist today.

After that gut-wrenching ordeal, I asked Wilburn to become the vice president of marketing and rebuild our sales force. I knew he could relate to the sales force, because he had "been there and done that" with the best of them, thus making his insights and leadership all the more valuable. Armed with a new marketing plan, Wilburn was off to the races and Pre-Paid Legal was back on track, growing faster than ever.

Over the years, Wilburn has held just about every position at our company and has stuck with me no matter what. If I gave him a task that I knew he didn't like, he would turn around and do it with enthusiasm, with the end result always a work of art. With this in mind, in 1995, my wife, Shirley, and I went out to dinner with Wilburn and his wife, Carol. After dinner, I asked Wilburn if he could be in my office early next Tuesday, as I had some good news for him. He said he would, and we waved good-bye. The following Tuesday I handed Wilburn a press release and asked him to read it; as he did, his eyes widened and his mouth dropped open.

I had come to realize over the years that through life's thick and thins, your parents, siblings and other family members are usually the ones who stick with you, enabling you to make it to the light at the end of the tunnel. But when you find a friend who will stick even closer than a brother, this is when you know you've found a very rare thing. And if you're smart, you won't let go of such a person! That is why I made Wilburn Smith president of our company.

Harland Stonecipher

EPILOGUE: *As with any new business venture, when Harland Stonecipher began Pre-Paid Legal in 1972, he was looking for those certain individuals who could help him develop his business into a viable and successful dream.*

Founder and CEO of Pre-Paid Legal, Stonecipher's entrepreneurial spirit definitely rubbed off on Wilburn Smith and his many other dedicated employees and independent associates. Today, the company continues to grow and is publicly traded on the New York Stock Exchange, providing legal services and identity theft protection to more than a million families and businesses in North America.

For more information, please visit www.prepaidlegal.com.

John Gardner

See Reality

My business partner, Rick Bacher, and I are not cereal fanatics. We're not restaurateurs, either. We are, however, two outside-the-box marketing guys who are keen observers of human behavior and fascinated with the passionate and often wacky, deeply rooted relationships people have with brand-name cereals.

Rick and I also consider ourselves pioneers and renegades. In creating "Cereality"—a cereal café that offers all cereal, all day, all ways—we took on the fiercely competitive and adversarial $11 billion cereal industry, and the even more cynical and entrenched $475 billion restaurant industry, turning some of their most basic assumptions and ways of doing business completely upside down. We listened to their positions: "People will never be comfortable eating cereal outside of their home kitchens," or "They won't spend $3 or $4 for something they can get in a supermarket for a fraction of that price," or "You can't build a restaurant around a menu of food from a box." But through sheer moxie, diligence, sweat and courage, mixed with a little bit of luck, Rick and I proved them wrong.

Cereality was built on the basic foundation that when it

comes to cereal and the 95 percent of Americans who enjoy it, the emotional ties surrounding the cereal meal—the rituals and habits, the loyalties to a particular product, the mood and ambience—are much more important than how convenient the container may be. Moreover, when it comes to cereal, unique in that it is an exclusively "branded" item, one can actually build a restaurant menu entirely around someone else's food if the focus is on making everyone feel like it's "Always Saturday Morning" rather than merely a restaurant that serves only cereal. That's a big leap and has tapped into the national zeitgeist with lots of people saying, "Why didn't I think of that?" Rick and I believe it's the hallmark of entrepreneurship at its very best.

For me, entrepreneurship was, and continues to be, a calling. For Rick, entrepreneurship was a freedom and a "zone" where he could be most expressive and empowered. We work especially well together and have for close to a decade, because Rick can quickly articulate an idea in a visually potent and meaningful way that speeds up the process of going from an idea to a product to a brand statement. The other reason our partnership has been so successful is that we are fully committed to authenticity in whatever we do. Our business philosophy is that in order to succeed, you must "bring who you are to what you do." It's the anchor of our corporate culture.

I see entrepreneurial life as a calling for a variety of reasons, some psychological, some financial. I've tested this over the years by taking often-challenging and prestigious, albeit traditional, jobs. Inevitably at the end of the day I would reach a brick wall, a "glass ceiling" if you will, when my creative spirit and drive to innovate and ask too many questions invariably resulted in someone above me being threatened. In the end, I was always made to be the scapegoat.

Going out on my own has been successful, like with Cereality or earlier in my career when I worked with Fortune 500 companies, helping them communicate around sensitive psychosocial issues in the workplace. I was in my twenties at that time, walking my career path of organizational psychology after receiving my master's degree from Harvard. But talking about depression in the workplace day in and day out just didn't seem to be a good fit for me. I was yearning for something else, and that something else was culinary travel.

But sometimes entrepreneurship can be more of a struggle. Following my dream, I entered the publishing world, starting a magazine for culinary travel enthusiasts like myself. I became inspired, focused, organized and made it happen. Just like that. I wore all the hats from CFO to editor-in-chief. The magazine won critical acclaim in the national press and had passionate and devoted subscribers, but because the topic was ahead of its time, I couldn't get the right level of financing to expand. After three years, the magazine died. While closing the magazine was devastating, it ultimately became the best learning experience of my life. I discovered later that prospective investors in Cereality viewed my experience with the magazine as a critical asset in my making Cereality a success. "First-time entrepreneurship is like riding a bike for the very first time," they would tell me. "You're now ready for a triathlon."

Unbeknownst to me, the first stop on my personal triathlon was at an office on Wall Street, where I was meeting with a colleague in the middle of the afternoon. During our conversation, my colleague was sneaking Cocoa Puffs behind his desk. I asked what he was doing and he said, "Oh, we all do this. Just look at our cupboards in our staff kitchen."

Leaving the meeting, I saw two different mothers walking down the street pushing baby strollers; both strollers had a diaper bag *and* a bag of Cheerios. Shortly thereafter, Rick was at an airport and noticed more than one parent feeding their child cereal while standing in line at a fast-food burger joint. And various friends shared with both of us their cereal-eating habits. It was then we realized we might just be on to a really big business opportunity.

The first thing Rick and I did was agree to explore the viability of a business that tapped into people's seemingly passionate cravings for their favorite cereal anywhere, anytime. We gathered up all of our savings, raised some outside capital from friends and associates and hired a research firm that told us a few salient things: (1) cereal was the third-most-purchased item in grocery stores; (2) 95 percent of the American public enjoyed it, and (3) cereal manufacturers were spending boatloads of cash on finding new packaging to make their products more convenient outside of the home and it wasn't working.

With these facts as our starting point, Rick and I developed the Cereality brand identity, put together a strong business model, then started raising operating capital. Two years later, after much grief, heartache, lecturing and hair loss, we found a very smart and visionary executive at Quaker who "got it" and agreed to support our initiative with cash and advice. Other high net-worth investors came on board, and we also hired some best-in-breed restaurant consultants. We were finally off to the races!

With inspiration from both *Seinfeld* and Martha Stewart, Rick designed a restaurant that looked like a home kitchen. We named our servers "Cereologists™" and dressed them in pajamas, put together a menu of well-known cereals, delicious and fun toppings plus myriad specialty cereal menu items, which allowed us to serve cereal all day long. We launched our first store at Arizona State University in August 2003.

Our original plan was to keep the store off the radar, because it was meant to be a laboratory to glean ideas of what worked, and what didn't, for future stores. But six months later, after receiving one too many calls from folks asking about franchising opportunities, or more alarming, others who alluded to opening their own cereal cafés, we knew we had to legally secure our idea. As any good entrepreneurs who create something truly original would do, we hired the best intellectual property attorneys in the country and then issued a press release that unequivocally claimed the business idea as ours. The headline read: "95% of Americans Like Cereal. 57% Like Sex. We've Got Cereal." It struck a chord. Behold, the birth of a brand.

Three years following the debut of the very first Cereality Café, we continue to build company stores. We have also expanded on our original model of a great restaurant chain: we've embarked on a major franchising initiative with best-of-breed partners; we're manufacturing our own specialty cereal bars for many companies, including a leading international apparel retailer; we're selling merchandise online; we're catering events for faraway movie companies and local accounting firms; and last, we have signed deals with major partners to license the Cereality name for all sorts of innovative products that will remind folks of our "Always Saturday Morning" spirit, regardless of whether or not they ever visit our cafés. Rick and I refer to it as our "Multi-Bucket Approach to Seeing Reality." I guess you could also say it's really just out-of-the-box thinking.

David Roth

[EDITORS' NOTE: *Cereality® is more than a place to get cereal: it's a new way of thinking about cereal, a new choice in fast food, and an idea whose time has come.*

To learn more about Cereality,® David Roth and Rick Bacher, please visit www.cereality.com, *where it's "Always Saturday Morning!"*]

Reprinted with permission of Jonny Hawkins. ©2006.

5

IT'S ALL RELATIVE

The only rock I know that stays steady,
the only institution I know that works,
is the family.

Lee Iacocca

Following Our Hearts

The only way to do great work is to love what you do.

Steve Jobs

I looked out the window and saw hundreds of troops pouring into the streets. When they saw me through the glass, some pointed their guns at my chest. A hotel attendant opened my door and directed me downstairs to the lobby where the glass was bullet-proof.

Funny how you think of your family at times like that. For eleven days there wasn't much else to think about; I couldn't go outside, there was no Internet or television, and I had one book.

How do you explain to your young children why you'll miss trick-or-treat despite your promise to be home? How can you explain why you spend so much time away to a cocky young teen who can't relate to your career?

I kissed the ground when I came home. And then we held a family meeting.

It was a huge moment of truth. Six years of college, ten years of rising through the ranks in a specialized field—

and my family wasn't happy about it. My cocky young teen had written a book report on Steve Jobs. Why couldn't I work in computers like him? It's what cool people do. No chance of that. I was a geophysicist, in Houston, age thirty-seven. The sensible thing to do was to say comforting words and explain that Dad needed to pay the bills.

But somehow we made the landmark decision during that meeting that would change the rest of our lives: I quit, we packed a U-Haul, and we drove to the Silicon Valley in California without a job. There was no Harvard MBA–like analysis. We simply followed our hearts.

Following our hearts meant listening to computer conference tapes in the U-Haul so we could speak the language when we arrived. It meant reading everything about Steve Jobs and Bill Gates. It meant somehow persuading a computer company to take a chance on a geophysicist, a very tough sell.

We had read that Steve Jobs would break the rules and hire passionate people other companies wouldn't. Joanna Hoffman left Middle Eastern archaeology to become the first Macintosh marketer. Steve hired Randy Nelson, one of the founders of the Flying Karamazov Brothers, jugglers who performed on the world's most famous stages, to teach computer programming. Randy is now dean of Pixar University.

Passion was the key that got me into NeXT, Inc., the company Steve started after being fired at Apple, and I suddenly became the coolest dad ever. I told breathless stories of Steve's legendary tantrums and magical demos, and my children hung on every word as they used to when I read *How the Grinch Stole Christmas* to them.

I was there when the first Internet browser software, written on a NeXT computer, was demo'ed to Steve. We were solving computing's most vexing problem—making the world's most powerful operating system (UNIX) simple enough for mere mortals. We had no idea it would eventually be the driving force behind Apple's renaissance. We were just following our hearts.

But there was a nagging problem. The Silicon Valley has a way of consuming your life, and we had moved there so we could spend more time together. Obviously, this wasn't happening. That cocky son of ours, Don, did something bold that changed our family's dichotomy again: he started Smugmug.com, an Internet-based company that offered customers a Web site for sharing digital photos. And then he hired me.

Once more we followed our hearts into what seemed like the jaws of death. We were hopelessly in love with the Internet and digital photography. What's better than priceless photos of life's best moments, summoned with a click? Everyone has a shoebox in the closet where irreplaceable photos decay, alone and unseen. We believed in our souls that a photo online is worth ten in the closet.

It doesn't take a Harvard MBA to recognize a problem. The world's most trusted brands offer Internet photo sharing, and they have good reasons to give it away free, as it helps them sell more cameras or more ads. Are you going to entrust an unknown brand with your priceless photos when so many trusted brands will store them for free?

It was a moment of truth for our belief that passion is the most important thing in business. We all know passion explains why Apple, Harley-Davidson and Starbucks thrive, but I swallowed hard when I considered the odds against us. Our competitors would be Microsoft, Sony, Canon, Kodak, Yahoo and HP.

But if you really care about your baby's photo, do you want an ad alongside it? You wouldn't clip ads from the paper and place them in your photo albums at home. The big brands can't resist inserting ads in your albums, or asking your visitors for their e-mail addresses so they can send spam. Our hearts led us to design ad and spam free albums. One point for passion.

They won't let you hide their logos and decorate your albums like you can at home. Two points for passion.

They won't let your mom in Atlanta download high-resolution versions of your photos to print at home. Three points for passion. No full-screen slide shows. Four points for passion. And there would be many more.

Three years after starting, SmugMug has become the Internet trustee for the priceless photos of fifty thousand families, the equivalent of a medium-sized city. Gone are the sharing sites of many trusted brands.

We did it without taking debt because we felt a great sense of responsibility for the photos we store. Our pay in the beginning was huge: the joy of working with each other doing what we love and the bonds that form when you struggle for a great cause. Delayed gratification was worth the reward.

Along the way the contagion spread to the rest of the family. They left their promising careers and two SmugMug MacAskills became seven, solving the Silicon Valley problem of not enough time for family. Our favorite activity is to work long hours together on exciting new features. The rest of the SmugMug team has become family, too, and even our customers consider themselves part of the family. We revel in seeing their photos of weddings, newborns, Peace Corps assignments, athletic triumphs, restored cars, dogs and travels.

It seems too good to be true.

I almost choked when I heard Steve Jobs would give the commencement speech at my alma mater, Stanford University. Had he ever been to a college graduation? Not that I knew of.

But he said something powerful there that I knew he

believed: "Your work is going to fill a large part of your life, and the only way to be truly satisfied is to do what you believe is great work. And the only way to do great work is to love what you do."

That's how my family's dreams came true.

Chris MacAskill

EPILOGUE: *The father-and-son team of Chris and Don MacAskill are legends in the high-tech industry; besides working at NeXT, Inc., Chris's past includes creating the legendary online book-selling site,* Fatbrain.com, *one of the Internet's first (and few) success stories. Fatbrain.com grew from the MacAskill family garage into a $100 million publicly traded company before it was purchased by Barnes & Noble in 2000.*

Don was the first nonfounding employee at Best Internet, the earliest, most respected and most successful Internet service provider in the Silicon Valley, which was eventually purchased by Verio. Don designed the networks at Best Internet that hosted Hotmail, eBay and Fatbrain before launching his sights on creating the current family business.

Smugmug.com *was founded in 2002 because the MacAskills could not find an industrial-strength Web site free of clutter for photos, where, as they say, "great sharing is the center of gravity." Besides being able to post digital photographs, the company allows customers to either print photos at home or via their high-quality lab at a reasonable cost.*

To fully appreciate the magnitude of this company and its offerings, a trip to the SmugMug Web site is a must. Over 53 million photos are displayed, free of obnoxious advertising and pop-up ads. As of last count, the site had over 50,000 customers.

To learn more about Chris and Don MacAskill and SmugMug, please visit www.smugmug.com.

Dahlynn McKowen

The Bag Lady Triumphant

When I graduated high school, I thought I knew it all. Therefore, when Daddy suggested that I attend school to become a dental hygienist, I let him know that I had no desire to smell people's bad breath day in and day out. I counteroffered with the suggestion that I attend a modeling school in Atlanta. Unfortunately, that went over like a lead brick.

Instead of pursuing higher education, I decided to marry my high school sweetheart. Momma tried to get me to reconsider, but I possessed greater wisdom than my parents. I was determined to be the perfect wife and mother, and my fiancé would surely be the perfect husband and father.

But life changes quickly, and my fairytale existence was soon a shattered dream. Daddy died just seven months after I married, and Momma passed away four years later. At twenty-three, I was the mother of two boys under the age of three and was also raising my sixteen-year-old brother. At times, the future seemed overwhelming.

In the years that followed, I also realized that I was not the perfect wife and that the man I had married was not the perfect husband. For nearly twenty years, I lived in a vacuum. At times, I was simply unable to leave my home and unable to be the perfect mother I still longed to be. I existed but seldom lived.

When my marriage finally came to an end, I was faced with the reality that I had to have a way to earn money. Though I had worked as a bank teller—coming face-to-face with an armed robber had served as the catalyst to pursue another career—what else could I do? I was essentially uneducated and talentless. The only skill I had was the ability to cook.

Growing up, I had spent hours in my Grandmother Paul's kitchen. At the time, I didn't realize that I was receiving an education. Amid the laughter that echoed around us, I spent hours watching Grandmother Paul stir, pour, mix and knead. I learned the intricacies and techniques of preparing Southern food. You see, Southern cooking is a hand-me-down art, not a skill taught in culinary schools. Instead, it comes from within. It is, in the South, how we show our love.

So, with two hundred dollars in my pocket, I followed my fledgling entrepreneurial instincts and went shopping. I purchased a thirty-six-dollar cooler, paid fifty dollars for food and spent the rest on a license to start a lunch-catering business. I marched up and down the streets of Savannah, Georgia, knocking on doors of businesses, requesting permission to sell meals to the staff. With the support of my two sons, Jamie and Bobby, who were by then handsome young men, The Bag Lady was born.

I was up and cooking by five o'clock each morning in order to prepare the 250 meals that my handsome sons would deliver. Soon, the three of us had established a brisk business. I never found it necessary to advertise, and it was just as well because there were no advertising funds in the budget. Instead, dependability, spirit and great food established our reputation.

It did not take long before customers began planting a seed in my head. "Why not open a restaurant?" they asked. Thus, I again laid it all on the line and leased a space in a local hotel. Now, my boys and I were not only running The Bag Lady, but we were also full-fledged restaurateurs—proprietors of an establishment called The Lady.

For five years, I worked twenty-hour days to keep the businesses going. It was the hardest five years of my life, but the people came and even waited in line to enjoy the food at our eatery. Like a proper Southern hostess, however, I made certain that we took care of them well. Passing out fresh cheese biscuits to those waiting became a tradition.

It soon became obvious that I was handing out many cheese biscuits. Believe it or not, we needed even more space. We closed the hotel café, moved The Bag Lady back to my cluttered kitchen and began renovating a former downtown teacher's supply store. For a year, my boys and I labored and struggled to create The Lady & Sons restaurant. Times were tough. In fact, there were days when I did not have change for the parking meter. By the time we finally opened, I was overdrawn in not one account, but two. My accountant was concerned, but I convinced him that if I could just get those doors opened, I could repay every debt. So I opened the doors, and thank God the people came.

These days, The Lady & Sons is at an even bigger location on Congress Street in Savannah. I still specialize in the comfort food of my youth, and people come from all over for classics made with Southern cooking staples like butter, salt, sugar, hot sauce, ham hocks and, oh yes, fat! In addition to The Lady & Sons, I have even managed to find the time to write a few cookbooks and host a televised cooking show.

Someone once told me that I possess an unfailing survival instinct, and I suppose that I do. It's inherent in all entrepreneurs. The last several years have been a wild and amazing ride, one that I could not have taken without the constant support of Jamie and Bobby. Why, I never dreamed that a mere two hundred dollars would take us this far. I am living proof that we must accept the challenges that life offers. Whenever one door closes, another one always opens!

Paula Deen
As told to Terri Duncan

EPILOGUE: *A trip to Savannah, Georgia, would not be complete without dining at Paula Deen's award-winning restaurant The Lady & Sons. One of the coastal area's most popular tourist stops, Paula and her two sons—Jamie and Bobby—frequent their establishment and enjoy visiting and serving Southern delectable delights to their loyal customers and tourists alike.*

In addition to the restaurant, Paula has ventured into other areas. She has authored five cookbooks, the most popular of which is The Lady and Sons Savannah Country Cookbook *(Random House, 1998). Paula also has the distinction of being QVC's all-time bestselling cookbook author. As if those weren't enough, Paula launched a bimonthly magazine last year—* Cooking with Paula Deen *(Hoffman Media).*

*Besides being a restaurateur, author and entrepreneur, Paula also hosts her own television show—*Paula's Home Cooking*—which airs twice daily on the Food Network. For those who prefer direct instruction from the lady herself, Paula offers a cooking school at Uncle Bubba's Oyster House.*

The flair for Southern cooking is definitely a family affair, as Paula and her brother Bubba Hiers collaborated and opened Uncle Bubba's Oyster House in December 2004. Also located in Savannah, the restaurant is known for its seafood, live music three nights a week and good old Southern charm. Check it out yourself: www.unclebubbasoysterhouse.com.

To subscribe to Paula's magazine, purchase her books and other items, or to just learn more about this famed lady and her boys, please visit www.ladyandsons.com.

Terri Duncan

Reprinted with permission of Mark Parisi and Off The Mark ©2001.

For the Love of It

We're brothers, who, on a hope and a dream, both quit our jobs in Corporate America on the same day.

It was 1998. We were following the path that was expected of us; we had attended private schools, continued on to respectable colleges and landed jobs on Madison Avenue. We were living at home with our parents in Connecticut, as most recent grads did, in order to save as much money as we could to eventually move closer to our jobs in New York City. We had decent jobs and were ascending our respective corporate ladders—on our way all right, but something was missing.

Growing up, we lived a dichotomy. Our parents were travel and lifestyle writers who specialized in the finest world resorts; however, as the children of writers, we learned how to live a modest life. We traveled together as a family and spent our summers on Martha's Vineyard. After traveling to the most remote, secluded places in the world, we always longed to return to the Vineyard. More than anywhere, the Vineyard became our home. It was our oasis, our place of relaxation.

So, there we were, all grown up and in New York City, dressing as if we had important places to be, riding the train to work so we could push paper along, making our clients happy. At the same time, we were missing the Vineyard and our old boat, one that we had worked so hard to buy the previous summer. We weren't happy; in fact, we were downright miserable.

That January, while on vacation with our parents in the British West Indies, neither one of us could bear the thought of leaving that tropical haven to go back to our jobs. While commiserating, we talked about starting our own business; we wanted to create a product—a brand—that represented this "good life" we loved so much. Over dinner that night, we came up with the idea to make a product that represented the finer things in life we had grown to love; we could create specialty neckties, made from the finest silk, and make them fun and colorful with patterns reflecting the place we loved most—the Vineyard. It was one of those ideas that many people have, but few ever act on. We were excited and confident that we knew what we *wanted* to do. We just didn't know *where* to start.

That very evening, the resort's general manager loaned us a New York City phone book. We looked up a few tie manufacturers, made a few connections and before we knew it, it was summer time and we had sample ties! In our minds, there was no doubt that there would be a demand for them. Our plan was to start selling the specialty ties on the Vineyard and see where it took us. We had nothing to lose; if all else failed, we'd just dock our boat and get back on the commuter train to New York City.

Our plan was to fund this venture with credit card cash advances. So before we quit our jobs and launched the business, we signed up for every credit card possible while we still had steady incomes and could qualify for the credit. We also arranged to have our wisdom teeth pulled—on the same day, mind you—while we still had health insurance, and we leased cars while the banks would still approve us. Once we had everything in place, we quit our jobs within five minutes of each other. We rode the commuter train home, clinking our glasses while celebrating in the bar car. That day, Vineyard Vines was born.

We were entering a new market with no experience, and people told us we were crazy. Looking back, they probably were right. It was the late 1990s, the height of "business casual," and ties were not in fashion. But we saw our lack of experience as an opportunity, an opportunity to bring a product we loved to the market. Our philosophy was simple: make great products that we love and other people will love them, too. Even with our grand vision, we knew we would make some mistakes, but we were going to listen to our customers and do whatever it took to make them happy.

Not knowing much about the fashion industry and the retail market worked to our advantage, as we were able to create a product without the parameters and procedures other companies followed. We made ties with color—icons of the good life—and were going to market them in a grassroots manner. Convincing a few stores to take our ties on consignment, we offered them a no-risk policy, simply saying, "If the ties don't sell, don't pay us for them, and we'll take them back."

That first summer on the Vineyard, the ties took off like wildfire. We peddled them from our old boat in the harbor, from our rusted-out Jeep in town, anywhere we could find an audience. In reality though, we weren't selling our ties; we were selling our story and lifestyle. We would often give our product away to whoever would take it, wear it, and who would ultimately become an ambassador of Vineyard Vines. We supported our retailers, doing whatever we could to make their experience with Vineyard Vines a good one. We had never sold anything before in our lives, and we simply did what felt right by delivering a quality product, sticking to our word and doing everything possible to ensure great service.

Before we knew it, that first summer was over. We hit the road, traveling throughout New England, building relationships everywhere we went. We won our accounts one at a time, appreciating those retailers who took a chance on us.

It is truly satisfying to both of us that we have helped our customers take a bit of "the good life" to work with them. Just eight years after opening Vineyard Vines, our products can be found in the finest specialty and department stores in the world. Our line has expanded to include full offerings for men, women and children. In addition, we've found that we've created a family at Vineyard Vines—a family of employees and customers. We value this aspect of our business more than anything else we do.

People always say that if you love what you do, you'll be successful. There is no doubt that we love being entrepreneurs. We're having fun, working hard and meeting great people. And we love the fact that we've provided our customers with more than just a product; we've shared a lifestyle with them. We're still just two normal guys living the American Dream, and it's more fun than we could ever have imagined!

Shep and Ian Murray

EPILOGUE: *Shep and Ian Murray—lovingly referred to as "The Tie Guys"—are cofounders and CEOs of Vineyard Vines. Established in 1998, the company, best known for elegant neckties and high-end sportswear for men, women and children, has a hundred employees and annual revenue in the tens of millions of dollars.*

Honors bestowed on the Murray brothers include the 2005 Ernst & Young Entrepreneur of the Year Award and the Inc. 500 list for 2005 (#202). The duo is also active with nonprofit and charity causes, receiving the 2005 Bear Necessities Pediatric Cancer Foundation HOPE Award and the 2005 Coastal Conservation Association Conservationist of the Year Award. The brothers also have been featured in the media, the most popular segment being NBC's Today show.

In their free time, the brothers can be found on one of their four fishing boats or racing their thirty-five-foot sailboat during the summer. Shep—the family man—spends as much time as he can with his young family, while Ian—the musician—just released his first solo album.

To learn more about Shep and Ian Murray, please visit www.vineyardvines.com.

Dahlynn McKowen

A Sign of the Times

There are many spokes on the wheel of life. We're here to explore new possibilities.

Ray Charles

There's a time in your life when you just know that things are going to change—that things just have to change—and you can't stop it from happening.

In December 1996, our daughter Leah was born. My husband, Aaron, and I were elated to be blessed with such a wonderful child. Everything about her was perfect: her cute little nose, her happy wiggling feet and her amazing little hands. She was our precious, darling girl.

When Leah arrived in this world, I was writing music and performing with my folk-rock band. Aaron and I would take our little Leah to band practices and concerts, and to our amazement, she quietly slept through much of it in spite of the loud music. When she was fourteen months old we discovered why: Leah was deaf.

Instantly, my priorities changed. I just couldn't find a way to rationalize spending hours working on my music, so I put down my guitar and picked up American Sign Language (ASL) instead.

Both Aaron and I quickly learned enough ASL to begin teaching Leah. We were astonished to see that within six months, Leah's sign language vocabulary far surpassed the speaking vocabulary of hearing children her same age. We realized this when Leah's little friends could only point at something they wanted, but Leah could actually tell us by signing for it. And because Leah had learned to use sign language so early, it was not long before she could read written words, even though she was only two years old.

My sister Emilie and her husband, Derek, also started teaching ASL to their hearing infant son, Alex, so he would be able to communicate with his cousin. Emilie was thrilled one morning when a very fussy Alex, then only ten months old, looked up at her and made the sign for "milk."

A few years later, we had a second daughter. Our little Lucy was born eight weeks premature, with spina bifida and cerebral palsy. Doctors worried that, due to her cerebral palsy, Lucy would never be able to talk, let alone use her rigid fingers to communicate in ASL with her older deaf sister.

In the midst of everything that was happening to our family, Emilie and I came up with the idea to create a video for hearing children that would be captivating and entertaining and would make sign language fun and easy for all children. If anything, the video would also teach our friends, family and neighbors how to communicate with Leah. We formed our company, Two Little Hands Productions, to produce and distribute our videos, and *Signing Time! Volume One: My First Signs* was completed in May 2002.

Well, after two years of no communication, Lucy began to sign along with *Signing Time!* in spite of her cerebral palsy. It wasn't long before she also started talking—in fact, she's still talking and signing to this day, and we can't get her to stop! She now goes to a mainstream elementary school, which blows me away. Lucy was the first of thousands of *Signing Time!* miracles.

The timing for our idea couldn't be more perfect. There has been an incredible amount of media attention focusing on how infants and toddlers communicate with signs before they can speak. Documented research, as well as firsthand experience of many parents, demonstrates that signing hearing children generally have higher IQ scores, are better adjusted and read at an earlier age. By learning to communicate earlier, the "terrible twos" are not so terrible. And, with millions of deaf or hearing-impaired Americans using ASL as their native language, communication through signing has become an important part of American culture.

While sign language can be beneficial for every child, I confess a more personal goal: my hope is that *everyone* will know a little sign language, just as most people know a little Spanish. If this dream could happen, when my child plays with other children at the park, there would be no awkwardness, no communication barrier, just three signs: "Hi—friend—play." This is all it would take to change her world.

After all those years of musical silence while helping my daughter learn to adapt to the world around her, I'm happy to say that I've picked up my guitar again, writing and performing all the songs for the entire *Signing Time!* series. I used to sing for myself and my fans, but now I sing and sign for Leah, Lucy and children everywhere.

Rachel de Azevedo Coleman

EPILOGUE: *When Rachel Coleman and her sister Emilie Brown came up with the idea to make a fun, musical video to teach American Sign Language (ASL) to Leah's hearing family members and friends, they had no idea the scope and reach their "little project" would have.*

When their first video became available for purchase in 2002 via a simple Web site, its popularity spread like wildfire through all fifty states and twenty different countries. Almost entirely by word of mouth, the video excited many, including educators, homeschoolers, speech therapists, pediatricians, daycares, providers, schools, librarians and families. By the end of 2005, the Signing Time! *series had grown to nine ASL vocabulary-building volumes, sing-along music CDs, board books and even a spin-off two-volume series just for infants called* Baby Signing Time! *In addition to even more volumes and products planned for release in 2006,* Signing Time! *is the first program of its kind to appear on public television stations across the United States beginning in January 2006.*

The message is clear: Signing Time! *is for* all *children and* all *families. Though its popularity has certainly grown among families with "typical" children, according to Coleman, the most touching testimonials have come from families of "exceptional" children such as those with Down syndrome, autism, speech delays and other developmental challenges. As was the case with Coleman's second daughter, Lucy,* Signing Time! *has been instrumental in making the miracle of two-way communication possible for many of these children.*

To learn more about Rachel Coleman, Emilie Brown and Signing Time! *please visit their Web site at* www.signingtime.com.

Dahlynn McKowen

The Wheels on the Bus Go 'Round and 'Round

High expectations are the key to everything.

Henry Ford

At Hemphill Brothers Coach Company, we know buses. As part of our family's gospel group, The Hemphills, the two of us have logged over 2 million miles on buses. We have been bumped, bruised and scraped by the sharp corners and edges of cabinets and equipment on those buses. We have waited patiently and not so patiently on the side of the road when a bus broke down, and we have inhaled noxious diesel fumes as we rolled down the highway. We have sweltered in the heat when the air conditioner blew anything but cold air, and one of us has peeled his face off of a frozen bus window when the heating system proved to be inadequate in frigid Canadian weather! In addition, by the time we were teenagers, we boys were not simply bus passengers, but we were also intimately familiar with washing, servicing and refurbishing buses because we worked at our father's coach leasing business. We have forty years experience with buses, and in our world, you cannot spell "business" without that one special word—bus.

Though tour buses were a natural part of our livelihood, Dad did not knowingly intend to become a pioneer in the bus industry. His was already an active and often hectic life; not only was he an active minister, but he was also a songwriter and the senior member of The Hemphills. And when it came to buses, keeping our group's 1962 Flexible on the road was his greatest concern. Then, in 1974, a haphazard chain of events occurred that included purchasing a bus from a financially strapped singing group and refurbishing it, selling it for a profit, having it stolen while the check was merrily bouncing and then repossessing the bus in accordance with a judge's orders once it was located. When all was said and done, Dad inadvertently found himself in the bus leasing business, and we soon discovered that we had new jobs in addition to our musical endeavors.

For several years, Dad added to his fleet of buses and drivers, and during that time, the two of us became involved in the coach business. Though we had no formal training, we were very enthusiastic and spent hours washing, designing and providing the labor to make those designs become reality. After all, we knew from personal experience what a tour bus needed. While our enthusiasm blossomed over the years, Dad's waned. In 1980, he decided that he had had his fill of bus leasing and made the decision to sell the shop.

Joel and I were twenty and twenty-one years old at the time. Though we were not experienced enough to drive buses, we were old enough to become business partners and start our own coach company. It was a natural transition. After all, we had always shared a room and had learned early on that by combining our wealth and talents, we could accomplish more! It was that frame of mind that allowed us to buy our first stereo together, to purchase our first car together, and now to start our own business together.

Dad helped our jump into entrepreneurship by cosigning on a $50,000 loan and loaning us an additional $500. He even sold us two of his buses—two 1965 Eagles—that he had been unable to sell. After we started our business, we continued to tour with The Hemphills, singing at night and running our coach company from hotel rooms around the country by day. We were young, eager to succeed and had nothing to lose.

From those meager beginnings, our company has grown from two buses and a backyard shop into eighty coaches and a 28,000-square-foot office complex on ten acres outside of Nashville, Tennessee. A 15,000-square-foot addition is in the final stages of completion. When we sold our first bus, it went for $35,000, an astronomical amount of money to us at the time. Now, it is not uncommon for one of our coaches to sell for a million dollars or more.

We never know who is going to wander into our shop or who may be on the other end of the line when the telephone rings. It could be Air Force One or the White House with a request from the president for buses that will need to be equipped in a manner that allows them to serve as rolling White Houses, or it may be a big-name entertainer requesting a coach equipped with a tanning bed, Steinway piano or a secured baby crib. It could be a major television executive who needs a fleet of buses equipped with the latest in technology in order to travel the country filming the stories that we all watch on daily newscasts. And we have learned from experience that when Ed McMahon calls us, we have not won the multimillion-dollar sweepstakes. Even Ed needs a bus now and then! Our coaches are designed with amenities and features that rival those available at any five-star hotel, allowing those on the road the comforts of home.

As brothers and business partners, we started out with absolutely nothing. Over a period of twenty-five years, we have built a company that is firmly rooted in Christian values and ethics. These principles have enabled us to be a stable source in an often-unstable industry. Even when all we had at our disposal was older equipment, we were able to compete because of our unwavering commitment to service and loyalty. We are also deeply rooted in family, which extends beyond those family members with whom we share genetic makeup; our employees are our extended family, and they are all as committed to the Hemphill Brothers Coach Company as we are. Each is loyal, trustworthy and proud of the product he or she helps to create.

Our journey to success has not always been a smooth ride. It was difficult for us to gain respect when we were younger, and situations sometimes forced us to survive through financially and emotionally difficult times. We have learned not to force things, that indeed, there is a natural rhythm that beckons us to follow, and that by putting our heads together and sharing opinions, big decisions can be made more easily. Our business is like a moving bus. It has momentum and is moving in the right direction. We are simply here to pave the way and let those wheels keep turning 'round.

Trent Hemphill and Joel Hemphill Jr.
As told to Terri Duncan

EPILOGUE: *Hemphill Brothers Coach Company is located in Nashville, Tennessee. Trent and Joel Hemphill believe in exceeding the expectations of their clients, and their client list is a who's who of entertainers, actors, political figures and athletes. A Hemphill*

Brother's coach is a custom-built rolling hotel suite.

In addition to customizing buses, Hemphill Brothers Coach Company also leases buses. They can provide one for a weekend or forty for a national tour. Their drivers are among the best in the business and make safety a top priority. Trent and Joel consider their drivers to be a key element to their company's success.

Over the years, Trent and Joel have established many strong, long-term relationships. With honesty and integrity as well as innovative ideas, they have established the industry standard not only in design but also in service. For more information, visit their Web site at www.hemphillbrothers.com.

Terri Duncan

"The wheel kept getting stolen—until I invented 'The Club'."

The Fair Entrepreneur

"What would you like today?" our teenage daughter Erin asked the next customer in line. The woman placed an order for an award-winning Country Fair Cinnamon Roll. "I always come to the State Fair to buy the cinnamon rolls," she said to Erin. Then, looking around, she asked quietly, "But does your mother know you're working here?"

Unfortunately, general fairgoers' perceptions of most people who travel and work at fairs is both demeaning and wrong. You know: "Lock up the chickens and hide the kids, the nomads are coming to town!" But working behind those fair booths is an ensemble of entrepreneurs who have combined their love for travel and meeting people with an ability to make very good livings serving not only their own home communities, but communities around the country. And, yes, we do have homes. For us, it's in a small California Sierra Nevada mountain community, except when we're at our villa (formerly owned by the founder of Tupperware) on the property in Costa Rica.

As the owners of Country Fair Cinnamon Rolls—a mobile food concession company—the lifestyle we have chosen for our family is not what most people would consider traditional or "normal." And in their view, from inside their safety zones, they're right, but a traveling business fits our personalities and has provided many positive opportunities for our three daughters.

Like any entrepreneur, we started small, changing products that better suited us and better matched our chosen markets. Fortunately, our businesses have been successful. My husband, Eldon's, background is in inventing and manufacturing coin-operated amusement machines, so placing them at fairs was a natural outlet. From amusement machines, we expanded into Fresh Squeezed Orange Juice, served from a seven-foot-tall fiberglass orange. Our next entrepreneurial adventure was renting baby strollers and wheelchairs to fair patrons; we built that business until we owned and operated the largest stroller rental business in the country.

For the past twenty-odd years we have focused on one product—our exclusive, made-from-scratch-as-you-watch, served-hot-from-the-oven Country Fair Cinnamon Rolls. It's a product concept now used successfully by other baking companies. Our mobile bakery is designed to showcase the full production process; the hypnotic aroma of fresh baked bread and cinnamon draws people to our fair locations like bees to honey. For thousands of families around the country, our delicious cinnamon rolls have been a fair tradition much longer than airport and mall franchises have been selling them. Per our company slogan, our exceptional cinnamon rolls "Bring Back the Memories®" of good times and cozy comfort.

Our "Mama-Papa" company started with one small mobile bakery, and we now operate multiple trailers at fifty or so events per year, often at multiple locations within each fair. And we travel in a modern recreational vehicle that provides our family with comfortable living facilities including bathrooms, showers, and a kitchen. These are big investments.

But there's still that perception that we are wandering nomads and that our children suffer because, from May to October each year, our family is on the road. In reality, we have the good fortune to be contributing members of many communities—certainly with our neighbors in California and Costa Rica. But we also consider the "fair families" a community whose members are our friends and whose kids have been the playmates of our three daughters for their entire lives. Our fair families provide many things for the local communities in which they travel and conduct business: entertainment, special exhibits, new products, lots of great-tasting food and much-needed money in way of rental space costs and sales tax contributions.

Entrepreneurs are independent thinkers, looking for that perfect opportunity to meld their personal beliefs and lifestyles with a business that allows them to be themselves. Our business has allowed our family the opportunity to work hard together, then have time to play hard together. Our May-to-October working season allowed us, as parents, to participate actively in our daughters' and their friends' school sporting activities. Our daughters had the only "Room Daddy" at the school. We became the permanent chaperones for field trips and dances. The Halloween carnivals had professional food booths, and the volleyball club used our cinnamon roll trailer to earn money for years, even after our girls graduated.

We know that our three daughters, Dara, Erin and Ryan, have learned hands-on life experiences from growing up and working at fairs. They are self-confident and self-sufficient. They learned how to work with the public and deal with emergencies. Owning and operating their own Frozen Fruit Bar concession at age twelve enabled them to learn business skills firsthand, from establishing valuable work ethics to how to manage money, from ordering inventory to learning how to handle and serve food safely. And they have learned how to accept responsibility, take business risks to grow their business and enjoy the financial rewards that come from hard work.

Our chosen career path has also contributed to our daughters' education in many other ways. The girls have learned lessons in geography, math, history, political science, ecology, agriculture and art through everyday life experiences, both at fairs and during our travels. World travel is our passion; our lifestyle has allowed us the time and financial means for our family to travel literally from Katmandu to Timbuktu. And the life-changing lessons gained by the girls through travel have been priceless, including swimming in the Amazon to witnessing the cultures of African tribes. We have visited "fair friends" and their families in Switzerland, Argentina, Peru, Zimbabwe and Mexico and made new friends, from Costa Rica to the United States, all of whom have given our family insights into many cultures.

Without any doubt, we love our nomadic lives. And now we are passing the future of our business to our daughters and their families, and many other "fair families" are doing the same. The next generation has been well trained and is eagerly prepared to face the challenges and rewards of our "unconventional lifestyle."

So to answer that woman's question to Erin, yes, I do know where our daughters are working, and we are proud of them!

Janis Dale

Thank You, Mr. Wayne

Ever since I can remember, my father was at the forefront of the curve. Before my four brothers and I were even thought of, he began his long journey from his homeland of China in search of a better life. Traveling to Hong Kong and Japan, he always led the pack by calling his friends to join.

In the late 1960s, it was easier to get a working visa in South America than the United States. So Brazil would be my father's next stop, where he would open a Chinese restaurant and the place we would call home for the early part of our childhood. In South America in 1976, devaluation hit, and 90 percent of the value of our money was lost. With luck on his side, my father led the pack and left one year prior to this turbulent time.

Among the first major wave of Asians to come to the United States in the 1970s, my father happened to be in the right place during a thriving time. Real estate was booming when he purchased a restaurant on Balboa Island in affluent Newport Beach, California, for $90,000.

As my brothers and I were forced to tackle the culture shock of meeting new people and learning to speak English, my father worked hard to build his business. But it was one particular event in 1972 that triggered a boom in our family's business and changed our lives forever.

A young lady named Gloria Zigner, the publicist for John Wayne's wife, was planning her husband's birthday party at our restaurant. As a favor, Gloria asked her client if John Wayne would make an appearance at her husband's birthday party. The day he accepted was the day the press would twist the event in such proportions that the myth would begin, and my father's business would skyrocket.

As the press got wind that John Wayne would be dining at our restaurant, news spread that he was there for his own birthday! Soon, everyone associated my father's restaurant with John Wayne, and so came the power of celebrity endorsement. Suddenly, our restaurant became a social place that was famous by association. People were coming in to have the chef, who supposedly sang "Happy Birthday" to John Wayne, sing "Happy Birthday" to them. They would say, "Wow, your dad is friends with John Wayne!"

As business did well and our lives in Southern California progressed, so did our social agenda. My brothers and I grew to love the ocean and the beach lifestyle. Surfing became our way of life, and we became known in the surfing world.

As we grew older, our father encouraged us to go to college and discouraged us from working in the restaurant business. He said it was just too hard. So we each went to college to pursue our respective degrees. As I pursued my engineering degree at San Diego State University, I found that being near the border allowed for better partying and better waves. I changed my major and went on to study finance and was the first in my family to get a job in Corporate America. Bouncing around within a few major corporate companies, I realized that the freedom and flexibility that my parents had was not an option for me. I was on a regimented and confined schedule; my life was about rules and regulations. I was not happy.

Knowing I needed to make a career change, I got with my brothers Bismark, Ed and Mingo, and together we decided to start our own restaurant. Our idea? To tap into a new category of restaurants that was developing in the 1980s—quick casual dining! It would encompass a laid-back, hip environment with good-tasting, healthful fast food. Many surf trips down to Mexico would influence our food of choice—grilled fish tacos—but with our own Brazilian/Asian flair!

As with my father's business, we knew we needed celebrity backing. So we strategically positioned the location of our first restaurant in pursuit of our very own John Wayne—the surf industry! We gutted an old pizza joint in the surfing town of Costa Mesa, California, within just one mile of the major surf companies. A week before the grand opening, our menu was created from borrowed recipes from friends. Wahoo's Fish Taco was born.

Being near the surf industry, we knew we needed to be embraced by them, but knew we couldn't ask. In the surf world, you don't show up at the beach and expect to surf a local break without being invited in. We had to build this relationship, then hopefully the invitation would come on its own.

After opening the store in 1988, things moved slowly; we were working hard and not making much money. One day Mike, my brother's former boss from Newport Surf and Sport, asked me why we didn't have uniforms. Before I knew it, I was going on an official "walkthrough" of their warehouse. He gave me Billabong T-shirts, hats and shorts in pink, yellow, green—every day-glow color you can imagine. We had uniforms! Only a week later, a friend from Quiksilver asked why we were wearing all Billabong clothes. Can you guess what happened next? More and more surfwear companies followed. Then came the decorations, paintings, posters and stickers. The John Wayne ball was officially rolling.

Another call from Mike invited us to cater a preview they were putting on for the industry buyers. There we were, cooking fish tacos in their parking lot! The buyers couldn't believe what they were eating. Word spread about our catering services, and Wahoo's began to expand outside of the restaurant walls. John Wayne couldn't be more proud.

That next summer, the local paper contacted me to advertise on their special insert that was profiling surfers. I knew our business couldn't afford it, but I bought the entire back cover for two thousand dollars. I called Mike and asked him if I could use the Billabong logo on the ad. He agreed, and Wahoo's Fish Taco became the "official restaurant to Billabong." Before long, Quiksilver, O'Neill and others were on board. Suddenly, within our first year of business, we were the official restaurant to seven surf companies. It was John Wayne to the max!

After the ad came out, the surf companies brought their top riders into the store. For two weeks, I had "John Waynes" walking around the restaurant every day. I'd hear kids saying things like, "Oh my God! There's a world champion! There's a world champion!" Famous surfers were at our place, and for the first time, I knew we would be a success. The following year, Wahoo's exploded in popularity, becoming the official restaurant of over one hundred surf companies!

It's been eighteen amazing years, and the myth continues to grow. With over forty Wahoo's locations and a loyal following in the action sports world, Ed, Mingo and I couldn't be more grateful—grateful to our mom and dad for having the vision to come to America and teach us about hard work; grateful to the people in the surf world who invited us in to surf their break; and, most of all, grateful for that special birthday evening in 1972 at Shanghai Pine Garden Chinese restaurant.

Thank you, Mr. Wayne. The myth lives on.

In loving memory of our brother Bismark,
we dedicate this story to you in appreciation
of your constant support of our dream.
Thanks for being there to catch us when we jumped!

Wing Lam
As told to Gina Romanello

[EDITORS' NOTE: *Wing Lam is a cofounder and owner, along with his brothers Ed and Mingo, of Wahoo's Fish Taco. The trio continue their entrepreneurial spirit, having opened an online store for Wahoo's merchandise, including designer clothing, wine and kitchen accessories. All three are also very active in their community, donating their time, efforts and money, as well as Wahoo's name and reputation, to help raise funds for charitable organizations and causes. To learn more about the Lam brothers and Wahoo's Fish Taco, visit* www.wahoos.com.]

6

NEVER GIVE UP

All of our dreams can come true—if we have the courage to pursue them.

Walt Disney

The Successful You

If your ship doesn't come in, swim out to meet it.

Jonathan Winters

You probably know me best as that *Chicken Soup* guy who, along with that other *Chicken Soup* guy (a.k.a. Mark Victor Hansen), founded the *Chicken Soup for the Soul* series in the early 1990s. Well, yes, you're right, and I'm extremely fortunate to have this extraordinary series be a part of my life over the last decade.

But before I became that "*Chicken Soup* guy," I was, and continue to be, one of America's leading experts in motivating, training and coaching entrepreneurs, corporate leaders, managers, sales professionals, employees and educators. For the last thirty years, I have helped hundreds of thousands of individuals the world over achieve their dreams. I love what I do—and I do what I love—and I wish the same for you. Thus, I'm excited to share some of my wisdom with you, to inspire you into action. Are you game?

* * *

One of the most pervasive myths in American culture today is that we are entitled to a great life—that somehow, somewhere, someone is responsible for filling our lives with continual happiness, exciting career options, nurturing family time and blissful personal relationships—simply because we exist.

But the real truth is that there is only one person responsible for the quality of the life you live.

That person is you.

If you want to be successful, you have to take 100 percent responsibility for everything that you experience in your life. This includes the level of your achievements, the results you produce, the quality of your relationships, the state of your health and physical fitness, your income, your debts, your feelings—everything!

And this is not easy, especially when you're either contemplating starting your own business or you currently own a business. But I can help you get from where you are to where you want to be.

In my 2005 book—*The Success Principles™: How to Get from Where You Are to Where You Want to Be,* penned with Janet Switzer (HarperCollins)—I write about sixty-four principles and strategies that will give you the courage and the heart to start living successfully today. For the purposes of entrepreneurship, I have selected ten principles from my book to share with you:

1. **Decide what you want.** If you are going to get what you really want out of life, you will have to stop saying, "I don't know; I don't care; it doesn't matter to me," or my current favorite of teenagers, "Whatever!" When you are confronted with a choice, no matter how small or insignificant, act as if you have a preference. Ask yourself, *If I did know, what would it be? If I did care, which would I prefer? If it did matter, what would I rather do?*

2. **Unleash the power of goal setting.** Experts on the science of success know the brain is a goal-seeking organism. Whatever goal you give to your subconscious mind, it will work night and day to achieve. Much of this can be obtained through visualization (Principle #3, below), but it is up to you to figure out what you want and desire. When you create your goals, be sure to write down some big ones that will stretch you. It pays to have goals that will require you to grow to achieve them. Why? Because the ultimate goal, in addition to achieving your material goals, is to become a master at life. And to do this, you will need to learn new skills, expand your vision of what's possible, build new relationships and learn to overcome your fears, your intellectual considerations and any external roadblocks you encounter.

3. **See what you want, get what you see.** Visualization—or the act of creating compelling and vivid pictures in your mind of what it is that you want—may be the most underutilized success tool you possess, because it greatly accelerates the achievement of any success in many ways. When you consistently visualize your goal as already achieved, your brain will do three things: (1) generate creative solutions for achieving your dreams, (2) perceive more resources that can help you, and (3) increase your motivation to act. Sports psychologists and peak-performance experts have been popularizing the power of visualization since the 1980s, and almost all Olympic and professional athletes now employ the power of visualization. Remember, to get what you want, you need to first visualize it in your mind.

4. **Take action.** The world doesn't pay you for what you *know;* it pays you for what you *do*. There's an enduring axiom of success that says, "The universe rewards action." It is as simple and as true as this principle; it's surprising how many people get bogged down in analyzing, planning and organizing, when all they really need to do is *take action*. Many people fail to do so because they're afraid to fail. Successful people, on the other hand, realize that failure is an important part of the learning process. They know that failure is just the way we learn by trial and error. Simply get started, make mistakes, pay attention to feedback, correct and keep moving forward toward the goal. Every experience will yield more useful information that you can apply the next time.

5. **Use feedback to your advantage.** Once you begin to take action, you'll start getting feedback about whether you're doing the right thing or not. You'll get data, advice, help, suggestions, direction and even criticism that will continually enhance your knowledge, abilities, attitudes and relationships. But what you do with that feedback is critical. Be it good or bad, favorable or unfavorable, it is up to *you* to absorb the information and use it in a positive manner that will help you constantly adjust and move forward.

   To ensure you get valuable feedback, ask for it. For example, the most valuable question you can ever ask as an entrepreneur is the following: "On a scale of one to ten, how would you rate our product/service/relationship/etc.?" Anything less than a ten gets a follow-up question: "What would it take to make it a ten?" Ask this question of your clients, employees and suppliers. Ask it often, and then put new policies and procedures in place to constantly get closer to a ten.

6. **Commit to constant and never-ending improvement.** In Japan, the word for constant and never-ending improvement is *kaizen*. Not only is this an operating philosophy for modern Japanese businesses, it is also the age-old philosophy of warriors, too—and it's become the personal mantra of millions of successful people. Whenever you set out to improve your skills, change your behavior or better your family life or business, start with small, achievable goals that can be easily mastered. By consistently taking little steps, your belief that you can easily improve in that area will be greatly reinforced.

7. **Exceed expectations.** Are you someone who consistently goes the extra mile and routinely overdelivers on your promises? A rarity these days, this is the hallmark of high achievers who know that exceeding expectations will help them stand out above the crowd. Almost by habit, successful people *simply do more.* As a result, they experience not only greater financial rewards for their extra efforts, but also a personal transformation; they become more self-confident, more self-reliant and more influential with those around them. Always ask yourself, *How can I give my customers and clients more? How can I surprise them?*

8. **Stay motivated with the masters.** The title of this principle sounds a lot like the title of an exercise video, and it is—but for your brain. So many of us are trained (or brainwashed) by the media, parents,

schools and culture to have limiting beliefs. *It's not possible. I don't deserve it.* Well, you do deserve it, and only you can make it possible, by reading inspiring books and listening to motivational and educational CDs. Did you know that the average person commutes a total of one hour each day? In five years, that's 1,250 hours in the car, enough time to give yourself the equivalent of a college education! Use that commute as a time for maintaining high levels of motivation, learning a language, honing your management skills or creating sales and marketing strategies. Use this time to learn virtually anything you want or need to know to succeed at a higher level. A comprehensive list of books and audio programs can be found on pages 441 to 451 of *The Success Principles.*

9. **Hire a personal coach.** Of all the things successful people do to accelerate their trip down the path to success, participating in some kind of coaching program is at the top of their list. A coach will help you clarify your vision and goals, support you through your fears, keep you focused, confront your unconscious behaviors and old patterns, expect you to do your best, help you live by your values, show you how to earn more while working less and keep you focused on your core genius.

10. **Mastermind your way to success.** We all know that two heads are better than one when it comes to solving a problem or creating a result. So imagine having a permanent group of five to six people who meet every week for the purpose of problem solving, brainstorming, networking, encouraging and motivating each other. This process, called *masterminding,*

is one of the most powerful tools for success presented in my book. I don't know anybody who has become super-successful who has not employed the principle of masterminding. If you are not already in a mastermind group, join or start one now.

* * *

I simply leave you with one of my favorite ancient Chinese proverbs—*"A journey of one thousand miles must begin with one step."* Godspeed.

Jack Canfield

[EDITORS' NOTE: *To learn more about* The Success Principles *and Jack's mentorship, training, coaching, audio and speaking programs, please visit* www.successprinciples.com *or call toll-free 800-237-8336.*]

"You're an entrepreneur, eh?
How long have you been trying to get ahead?"

Pride and Prejudice

I never wanted to be an entrepreneur. I just wanted to have a newspaper.

It was 1974, and the news of Watergate had just broken. Immigrants in Seattle's Chinatown were lining up outside grocery stores to buy Chinese newspapers from San Francisco, so they could read about the news. In those days, the Chinese immigrant community had to rely on rumors and gossip. I wanted to help the community by providing them with information and facts. Starting a newspaper seemed like the right thing to do.

Despite objections from my parents and friends, and a touch of skepticism from my husband, I began my marketing campaign. I distributed flyers announcing a new Chinese-language newspaper throughout Chinatown. I told everyone on the street that I was starting a newspaper. People thought I was crazy. One man pulled me aside and said, "You keep on telling people that you are starting a newspaper. What if, in the end, you have no paper?"

Failure was neither an option nor a concern. I completely ignored the statistics that four out of five newspapers in this country fail because of lack of revenue and insufficient advertising. Although my only prior sales experience was a three-week stint in a boutique, I was not to be deterred. *Why should I let anybody else determine my fate?* I asked myself. Whenever I felt discouraged, I would think about those people waiting in line just to get a copy of the newspaper. I could not turn my back on them. If I met rejection, I would look at it as the entire group of people facing rejection, not just me alone. All along, I saw the endeavor in terms of "us," as opposed to just "me."

We—us in the "us" I envisioned—were forced to deal with rejection a little sooner than I expected. After putting together a selling strategy, I decided to target the oldest, most successful restaurant in Chinatown. I thought that I would have the best chance at selling an ad because the owner would certainly have enough money to afford advertising. Mr. Quan was a well-known citizen, respected for his straightforward approach to business. Confidently, I walked into Tai Tung Restaurant and asked to speak to him. The hostess looked me up and down, surprised that a young woman dressed in jeans and tennis shoes would make such a request. Puzzled, she disappeared into a back room and returned with Mr. Quan. I was oblivious not only to proper business attire, but also to business etiquette. Looking back, I should have commented on the fabulous décor of the restaurant or on the success of his business, but I had only one intention: selling ad space for my newspaper.

"Mr. Quan, my name is Assunta Ng. I am starting the *Seattle Chinese Post,* a Chinese-language newspaper. I want you to buy an ad."

Mr. Quan, charmed by my boldness, asked me to join him at a booth. "Assunta, I have not advertised for thirty years, and I'm doing great," he explained earnestly. "Why should I advertise now? And why with you?"

I explained the benefits of advertising in my newspaper, but to no avail. More than ten minutes passed, and still

Mr. Quan did not budge on his decision. This was going to be harder than I thought. Mr. Quan had no desire to advertise, and he had no problem telling me so. The community had not had such a newspaper in more than fifty years, he explained. If he decided to advertise now, people might assume that his business was failing. I knew I was in trouble. The Seattle Chinatown community had forgotten the purpose of advertising.

"No," he said adamantly. "I will not advertise in your newspaper."

Frustrated, I began to gather myself and leave the restaurant, but something stopped me. I recalled my childhood: "No" was an all-too-familiar word. Growing up in a traditional Chinese family in Hong Kong, I had heard it far too many times.

As a young girl, I was not allowed to dream. My life had already been planned for me, and there was no possibility for variance from that path. I would do all of my family's cooking, washing and housework until I was old enough to find a husband of my own. That was it—nothing more. My two brothers would be given everything and would never have to lift a finger around the house. They were first-class citizens, and I was not.

Little girls could not create anything for themselves; they could not imagine becoming doctors, lawyers, entrepreneurs or anything else. We were expected to be obedient and subservient. I was timid and shy, never questioned authority, always followed all the rules. The only role models I knew were housewives, secretaries and teachers. Although I loved my mother dearly, I knew one thing for sure: I never wanted to end up like her. As a housewife, her life was as predictable as the sunrise, void of excitement and change. My father was a businessman involved in the import and export of commodities, but he was never a role model. I was not allowed to ask him any questions about his business, and would have been mocked had I tried.

As the eldest child, I felt a compelling need to be independent. My culture, I knew, would never permit this behavior from a young woman. My spirit was too wild and free for the restrictive chains of traditional society to contain me, and I began looking for a way out. I spent my free time reading works of literature from the American Cultural Exchange Library in Hong Kong. I admired the free spirit of American authors such as Pearl S. Buck, and decided that America was the place for me.

Although my parents had low expectations of me, they believed in the value of a good education. They sent my brothers and me to the best Catholic missionary school in Hong Kong. My unhappiness prevented me from excelling in high school. When I passed the national standardized exam with flying colors, everyone was surprised. It came as a shock to everyone, including my parents, that I was intelligent. I scored in the top tenth percentile, and suddenly I became college material. Immediately, my parents and peers perceived me differently. *And so did I.* Convinced that America was the road to a new and better life, I mustered up the courage to tell my parents that I wanted to go. "No," they said without discussion. "Get those ridiculous thoughts out of your mind."

During the six months that followed, I acted in absolute rebellion for the first time in my life. I did not utter a word nor did I express any emotion. My parents were standing in the way of my dream, and I was determined to let them know of my disapproval. Finally, my parents realized that my heart was truly set on going to America, and they agreed to give me the money for one year's university tuition. After that, I would be on my own. At the age of eighteen, I boarded a plane from Hong Kong to Portland, Oregon.

Recalling my childhood forced me to remind myself that I was in America, the land of dreams and possibilities. I could not take "no" for an answer. I remembered the faces of the people standing in the long line.

"Mr. Quan, forget about advertising. I am not asking you to advertise," I said, changing my strategy.

"You are not?" His face showed relief.

"You'd like to see a Chinese-language newspaper in this community, right?"

"Right," he replied.

"I am asking you to put a congratulatory message from the staff of Tai Tung Restaurant to the *Seattle Chinese Post* on its grand opening," I said.

"So this is not an advertisement?" he inquired.

"Oh, absolutely not," I assured him.

"How much is half a page?" he asked.

"One hundred seventy-five dollars."

Mr. Quan reached into his back pocket, counted out $175 in cash and laid it on the table. My first ad!

From there, I went to every business in Chinatown and said, "Mr. Quan is advertising, so would you like to also? And by the way, he paid cash." I must have worn out five pairs of shoes going door-to-door selling ads, but the reward was awesome: I was able to collect four thousand dollars in advertising for my first issue and signed up hundreds of subscribers.

If you believe in your dream, never, ever give up. "No" may mean "not now" or "maybe later." But in the world of business, "no" is never final—and it is where the real fun begins.

Assunta Ng

EPILOGUE: *Assunta Ng is the founder and publisher of both the* Seattle Chinese Post, *published in Chinese, and its sister publication, the* Northwest Asian Weekly, *published in English. Both papers serve the Asian community of Seattle and its neighboring cities.*

According to Ng, the Seattle Chinese Post *was a relatively early participant in what has become a significant trend in the publishing business and the proliferation of Asian-language media in the United States. Per Ng, the growth is fed by demographics, because Asian and Pacific ethnic groups make up the fastest-growing segment in America's population.*

To learn more about Ng and her papers, please visit www.nwasianweekly.com.

Dahlynn McKowen

Thirty-Five-Minute Miles

In the early 1990s, at the age of twenty-seven, I founded Earth General, one of the hottest environmental retail stores in the country. I was featured on the front page of the *New York Times* and then profiled in *Mademoiselle* magazine's "Who's Hot Under 30" section. Me . . . on the same list with Michael Dell, Julia Roberts, Brad Pitt and Michael Jordan.

With the business booming, I decided to open a second store, never bothering to ask anyone else's input. *Hey, why mess with success?* I thought. My store was rocking, and I was the one who made it happen. Unfortunately, I didn't have a handle on what was making the first store so successful or a solid infrastructure to expand. And while I had some incredible entrepreneurial skills, I was sorely lacking some foundational skills.

Within a year, the business went bankrupt and I was getting divorced. My entire life felt like it was crashing down around me. In just seven years I had raised and lost almost a million dollars of my investors' money—including my mother's—and I couldn't even look at myself in the mirror. My over-inflated ego was reduced to incredibly low self-esteem. The only thing I found joy and peace in was running. I ran several times a week and had it down to a seven-minute mile. But other than my five-mile runs, my life was at rock bottom.

One day I was walking across the street near my home in Brooklyn. Out of nowhere a car came barreling around the corner and hit me head-on, catapulting me onto the sidewalk and fracturing my skull. While I lay in a coma for weeks, the doctors told my family they didn't know if I would live or die; and if I lived—whether I would be able to walk again.

When I woke up three weeks later, I had no memory of the accident. In fact, I didn't remember anything. One night I was at my parents' house with some family and friends. I thought, *Wow! A party. I wonder what it's for?* They told me the party was for me . . . to celebrate the fact that I was alive. At that moment I began to piece together what happened.

During the next few months I went through the most intense hell you could imagine. I had lost almost all of my hearing and vision. The doctors said I might never be able to walk again, let alone run.

Before the accident, I had started a mastermind group of people who supported each other in making things happen in our lives. After hearing the doctors' grim prognosis, I told the group, "I'm going to come up with an unreasonable goal. Ninety days from today I'm going to run five miles in Central Park." They looked at each other as if I were crazy, but then said, "Okay, we'll support you."

And so I began to train. And every time I became discouraged—and there were a *lot* of times during my new "thirty-five-minute mile pace" that this would occur—my hope and faith were tested to the nth degree. I was determined to prove my doctors wrong and to prove to myself that I could pick myself up and make something positive out of my life. Every time I would fall down or want to give up on my dream of running again, the group encouraged me to keep going.

That's when I learned the value of a team and the necessity of a strong support structure. I realized I had failed in business because I was too arrogant; it had been all about *me.* Now I realized that I was only as strong as the team around me. They gave me inspiration.

On December 28, 2002, eighty-seven days after I set my ninety-day goal, I met twenty-two friends and family in Central Park. Together we ran five miles, six months after doctors said I might never walk again.

As I crossed the finish line, I realized the power of a crystal-clear vision, intense determination, and most important, an awesome support structure. I came to realize that there is absolutely nothing that we can't accomplish if we set our minds to something and it resonates deep in our core.

I took the same strategy I used during my recovery and applied it to my future businesses. Within two years of the accident, I created two healthy and thriving companies, one of which now allows me to share my passion and lessons learned with other entrepreneurs. Many people said that this terrible accident would change my life forever, and they're right. I'm one lucky guy.

Stefan Doering

EPILOGUE: *Stefan Doering, president and founder of BEST Coaches, Inc., creates and facilitates breakthrough "90-Day Dream Teams" specifically aimed at entrepreneurs. A groundbreaking process, Doering brings to the table nearly a quarter-century of hard-earned business savvy and four decades of pure heart, helping other entrepreneurs achieve equally ambitious and outrageous goals in their businesses and personal lives.*

The entrepreneurial spirit became evident in Doering when, at age of seventeen, he started his first business—Doering Housepainters—with the motto of "Help us paint our way through college." After receiving an MBA from Pace University in New York and rising to vice president at Citigroup, Doering launched and managed four more companies, two of which were firsts of their kind: Earth General was a one-stop retail store for more than 3,000 environmental products and became one of the largest environmental outlets in the nation, and VentureMate, an innovative Internet business that traded shares in private companies before going public. VentureMate was designed to make investing in private companies easier for investors.

To learn more about Doering and BEST Coaches, Inc., please visit www.BestCoachesInc.com.

Dahlynn McKowen

The Candy Man Can

You can tell a lot about a fellow by his way of eating jelly beans.

Ronald Reagan

When I was thirteen years old, I started working with my dad at our little family candy company located in Oakland, California. I learned a lot from my dad, as he did everything there was to do in the company. Then in 1960, I went to work for the family business full-time. I started at 5:30 A.M., turned on the boiler and had candy ready to process for the crew who arrived at 7:00 A.M. I was paid sixty-eight dollars a week and was very proud to be a candy man, just like my father, my grandfather and my great-grandfather.

Gustav Goelitz—my great-grandfather—came to America in 1866 from Germany. He bought a little shop in Belleville, Illinois, and started producing candy. Having learned to make candy from his father, my grandfather Herman Goelitz started his own candy company in 1921 in Portland, Oregon. Candy corn was his company's main product, but the damp weather and humidity weren't good for making butter crèmes like candy corn, so he moved his company to Oakland, across the bay from San Francisco.

My grandfather had one child, Aloyse Goelitz, my mother. She married my dad, Ernie Rowland, who came to work in the candy business, too. He had a real knowledge of engineering and kept the machinery running even when it was past its prime. My mother ultimately worked in payables and receivables and was a wise advisor to me.

In the 1950s and '60s, it was difficult to make a penny from a seasonal product such as candy corn. Some years we even lost a few pennies; we had to start making candy six months before Halloween and often had to get extended terms for payment to purchase the raw materials from our suppliers. Fortunately, we had very good working relations with our suppliers, like Al Saroni, who would advance us the sugar, saying he knew we were good for payment later on.

My folks and I decided it was imperative to expand so we could sell a higher-quality product line at a higher margin. We needed to do this in order for the company to survive. When things were really tough, I wondered what I would do in order to feed my family if the business did not survive. I felt that if the company failed, I would not be capable of working any other place. After all, I had only a high school education and a year of college. As such, I poured my life and soul into making the business grow. We began to dream up new candies, and then we hired a European confectioner to help us. The result was the "Dutch Mint®," which is one of our best products even today. Continuing to expand our candy product line led to our company making the first American-produced gummi bear, and we also started making jelly beans.

In the early '60s, I read an article about Small Business

Administration advisors who could help organize a business. I got in touch with Mr. McDaniel, who was a businessman working through SCORE (Service Corps of Retired Executives). He worked every Saturday with my parents and me for two years and educated us on running our business more efficiently. After a few months, his recommendation was to add on to our cramped 10,000-square-foot factory to increase capacity. As payment for his help and advice, all Mr. McDaniel would accept was a tuna fish sandwich for lunch each day.

With an SBA loan guarantee for 90 percent and Mr. McDaniel in tow, we went over to the Bank of America in San Francisco and showed the loan officer our financial statement and told him our story. He took one look at our statement and said to sell off all the assets and close the business because we would never make a go of it. We left in shock. Thankfully, that afternoon our local Bank of America branch manager offered us a portion of the finances we asked for in San Francisco, a loan that would allow us to at least construct the building.

Driving to work one day, I heard a gentleman by the name of Ronald Reagan, who was running for governor of California, on the radio. I was impressed with his political ideas and thought that he was someone who could make a difference in the world. From that moment on I became an admirer and supporter of Ronald Reagan. Little did I know he would learn about us in the years ahead.

My good friend and mentor Russell Albers, who was president of a confectionery retail chain, was introduced to Ronald "Dutch" Reagan at a political reception in Los Angeles in 1966. There, he learned from an acquaintance that Reagan was attempting to give up his pipe smoking habit by eating jelly beans. Russ began sending him our mini gourmet jelly beans as a courtesy. This was ten years before Jelly Belly jelly beans were born.

When Reagan won the election for California's governor, Russ suggested we send the jelly beans directly to Sacramento, which we continued to do throughout his term as governor and in the years following. It wasn't long before we received a very gracious letter of thanks from Governor Reagan, who mentioned the jelly beans were served at meetings in the Capitol. That letter is on public display at our tour center in California.

In the summer of 1976, I received a call from an employee of a distributor in Los Angeles who knew we made quality candy. He was a very creative guy and had an idea for a jelly bean made with "natural" ingredients. We started with eight flavors of jelly beans, which were named Jelly Belly. They were sold in single flavors, not in assorted mixes like we had been doing with the mini jelly beans we produced at that time. Orders started to roll in for this new product.

When we sent Governor Reagan his usual shipment of jelly beans, we substituted our newest candy creation, Jelly Belly jelly beans. Then something remarkable and unthinkable happened. In 1980, Ronald Reagan was on the campaign trail for the presidency and was photographed by *Time* magazine with a bowl of our Jelly Belly jelly beans on the table in his hotel suite. The national press became aware he ate jelly beans, and then the *San Jose Mercury News* broke the story that those jelly beans were made by our California company. In January 1981, all the media wanted to know our story. For two days I sat in my office afraid to let the media in, but I finally had to. We did back-to-back interviews from 8:00 A.M. to 7:00 P.M. for days with reporters from around the world. Once that story hit, our phone kept ringing with people who wanted our jelly beans.

During that time, we received a call from the

Presidential Inaugural Planning Committee inquiring whether it would be possible to supply red, white and blue jelly beans for the inaugural parties in Washington. This was not a problem as a blueberry-flavored Jelly Belly had been created that summer to make up the colors of the American flag with red (very cherry) and white (coconut), which were regular flavors. We sent three and a half tons of Jelly Belly jelly beans to Washington. The privilege of supplying the Inaugural Committee with candy was overwhelming, but then upstaged by the shock of receiving an invitation to attend the Washington celebrations. In a whirlwind trip, my wife and I attended the celebrations, being even more surprised to see Jelly Belly jelly beans photographed in the official inaugural book.

As time went on, it seemed all of America wanted to taste the jelly beans President Reagan loved. We were backlogged in orders for well over a year. We were thrilled by press reports that President Reagan gave jars of Jelly Belly jelly beans to visiting dignitaries. One day I was watching the news reports of the space flight of the shuttle *Challenger* when the astronauts opened a surprise package sent by President Reagan. It was filled with Jelly Belly jelly beans, and those beans were floating in space!

Today we're still making candy corn and Dutch Mints, as well as Jelly Belly jelly beans and our newest sensation, Sport Beans™ (formulated with carbohydrates, electrolytes and vitamins, the jelly beans are the ideal Portable Power™ for endurance athletes, weekend warriors and sports enthusiast of all types). We also make approximately one hundred other candies. And we have two manufacturing plants—the one in California and another in Illinois—and over 600 employees.

I wish I could remember the name of that San Francisco banker who turned us down, so I could send him a complimentary bag of Jelly Belly jelly beans; I'm curious what he would have to say today.

Herman G. Rowland Sr.

EPILOGUE: *Herman G. Rowland Sr. is chairman of the board of the Jelly Belly Candy Company. More important, Rowland is a fourth-generation candy man.*

More than just a hill of beans, Jelly Belly jelly beans are the world's number-one and best-loved gourmet jelly bean. Today, Rowland oversees every aspect of the business, which includes major production facilities in both California and Illinois.

California factory tours and Illinois warehouse tours delight young and old alike. In 2005, the California facility, located in the Bay Area city of Fairfield, was named "Best of America" by Reader's Digest *magazine for its factory tours. The Fairfield location features an extremely popular visitor center and gift shop and an elevated walkway through the manufacturing plant, accommodating close to a half a million visitors annually.*

Family legacy lives on at Jelly Belly; the fifth generation of candy makers is active in the company's operation. Rowland's daughter Lisa Brasher serves on the board of directors and is in senior management; son Herm Rowland Jr. is a vice president; youngest son, Christopher Rowland, works on various assignments in shipping and event organizing; daughter Becky Joffers serves on the board of directors; and son-in-law Andy Joffer is vice president of sales. And some of Rowland's nine grandchildren—the sixth generation and the future of the company—spend their teenage summers learning the family business.

True to his roots, Rowland makes sure that the company still cooks up candy corn based on the family's original recipe. His grandfather would definitely be proud.

Dahlynn McKowen

A Promise to Keep

When I reflect upon my personal journey, I see the many crossroads I have confronted. Rather than standing still, the opportunity to choose a new direction propelled me forward, granted me the chance to see new landscapes and to embrace the life I was blessed with, regardless of the myriad challenges along the way. I now vividly recognize how the road I chose guided me to the life I know today.

As any young child, my earliest memories revolved around my family. My parents were high school sweethearts who married young and settled down in New Jersey. Surrounded by our large clan of relatives, I spent my days with my maternal grandparents—Nannie and Papa—and playing with my cousins.

The Antonetti name was a proud one, a testament to our strong Italian heritage. My father came to America from Rome in 1954 with nothing in his pocket except the dried sausages his mother had packed so he wouldn't starve. He arrived with the American Dream in his heart and a belief that if he worked hard he, too, would achieve that dream.

My father chased his dream, working tirelessly to rise

up the ranks of Corporate America. His goal was to give his family what he never had, but his dream became the monster that took him away from us and consumed him. His corporate job forced him to travel for extended periods and uprooted our family from its foundation over and over again. His job spit him back at us beaten up, exhausted, feeling unappreciated and inevitably filled with disappointment as the promise of the traditional gold retirement watch turned into the reality of downsizing.

My mother, a gifted artist, lived for her family, but soon became lonely, bitter and depressed during my father's long absences, eventually grasping for anything that would numb her pain. Addiction took control of her life and changed her from a loving, beautiful woman into something quite different. The "safe place to land" that a child's home should be was something my brother and I had for a brief moment in time, but was shattered as our parents' choices began impacting our family. This hurt me to the core and left the two of us to fend for ourselves. I spent much of my childhood dreaming of "normal," envisioning a day when I could have a home and family of my own. I wanted to feel safe, accepted and loved for who I was.

When bad looked like it could not get any worse, the unthinkable happened: my mother committed suicide. This proved to be one of my life's critical crossroads; I was only seventeen, and my mother, in that one final, desperate moment, had ended the path of her own life and redirected the course of mine.

While my mother's death had crushed me, it also pushed me to break away from all that I knew. I no longer dreamed and waited for life to come find me. I struck out to make things happen, and although I had no idea where I was going, I felt I already had met with life's bottom.

Nannie, the light in my life, was also my compass for life. When I left home, I took her voice with me: *You have a strong spirit and you will have a great life if you don't weaken. But if you do hit bottom, at least learn something while you're down there.*

I vowed to follow Nannie's words, regardless of the roadblocks and dead ends that challenged me. I was determined not to weaken and succumb to what I feared was my life's original road, a road paved with sad memories. It was those memories of my father that caused me to never trust Corporate America or to be satisfied with only one job. I often held several jobs at a time, working days, nights and weekends, whatever it took to move my life forward.

Then, at twenty-six, I thought my dream of a "normal" home and family was finally close at hand! Newly married to a man from a good family, we were soon blessed with a child. Feeling our baby growing inside of me was one of the most exciting times of my life! I was ready for that perfect life, the one I had dreamed of as a child.

Determined to be the great mom, I dove into learning. I read books, took classes and sought advice. I was determined to create the ideal place for my family to grow. We named our son David, and life was wonderful for a moment.

The joy I felt in David's birth was my most perfect blessing. I have never in my life felt more close to God than during this time. But when we took our newborn son home from the hospital, David's crying turned to agonizing screams of pain. The minor rashes that most babies get covered David's entire body. A familiar feeling began to stir inside me—life was taking a U-turn back to my days of fear and desperation.

David was sick, and I was petrified. We struggled through months of health issues as I turned to doctors, nurses and specialists, none of whom seemed to be giving us answers. Physically and emotionally exhausted, alone and beaten, hopelessness was closing in around me, and I believed it was coming even faster for David. What I had thought was going to be my "happily ever after" was turning into the hardest struggle of my life. Besides trying to help David, my marriage was falling apart. I was facing an all-too-familiar crossroad.

But Nannie's words echoed in my head, *If you hit bottom, at least learn something while you're down there.* I had no idea what I could learn from losing David, the most important gift of my life, so instead I made a promise out loud to God and myself: "If you let me keep him, I will do something to give back. I'm not sure what, but I will die trying."

I started journaling as much as I could. I soon discovered that David only had very severe reactions on Tuesdays, the day I cleaned house! Dumbfounded that my conclusion could not possibly be true, I went to the library on a mission to find answers. I was shocked to learn how toxic our homes had become over the years. In a panic, I raced home and threw out every cleaning product and anything I thought could be toxic. Then I opened the windows, sat down and cried. I had no idea if I was either right or insane, but I knew for the first time in months I took back my power and made a choice to do something. David didn't get sick that day, or the next, or any day that week. The sink was filling up fast with dirty dishes and the floor was piled with soiled laundry, but David was getting better. I saw hope for the first time.

Feeling that my son was safe, I looked at my home, which now was an absolute wreck. I had to get my home and life back in order. I reached out for knowledge to the most constant and reliable person in my life—Nannie. She shared with me that in her era people, not companies, made products. She gave me her own recipe on how to make soap and it was a simple mixture, with love as the most important ingredient.

I began using her recipes and sharing the results with friends and other moms. Word spread, and I found myself making more and more soap. Slowly I learned how to get more uses from the soap by grating a bar on a cheese grater; I was now able to wash clothes and used the gratings for a variety of other household cleaning chores.

Once again I found myself at another of life's cross-roads. Keeping my promise to God and myself, I knew I had a responsibility as a parent to tell others about what I had learned. Corporate America was leading women down a road of "fresh scent" and "concentrated cleaning power" without sharing any knowledge about safety and long-term health consequences. If I so easily made these mistakes, so would others.

With nothing but faith and my promise, I took my Nannie's recipe and began making vegetable-based products for moms like me. Without really knowing it, I stepped into the multibillion-dollar cleaning industry. I was determined to speak up for what I believed were the new choices needed for today's families. At the time, no one could have known how difficult this chosen crossroad in my life's journey was going to be. I had no idea how much would be asked of my family, my friends and myself. It came down to trust—trusting that I had enough in me to give it all back, knowing that I might lose everything I had ever known.

My journey continues to unfold and brings with it new challenges and new roads to explore. Yet at the end of each day, I remain connected to my promise, to my purpose, to my son—and always to helping people make better choices for their families. I believe there is a human-friendly lifestyle that offers better choices for everything and everyone around us. I consider my role and my life an honor and a responsibility. I take this journey down my personal road very seriously, and am truly grateful for each and every step.

Amilya Antonetti

EPILOGUE: *Besides being the mother of David, now a happy and healthy preteen, Amilya Antonetti is the founder of Amilya's Soapworks and president of AMA Productions.*

Inspired by the love for her son, created with her grandmother's wisdom and using the finest ingredients available, Amilya's Soapworks offers cleaning products that are certified hypo-allergenic, family safe, nontoxic, cruelty-free and biodegradable. Her products can be found at stores throughout the nation, including Hudson Bay Companies (Canada) and Linens 'n Things.

Outside studies show Amilya's Soapworks work as well as, if not better than, the harsh chemical products the majority of Americans use today. Using her entrepreneurial prowess, motherly instincts and life experiences to compete, and succeed, against the tightly knit world of America's mega-cleaning industry conglomerations, Antonetti's products are also very price competitive compared with those other brands.

Coined the "Better Choice Mom," Antonetti has been a featured guest on Oprah, Extra *and the* The Early Show on CBS, *to name a few. She is a nationally known speaker to both mothers and the business world, and an author as well, having penned* Why David Hated Tuesdays: One Courageous Mother's Guide to Keeping Your Family Toxin and Allergy Free *(Prima, 2003) and a self-published book entitled* The Broken Cookie—Life Can Be More Than Crumbs. *A frequent radio guest, Antonetti reaches out to the masses, teaching people how to live a fun, cost-effective and easy human-friendly lifestyle, and offers advice on making "Better Choices" for themselves and their families.*

Antonetti's business is worth millions. Albeit small in comparison with the billions that the "big boys" of the cleaning industry bring in, it's not bad for a single mom who made a promise to God and herself to help others find their way back to a simpler and more trusted way of life. She kept her word.

To learn more about Amilya's Soapworks, please visit www.soapworks.com *or* www.betterchoicemom.com.

Dahlynn McKowen

Lemming entrepreneurs

The Nose Knows

We can't become what we need to be by remaining what we are.

Oprah Winfrey

I like to say, "I'm alive and kicking!" Not many people are inclined to say something like that. I was living in New York City and working on my master's degree in food studies at New York University, studying the social, cultural and historical aspect of food. My goal was to become an academic and study the history of the restaurant and the humanistic element of dining.

Then, at age twenty-five, just two days before September 11, 2001, I lapsed into a coma. While I was taking a three-and-a-half-week nap, the rest of the world was in shambles. I awoke to find myself blind and paralyzed, but I had survived bacterial meningitis.

Sometimes, life's goals change quickly. After awaking from my coma, I found myself back at infancy, learning such basic tasks as bathing, dressing and feeding. Eating was the worst; I had to rely on a feeding tube for four months, and when I was wheeled around the hospital in my wheelchair, my nose would catch the aroma of what others were eating. My sense of smell became so acute that I would call out what people were eating as I passed by. When I finally got to actually eat something, the hospital staff fed me pureed spinach! I spit it out! Being in that hospital was bad enough, but they also wanted to kill me with their food!

I really love food and discovered my fascination with it from baking with my *safta* ("grandmother" in Hebrew). Thanks to my *safta,* cooking turned into my creative outlet. I have an identical twin brother named Ron, and when we were younger, we shared household chores. One of us would clean, and the other one would cook. We always ate much better when I cooked.

I began my professional exploration of restaurants in high school; I joined an after-school program that provided training in many different vocational disciplines. Originally, I had planned to attend culinary school after high school, but backed out at the last minute. Instead, I went to San Francisco State University where I graduated with a degree in hospitality management. My first management position was at the Millennium Restaurant. It was here, while hosting a wine dinner with Bonny Doon Vineyards, that I first got the wine bug.

As my career progressed so too did my fascination with wine. I studied at the University of California at Davis in the sensory evaluation of wine. I also completed my first course toward becoming a master sommelier. The Court of Master Sommeliers is an organization dedicated to educating the world's wine professionals.

After my illness, I found that job opportunities in my chosen field were almost nonexistent for someone who was blind. Frustrated, I reflected on the positive side of my blindness and literally followed my nose, right into the wine bar business.

In 2004, I risked everything I had and became an

entrepreneur, opening the Symposium Wine Bar, located in Irvine, California. At Symposium, we focus on taking the snobbery out of the wine experience. Located in a hip, modern industrial space designed for sensory enjoyment, we offer wine flights—three tastes of wine—which I call Threesomes.

What's different at my bar is that guests learn by experiencing the different elements that wine offers. They learn to use their sense of taste and, of course, smell! Besides wine, Symposium serves food—mostly cheese and chocolate—which stimulate our guests' taste buds, palettes and other senses, helping them to become better versed in the history, pleasures and subtleties of wine tasting. And I giggle to myself sometimes when I share tasting techniques with guests, because when wine critics talk about wine, they always emphasize doing blind tastings. I truly do blind tastings!

Owning a successful new business is hard work. In fact, sometimes I'm not sure which is harder, being an entrepreneur or overcoming my paralysis. I continue physical therapy to this day. Some people go to the gym to look good; I go so I can walk. I have gone from a wheelchair to a walker, to a quad cane to a single point cane, and now to only a guiding cane, yet I still have balance issues from the brain surgery.

I must thank my parents for their love and support during my long recovery; my mom is a medical doctor, and if it wasn't for her, I probably wouldn't be here. And my father was my coach—he always pushed me just a little more, especially when I was thinking about risking everything on a new specialty business without an established customer base. He believed in me, and I am honored to have him as my business partner, in charge of the finances. I don't want anyone to rob me blind!

Don Katz

EPILOGUE: *According to Katz, Symposium Wine Bar takes its name from the ancient Greco-Roman parties of abundant wine, conversation and entertainment, a maxim that holds true for his establishment. The bar offers American, French and Australian wines.*

Business is booming, and Katz plans on opening Symposium Wine Bars throughout the world and then traveling abroad, choosing wines for his restaurants. His business has been featured in many publications and business venues, including Entrepreneur.com.

To learn more about Symposium Wine Bar, please visit www.symposiumwinebar.com.

Dahlynn McKowen

Diving Head First into the Mud

It's not whether you get knocked down; it's whether you get up again.

Vince Lombardi

It was August 1984, and I had much to be thankful for: a wonderful life with a very special family and a great job as an administrator for the University of Missouri. Having been in education for over twenty-five years, I was well established and comfortable in my chosen field. I planned on being in academia for the rest of my working days.

It never occurred to me to upset the apple cart and try something off the beaten path . . . until that fateful autumn day. One of my staff members came into my office and handed me a couple of tapes by a motivational speaker I had never heard of named Jim Rohn. While I doubted he had anything to say that would be applicable to my life, I took the tapes home and listened to his message with my wife, Betty. To my surprise, his words had a significant impact on my outlook and caused me to reevaluate my life's purpose and goals. I realized that I was not living up to my potential, even though I was financially stable and working toward retirement. But with a doctorate in education and a lifetime in academia, what else could I do?

Over the eighteen months that followed, this realization weighed heavily on my mind, and I became more and more restless. No longer was I fulfilled or satisfied. I felt that I wanted to leave the university and try my wings in business, but I did not know where to begin.

In January 1986, Betty and I went to Atlanta to visit my old college roommate. I shared my frustrations and my feeling that there had to be something else I could do in life that would be more fulfilling. He suggested that I join his real-estate company and take a shot at selling franchises in Georgia—this, in spite of the fact that I had no sales training or experience. I would be on a fifty-fifty split and be responsible for my expenses. If I proved I could sell the franchises, then we would try to purchase an exclusive region from the franchiser in Denver.

The offer was appealing, but a far cry from becoming reality. It would mean cashing in more than twenty-six years of retirement monies, selling our house, and moving a thousand miles away from our children and grandchildren—all of this at the ripe age of fifty. In other words, we would have to take a leap of faith and risk losing every material thing we had accumulated over the course of a lifetime.

On March 10, 1986, I did just that. I left Missouri for Augusta, Georgia, to launch my career selling real-estate franchises.

They say that in every successful adventure there is a defining moment—an event so dramatic, it either makes you or breaks you. My moment came ten days into my new career.

My first week and a half of selling was an absolute nightmare. I had never had a real-estate license nor did I understand industry lingo. (*What in the world is an FSBO?* I wondered.) Now, let me just say that I did not go into my new career with unrealistic expectations. I had come to terms with the fact that understanding real estate was going to take some time, but I figured that, until I learned the ins and outs of the industry, my people skills would pull me through. *Boy was I wrong!* I had never heard the word "no" as many times in the course of a week in my whole life. With every rejection, I doubted myself more and more. To make matters worse, after a long day's work, I had to come back to the run-down trailer park I was temporarily living in. *Why in the world did I give up my nice home and career for this?* I asked myself each and every night.

So by day ten of my new life, I was really discouraged. This particular morning, the sky was even grayer than the hair on my head. Rain blanketed the ground, and I cynically acknowledged that it was appropriate weather for my gloomy mood. Late for an appointment that I was dreading, I gathered my sales materials and rushed out the front door of the trailer. With my first step onto the top metal stair, wet with rain, my slick-bottom dress shoes lost traction. Suddenly, I was flailing helplessly, spread-eagle above three rickety metal stairs, and aiming head first for a muddy destination. At the bottom of the stairs I landed, face first, in a sloppy soup of mud and water. As mud seeped its way into my brand-new suit jacket and pants, I questioned my sanity and the decisions that brought me to this place so far away from all that was familiar to me. I thought back to the warmth, security, and stability of my old life. Why had I let go of everything? At fifty, I had jumped out of the nest that I had worked so hard to build and landed face down in the mud.

My thoughts went wild, racing with pent-up frustration: *You have lost your mind! You left a great job with a major university. You have faced more rejection in the past ten days than you have received in your entire lifetime. Why? What did you think you could accomplish?* If this morning was representative of things to come, I was in for a bumpy ride.

At that moment, I could have easily packed up my belongings and headed back home. It would have been the easiest thing to do. Instead, even as all of the doubts raged within me, something new had stirred. I got mad. I got so mad that I decided that if life was going to keep on knocking me with hard blows, then I was going to stand on my feet and take them. As the rain beat down upon my back, a feeling of freedom enveloped me. I had survived so far, and it couldn't get much worse. I was determined to find and fulfill my potential. At ground level, I couldn't get any lower; the only way to go was up. With that, I dragged myself out of the mud, showered, and put on a clean suit and a new attitude. Late as I was, I set out to meet my prospect.

On the way to the meeting, I got lost. In an unfamiliar city, there was little hope of finding my way. When I spotted a man in front of a small office building, I stopped and asked for directions. He invited me into his office to use the phone. Within just a few short minutes of conversation with him, I was surprised to discover that he and his wife were both real-estate agents. Because of our common interests, we kept in touch, and within a couple of months, they became one of my first ten franchise sales.

Within two years, I became a successful co-owner of three RE/MAX regions. This was far, far beyond my wildest dreams. When I left Missouri and all the security I had known to set out in search of fulfillment, I never expected to achieve that kind of success so quickly. Looking back, I thank my lucky stars for that rainy Georgia morning. I thank God that I did not run. I thank God that I did not pack my belongings and head home, deciding that my career change had been a terrible mistake. The freedom I have today would not have come had

I decided not to pick myself up from the mud and keep going. I am so thankful for the obstacles I have had to overcome, for they have been my greatest allies in my search for personal fulfillment. In hindsight, I highly recommend taking a good leap, "falling from grace" and getting a little dirty to everyone.

Tom Hill

Blueberry Thrills

Don't aim for success if you want it; just do what you love and believe in, and it will come naturally.

David Frost

In high school, I set a goal for myself. I was determined to be a millionaire by my fortieth birthday. When you are in high school peering at the world through rose-colored glasses, anything is possible.

At that time, I didn't realize that youth can cause the mind to play tricks on you, cruel tricks that are seldom revealed until later in life when you are suddenly faced with reality as I was in 1989. There I was, recently divorced, standing in line at the grocery store with my two daughters, amid friends and neighbors, food stamps in hand. Day-to-day survival was the new goal, not a million dollars.

Though I was dependent on government assistance, I did work hard. I was a licensed cosmetologist and also drove a school bus. I had no social life, and frankly, could not afford the luxury of thinking of one! Then I met Dennis

Hartmann. We had known each other for some time, but it was not until we were both facing similar situations in our personal lives that our relationship blossomed. In 1990 we married, and I suddenly found myself wed to a third-generation blueberry farmer—a real blue blood!

Dennis had been involved in the blueberry industry his entire life and owned a ten-acre blueberry farm that he called True Blue Farms. Though my new husband had a full-time job, he spent his spare time in the fields. After our marriage, that, of course, is where I spent what little spare time I had as well. Don't all newlyweds spend their time together amid blueberry bushes?

After we married, Dennis adopted my two girls, then we had one of our own. We had only fifty dollars a week for groceries. There was no money for anything else; every penny we made either went back into the farm or paid tuition for the girls' education. We were determined that they would receive the best education available, and we were willing to make every sacrifice needed in order to ensure this.

By 1993, we were still just one small blueberry farm among several others in our rural Michigan community. We were not originally one of those "U-pick" operations, but sometimes when the other nearby farms were closed, tourists would stop by the house and ask if they could pick from our fields. Of course, we let them pick. Little did we know what we had started, and business boomed. That same year, we expanded the business and our production tripled, as did our workload.

While we were in the midst of this blueberry expansion, I listened and watched everything our customers were saying and doing when they came to our fields. They appreciated the fact that we welcomed them to pick their own berries. While other farmers were inconvenienced by the pickers' presence in their fields, we treated our visitors as honored guests. In retrospect, I feel that this simple attitude that came so naturally for our family was, and still remains, one of the greatest reasons for our success.

We marketed our place as a travel destination, featuring lots of down-home, country fun for everyone! Most of our customers traveled from the city; while chickens, kittens, goats and a host of other creatures great and small were familiar sights to us, they certainly were not for our city customers. They loved the opportunity to bring their families to a real farm where they could wander the fields picking round, ripe blueberries and experience the pure joy of getting a slobbery greeting from a very friendly farmyard animal. Our goal was to ensure that our customers headed home not just with a basket a blueberries, but with big smiles and cherished memories in their hearts.

Over the next few years, while farms around us closed, our operation thrived. During this period we also learned the business benefits of collaboration. After some very serious discussions with a neighboring blueberry farmer, Harold Wright, we decided that it would be advantageous for the two farms to work together and start a packing facility. The idea was brilliant! It taught us to partner with other entrepreneurs any time the opportunity presented itself, advice we follow to this day.

By 1997, I was working full-time at True Blue Farms. Whenever we had a question, rather than getting bogged down, we sought answers from reliable experts in that particular field. In the months that followed, we purchased an additional fifty acres, but we did not stop there. When Mr. Wright decided to retire, he not only sold us his share of the processing plant, but he also offered us his blueberry farm. That acquisition brought our facility to 160 acres of blueberries.

In the ensuing years, True Blue Farms has continued to grow and explore new ventures. We now have seventy-five people on payroll, and last year we packaged approximately 4.5 million pounds of blueberries. In addition, we have opened True Blue Farm's Country Store, which sells everything you could ever want or need, all made from blueberries! And our mission at True Blue Farm remains steadfast: to provide blueberry lovers worldwide the opportunity to enjoy quality-grown blueberries in a fun-filled, family-oriented, yet professional environment.

Traveling this road has not been fast-paced nor has the journey been easy, but True Blue Farms has proven to be tremendously rewarding. It thrills me to know that I have indeed accomplished a goal that for a while did not seem attainable. When I turned forty, I was a millionaire. I guess that is what you call a blueberry thrill!

Shelly Hartmann
As told to Terri Duncan

EPILOGUE: *True Blue Farms is owned and operated by the Hartmann family. The operation is located in Grand Junction, Michigan, a small town situated near Lake Michigan. Blueberry season runs from April until September, and during peak season, visitors are invited to pick their own berries.*

In addition, True Blue Farms has a country store on the premises that showcases products made from blueberries, including jams and juices. True Blue Farms has earned a superior rating from the American Institute of Bakers, and their blueberries are approved by the USDA. Many items are also certified kosher.

For more information on True Blue Farms, visit www.truebluefarms.com.

Terri Duncan

No Dream Is Too Big

Almost eight years ago, I was on the beach watching my four-year-old son, Brendan, play in the sand. As a single mother, I knew that taking my son on vacation was a blessing, and I savored the moment. He was all I had. I had been working odd jobs here and there, always improving my position. But in terms of a career, I had no idea what I could do.

When I found out I was pregnant at age eighteen—during my freshman year of college—I decided to drop out to raise my son, which I was forced to do alone. Most people told me I was making a mistake. How could I be a mother with no clear path toward a career? How would I pay for everything when I could barely pay for myself? Now, four years later, I was no closer to figuring out what I wanted to do with the rest of my life. Feelings of self-doubt were always looming in the corners of my mind. I was an unwed mother, a college dropout with a ridiculous dream that would never come true.

Then I reached into my beach bag and pulled out a copy of the new *Chicken Soup for the Mother's Soul.* As I read, the same feeling that millions of others have gotten from these books washed over me. I realized there on the beach that being a mother was the most challenging role anybody could ever play. Whether I chose to be a doctor, a lawyer, a teacher or a magazine editor, it didn't matter. Those professions would not require me to, as the book said, "let my heart run around" outside of my body. Although I was making under $17,000 a year at my job, the book empowered me with the feeling that I could do anything!

Upon returning home, I quantified my goals. I wanted to start a magazine. So I wrote my dreams down on a piece of paper and kept it on top of my dresser. When I had to sell the dresser along with some of my other furniture just to make ends meet, I kept the piece of paper in my pillow.

It would take almost three years of working odd jobs related to magazines, such as writing for the society pages, taking photographs for a local real estate company and learning sales from a local radio station, before I felt that I had gathered enough experience to step out on my own. I started a local publication in April 2000 and really learned the ropes the hard way, by literally jumping right in the middle of my dream. I made a lot of mistakes, but it was all a part of the process. I learned that nothing worth having comes easy, and it was the tough times that made the good times worthwhile.

But I decided to dream bigger. What about a national magazine, one based on the *Chicken Soup for the Soul* series? I was so motivated by the *Chicken Soup* books and so wanted to be a part of motivating other people. I could start a monthly magazine that would accomplish this same thing, but on a smaller scale than that of a mainstream book, I thought. The magazine could point out the funny things in life and connect with readers on a very personal level, just like the *Chicken Soup* books.

Once again the seed of doubt crept in. What did I know about a national magazine? Where would I start? Who do I call? How do I get it in stores? Once again, I pulled up my sleeves and thought, *This is going to be a bumpy ride.* And I jumped smack in the middle of my dreams again. I named the magazine *American Magazine* and made a deal with Wal-Mart to carry it in their stores. I made sure the tone of our family oriented magazine was inspirational, funny and motivational, just like the *Chicken Soup* books.

One year later, in October 2003, I was sitting at my desk working on the fifth issue of *American Magazine* when the phone rang. "This is the COO of *Chicken Soup for the Soul Enterprises.*" After overcoming the initial shock of this dream call, I learned from the COO that *Chicken Soup* fans had been asking for a magazine for a very long time. The COO had seen my magazine and said that *Chicken Soup* wanted to partner with me on this project. That phone call eventually led to my partnership with series founders Mark Victor Hansen and Jack Canfield, and *Chicken Soup for the Soul* magazine released its inaugural magazine in August 2005.

Looking back at my day on the beach, I felt as if my dream was like a grain of sand, tiny, unnoticeable and lost among thousands of other dreams. I am still a single mother and a college dropout, but today I look back and know that dreams are like the ocean—you can float on top as long as you want, but it's not until you face your fears, dive in and start swimming hard against the waves that you'll discover a whole new world. And only then will you realize your true purpose and potential.

J. Mignonne Wright

7

LISTEN TO YOUR GUT

There's no reason to be the richest man in the cemetery. You can't do any business from there.

Colonel Sanders

The Idiot Entrepreneur Theory

Our modern age has romanticized the concept of "entrepreneur." The idea is that the best and the brightest of each generation sets out to change the world by building world-beating innovating corporations. Mr. Hewlett and Mr. Packard built Hewlett-Packard (HP to the rest of us) into a multibillion-dollar computer company. Mr. Dell started Dell Computer in his university dorm room. Bill Gates, the quintessential nerd, started Microsoft with equally nerdy friend Paul Allen after dropping out of Harvard. They all became heroes and are studied in the nation's leading business schools.

The problem with all of these examples is that they are exceptions to the rule. All three of these companies were founded by really smart guys who either got, or were on track to get, advanced degrees from leading universities.

The fact is that most new companies are started by guys more like me. We are the guys (and women) who drag along in the bottom of the class academically. We have few, if any, accomplishments outside of the classroom. During job interviews, panel members roll their eyes, wondering, *How did this idiot get past our résumé screeners?*

The reason I founded my first company was to actually

get a job. My reasoning was that if you start your own company, you can employ whomever you like. So in order to reassure my mom that I was not completely destitute, I made a trip to the courthouse, filed incorporation papers, then went to the local quick-copy printing shop and ordered business cards that read "Bob Young, President." My new unpaid job came with a good enough title that my mom could brag about me when talking to my aunts on the weekend, aunts who had always liked me, but who worried about whether there was a government program that would look after a likable, but obviously unemployable, idiot of a nephew.

The first two companies I helped build were in the computer rental and leasing business. They went okay for a while. But I was not very smart, so I didn't realize that the computer rental and leasing business is a bad business. I defer to the definition of "bad" in the way that Warren Buffet, arguably America's greatest businessman, would use: Mr. Buffet defines a "good" business as one for which he can hire mediocre managers and still turn a profit.

While working the computer rental and leasing business, four out of five of our competitors went out of business. At first we thought they were just not very smart. But when we also ran into financial difficulties, our respect for the talents of our former bankrupted competitors rose immeasurably.

With this in mind, an interesting question was posed: how do so many people who fail at school eventually become competent and successful entrepreneurs? My thesis is as follows: Those of us who work well within the system learn to do so at a young age.

Let's begin in kindergarten. Because you are able to complete kindergarten reasonably well, minding all the rules and expectations, your teacher passes you with a glowing recommendation to the first-grade teacher. The first-grade teacher is already predisposed to liking you because you showed up for the first day of class on time. Given that all the great class behavior skills you learned in kindergarten are easily transferable to first grade, you do well there, too. So the first-grade teacher passes you with good marks and a glowing review onto second grade. As long as you continue to learn to work the system throughout your school years, your marks and your reviews continue to reinforce those system-approved behaviors.

Now consider the idiot. I, ah, wait, *he* typically starts out badly in kindergarten. He then graduates to first grade with a whispered warning from the kindergarten teacher to the next teacher: "Look out for this kid; he's an idiot." He isn't really sure what he has done wrong, because he's only five years old at the time, but it's obvious already that the "system" does not work for him. So he daydreams and goofs off and otherwise looks like an idiot to the first-grade teacher, who passes him along to second grade with a similarly poor review and warning, and so on and so forth.

So after twelve years of these constant reminders that he is not as talented, smart, or accomplished as the kids who get great marks, he graduates from high school knowing only one thing—namely, that he is an idiot.

But here is where it gets interesting. Knowing that you are an idiot is, believe it or not, a huge competitive advantage in business. The advantage is simply due to the fact that all your competitors don't know that they're idiots, too.

In the early days of the Open Source software movement, there were only a few companies trying to build a business selling "free" software. Open Source software consisted of software that was built collaboratively by engineers cooperating across the Internet and was shipped with both binaries and source code, all under a license that allowed anyone to modify the software. This was a very different model for software than that found in the existing software industry. Software was previously sold without source code (which you need in order to make changes) and came with a license that threatened to put you in jail if you even attempted to make any changes to the software.

At Red Hat, we were one of the few companies who thought we might be able to build a business supplying this Open Source software to our customers. We supplied an operating system called Red Hat Linux, made out of the Open Source software that was being worked on by engineering teams across the Internet. We collaborated with this community of Open Source software developers by giving away all the software we wrote under the Open Source license, as the software we were using. We believed corporate customers would want the benefit of having control over the software they were using to build their networks and infrastructure on, which the Open Source software model gave them.

Suddenly and out of nowhere, a well-funded competitor appeared, led by a couple of very talented and very experienced software industry executives. Without going into any of the details, our little company (funded via our credit card balances) had, within three years, run circles in the market around our larger, much better funded, competitor.

As near as we could tell, we were able to achieve this success not by being smarter than our competitor, as we were measurably less talented and less experienced. We simply avoided the mistakes they made. This competitor, trained in the existing software industry, chose to surround the Open Source software they were using in their products with proprietary binary-only software. They believed this additional software added functions and uses to their software that made it more complete and useful. But as it came without source code and with a proprietary license, it also meant the customer could not make any changes to their software. As a result, this deprived their customers of the unique benefit Open Source software offers—namely, control over the software they are building their businesses around.

Our competitors' success earlier in their careers in the existing software industry blinded them to the rules of the new environment they found themselves operating in. Hence, a perfect example of my original theory—in effect, our competitors did not know that they were idiots. Good students are taught to believe that they are clever. Sixteen years (they all went on to college) of having teachers and parents tell them how clever they are results in them thinking they are actually clever. They can't help not knowing they are idiots, because no one in their entire academic careers ever pointed that obvious fact out to them.

Yet given the pace that business operates at, which is several times the pace academic studies operate at, we are all idiots when we first launch our business careers. We have few if any skills that are transferable to the business world. It is why smart, talented guys like Sam Walton of Wal-Mart fame failed until he was forty years old. He had to unlearn all the bad advice and bad feedback he'd received in his star-studded childhood when he was the best athlete and smartest guy in his class.

But it is also why so many of those expensive retirement properties in Florida are owned by entrepreneurs who never graduated from high school. They knew they were not very smart when they came out of school, and on top of that no one would hire them, so they had to start their own businesses to get a job, just like me. And it can be a very badly paid job at that, because when you start a business, by definition you don't have any customers or any revenue or profits in order to pay yourself a salary.

Again, we dumb students knew one thing our smarter classmates didn't learn: we were idiots. But many of us were paying attention to the teachers who drummed into our heads that the only way to get smarter was to work harder. So we kept on studying in our own academically challenged way, too dumb to realize that we were too dumb to succeed.

But sometimes, just sometimes, we did go on to achieve remarkable success.

Bob Young

EPILOGUE: *Robert "Bob" Young is the founder and CEO of Lulu.com. A true technology entrepreneur with four successful, multimillion-dollar start-up companies on his résumé, Young also knows how to have fun; he is the owner of the Hamilton Tiger-Cats, a Canadian Football League team based in Ontario. Young and his champion football team are very active in their Canadian province, sponsoring and supporting many charity events and causes.*

As cofounder and former chairman of Red Hat Software (1993–2000), the largest provider of fee-based Linux products and services in the world, Young was responsible for the early success of the company. A true Open Source visionary, Young's success in developing Red Hat into a household name won him prestigious honors, including having been named one of Business Week *magazine's "Top Entrepreneurs" in 1999.*

Before founding Red Hat in 1993, Bob spent twenty years at the helm of two computer-leasing companies he founded. That experience as a high-tech entrepreneur, combined with his innate marketing savvy, gave rise ultimately to Red Hat's success. His book, Under the Radar: How Red Hat Changed the Software Business—and Took Microsoft by Surprise *(Coriolis Group Books, 1999), chronicles how Red Hat's Open Source strategy successfully won wide industry acceptance in a market previously dominated by companies that offered proprietary binary-only systems. After Red Hat went public in 1999, Young founded The Center for the Public Domain, a nonprofit foundation that supports the growth of a healthy and robust public domain of knowledge and the arts.*

*Then in March 2002, Young launched Lulu.com (*www.Lulu.com*), a Web site that allows businesses, educators, artists, musicians and others to publish and sell their own books, images, multimedia and music. According to Young, Lulu challenges conventional publishing models by allowing content creators and owners to bring work directly to market without surrendering control of their intellectual property. The enterprise is driven by Young's strong commitment to information access as a foundation for knowledge advancement, whether in education, computer code or other realms.*

To learn more about Bob Young, please visit www.Lulu.com.

Dahlynn McKowen

Moment by Moment

We do not remember days . . . We remember moments.

Cesare Pavese

Wow, 230 names. Jotting down a quick list while composing this story, it's hard to fathom the number of entrepreneurs whom I have worked with over the past decade through my company IMS, a marketing communications firm based in Arizona. And I know I'll remember some more as I write my story.

Scanning my list of entrepreneurs, I can't help but reflect on the companies and people who succeeded, and those who didn't. It wouldn't be the first time. Working with small to medium-sized entrepreneurial companies, I've spent hours in my car, on planes, even cooking dinner, trying to arrive at what the magic is that makes one entrepreneur wildly successful, time and time again, and another quite the opposite.

Entrepreneurs by their very nature are energetic, passionate and motivated, so why is it that some have legions of people who will leap off the tallest of cliffs for them, while others have employees who are hardly that brave? For those entrepreneurs who want to be remembered for the next iPod or the next Google, they better have followers of the cliff-leaping kind.

Extremely successful entrepreneurs are leaders who can make great things happen in their companies. No, strike that. They can make *extraordinary* things happen, and often they do so just for the thrill of saying they did. Many think that entrepreneurs who have devoted, intrinsically loyal staff hire better than those who don't, but I disagree. While they hire the same, they inspire better. But how?

The Truth of the Two Circles

Every organization has two circles, the "heart" circle and the "mind" circle. The heart circle is the excitement, the passion, the thrill. The mind circle consists of spreadsheets, forecasts and checklists. Entrepreneurial companies become great companies when they successfully bring together the heart circle *and* the mind circle; they have gracefully placed the rules, regulations, spreadsheets, budgets and all the other mind-focused endeavors within the creativity, caring, passion, purpose, fulfillment, achievement and pride of the heart circle.

There's a solid reason for this. When the circles come together, people understand *why* there are rules. People also *expect* to be held accountable to goals and results, because they are symbols of caring and passion; through them, a higher purpose is achieved. And about achievement: loyal employees look forward to achieving great things, big things, rather than simply accomplishing daily office tasks and then going home. It's the attitudes and beliefs of the people within heart-mind centric organizations that allow great things to happen.

Putting It All into Action

At IMS, we've discovered that the vehicles that create and nurture an entrepreneurial heart-mind centric organization are "moments," those brief instances of time that change lives. Those companies that do extraordinary things or deliver amazing products and services to their customers create moments for their employees at every turn. They make productions out of staff meetings with simple things like playing music to liven up the room when people walk in. They celebrate their successes and even make a scene. One company celebrated a big milestone with a party that included a "history walk" that let people reminisce about what it took to get there. They thank those around them, often not with HR programs, but with a sincere, "Thank you." They communicate their mission and their vision not with a poster on the wall, but with impassioned speeches and videos about what the world will look like when they get there and then rally the team with how much work it's going to take.

Why are moments so important? Because moments allow you into a person's heart. Moments can be formal or informal, but the key is to seize every opportunity to create positive, memorable, life-changing moments for the people around you.

Entrepreneurs must realize that moments will happen whether they intentionally create them or not. Why are you venturing out on your own, or at least thinking about it? It's probably because there were too many not-so-great moments at the places you've worked. Lots of good moments inspire greatness, and lots of bad moments inspire, well, not much more than a nine-to-five effort—not nearly good enough in today's dog-eat-dog world.

The impact can be huge. Moments connect people, and people who are connected to other people tend to be more loyal. They do things for each other and go out of their way to strike mutually beneficial partnerships. They also collaborate more and work harder, giving their company that competitive edge. These people are walking, talking, living and breathing embodiments of their company's heart and soul.

Opportunities for Moments Are Everywhere

Every organization has opportunities for moments. In the beginning, it's the entrepreneurial leader who creates them through inspiring words, often with hands waving in the air! From there it happens continually through actions and work.

So how do you know if you're creating good or bad moments within your company? Take a confidential "moments" inventory. Ask yourself first (your own answers may say it all), then ask your team to think back over the last year and jot down their most memorable moments. If the lists look like this, you're well on your way to greatness:

My Most Memorable Moments of the Year

- The annual user group conference where we revealed our latest product to thunderous cheers! Yeah!
- The team meeting where our founder opened up and told us why she decided to start our company: a dear friend of hers suffers every day with the illness she wants to cure.
- When we all pulled together and pulled off a huge presentation that got us the biggest contract in the company's history. The pizza party afterwards was great, too!
- The wonderful dinner my husband and I had when we used the $100 certificate my boss gave me for, as he put it, "going above and beyond" on that last project.

On the other hand, if the moments are looking more like this, problems are afoot:

My Most Memorable Moments of the Year

- Last month when Roger in Sales was let go for no apparent reason.
- Being forced to work the weekend and missing my son's first Pee Wee football game.
- The political games that cost me a promotion and a $20,000 pay raise.

That's enough to get the idea. Entrepreneurs who lead companies of all shapes and sizes must realize that good and bad moments happen daily. Your goal is to have the good outweigh the bad, either in intensity or number.

Understand that in every entrepreneurial company you have to keep your nose to the grindstone. But have two grindstones—one for the mind and one for the heart—and keep your nose to both of them. It's that simple, so take it moment by moment.

Kathy Heasley

EPILOGUE: *Kathy Heasley is the founder and principal of IMS, Inc.*

Located in Scottsdale, Arizona, IMS is a marketing communications company that is in the "moments" business.

Heasley and her team have successfully helped both small- and medium-sized businesses and Fortune 500 companies discover their hearts, align them with their minds and make it all come to life inside and outside their organizations. Current and past companies she's helped include Cold Stone Creamery, Make-A-Wish Foundation, Cole Companies, Realty DataTrust, Rich Dad Company, CSP Magazine, *Able Information Technologies, Coca-Cola, Procter & Gamble, Kraft, Hershey Foods, WaWa, Couche-Tard, and numerous other companies and independent entrepreneurs.*

An entrepreneur herself, Heasley is a twenty-year veteran of the marketing communications industry, and also is a published writer and video producer. She coauthored Seize the American Dream: 10 Entrepreneurial Success Strategies *(JaGrand Ventures, 2002) with health-care entrepreneur Jim H. Houtz and has ghost-written books, articles and columns for her clients. She has produced hundreds of corporate videos and has received Telly awards for her video work. Her company was also awarded finalist in the 2005 Better Business Bureau's Business Ethics Awards.*

Heasley plans to continue helping companies worldwide through speeches, books and videos. Heasley is a member of Entrepreneur's Organization (formerly YEO—Young Entrepreneurs Organization) and helps mentor young people through Penn State's Lion Link program. She is the founder of the Best Friends Brigade of Scottsdale in association with Best Friends Animal Society. The Brigade supports the No More Homeless Pets initiatives in the Phoenix metro area.

To learn more about Kathy Heasley and her company, please visit www.imsbreakthrough.com.

Dahlynn McKowen

The Dancer in All of Us

If you do work that you love, and the work fulfills you, the rest will come.

Oprah Winfrey

I knew from a very early age that I would be a dancer, but there was one little problem: I was pigeon-toed.

My parents told me that I began dancing even before I could walk. At the age of two, my mother and I were walking down the street in San Diego, where my family was stationed due to my father's navy job. Suddenly, I heard amazing, rhythmic music coming from a dance studio. I wandered into the studio and started dancing my heart out. Surprised by my half-pint talent, the owner said to my mother, "You know, this little girl has a gift, and you need to enroll her in a class." My mother thought it would help my foot problem, so when my family returned home to Iowa upon my father's retirement, she enrolled me in a dance class.

Flash forward through fifteen years of dance classes and recitals—and, I'm happy to report, sans my pigeon-toe issue that was corrected through dancing—to 1969 and the city of Chicago. I was dancing professionally with a company that also happened to own a dance studio. For extra money I taught traditional jazz dance classes at the studio. In one particular class I realized that my students were there to simply drop a few dress sizes in anticipation of a high school reunion or special event, not to become Broadway dancers. But I was trying to teach them formal jazz steps and movements.

Typical of traditional dance studios, a mirror lined the entire wall behind me. As the students followed my moves, they couldn't help but watch themselves in that long mirror, and it was very intimidating to them. I noticed that they were critical of how they looked as they tried unsuccessfully to match my moves. Attendance wasn't great, my students were frustrated, and I wasn't sure how to help them.

I evaluated my teaching style, trying to figure out how I could motivate my students, when suddenly it hit me: because my students were focusing on how bad they looked in the mirror rather than on me, I simply reversed dance tradition in my next class. I faced the mirror so my students would have *their* backs to the mirror. Now I became their mirror, and they loved it!

On the dancing heels of my room reversal debut, I thought about what I was teaching them. My students came to class to experience that special womanly camaraderie of working together toward a common goal—to get thinner and to feel that wonderful joy that comes through dance. *Okay,* I thought, *I have to make this simpler and easier and more fun.* Again, I challenged tradition. I replaced the professional dance steps with easier dance steps that even a beginner could quickly master. My new goal was to teach them to focus on the joys of the class itself and not worry about fancy routines and steps. If they were able to do this, I knew they would get fitter, lose weight and inches, tone muscle and, most important, not be so critical of themselves.

So I made my dance class much simpler, used lots of positive encouragement, and, of course, kept their backs to the mirror. My students enjoyed this new way of dancing, as did I, and the news spread; my class quickly went from a few students to fifteen, then thirty, then sixty! The room couldn't hold any more people! I knew I was onto something, something that would come to be known as Jazzercise.

Flash forward yet another thirty-seven years. Today, Jazzercise has evolved from that small Chicago studio to 6,300 amazing and talented fitness instructors who teach a total of 20,000 classes a week to over 200,000 students in more than thirty countries! My daughter Shanna has followed in my footsteps and is executive vice president of the company; she has a great business mind and is a beautiful dancer. Her toddler daughter, Skyla—my granddaughter—loves to dance and I hope will join us in the business one day. But mind you, I'm not ready to retire my dancing shoes just yet! I still enjoy teaching classes, choreographing and appearing in our instructional videos, leading Jazzercise in numerous philanthropic endeavors such as raising money for breast cancer awareness as well as the arts ($26 million and growing), and offering our fitness programs to schools to help curb childhood obesity.

One of my proudest achievements is that Jazzercise has provided hundreds of thousands of women the opportunity to become entrepreneurs themselves; Jazzercise instructors, women from all walks of life, from all over the globe, are teaching their students the value of exercise and fitness, and to feel good about themselves and their bodies. And to this day, no mirrors are allowed!

Judi Sheppard Missett

EPILOGUE: *As founder and CEO of Jazzercise, Inc., Judi Sheppard Missett is an aerobic dance pioneer, having led the way in women's fitness. Missett has parlayed her entrepreneurial savvy and tremendous success in the fitness industry into an apparel line, aptly named Jazzertogs, and founded JM DigitalWorks, a very prominent and award-winning video production studio.*

Besides her primary Jazzercise program, Missett had a desire to help children learn the values of a fit lifestyle. With this goal in mind, and also at the urging of a fellow fitness buff, she created two similar programs for our nation's youth. The first was "Junior Jazzercise," an after-school fitness program that continues to be a popular offering for youth and teens today. The second was the "Kids Get Fit" program. As an advisor to the President's Council on Physical Fitness and Sports, then-chairman Arnold Schwarzenegger challenged Missett and the other advisors to address the growing problem of childhood obesity and to find a way to help kids get fit. Utilizing Jazzercise as the foundation for the program, Missett, along with her network of fitness instructors, introduced the program with great success to the nation's schools.

An entrepreneur, much-sought-after motivational speaker and business leader, Missett exudes enthusiasm and boundless energy in her lifelong journey to help and encourage others. As Missett says, "Always challenge yourself and be willing to change and try new things, because life is too short not to do that." Well said, Judi.

Dahlynn McKowen

"It was a natural spinoff."

American Dreamin'

It was more than a decade ago when I got my first taste of the American Dream. While most of my friends were still folding sweaters at the Gap, I was wearing a business suit and reporting to my first job in an office building that looked as big as Disneyland. The monthly salary was handwritten on a Post-it® note. I unfolded the golden slip and revealed a number that would not even cover my mortgage today—I was elated! I nodded my acceptance and reveled in the fact that my days of hourly wages were behind me.

My new, prestigious career began in a customer service center where two dozen robotic agents answered an endless stream of incoming phone calls. The only window looked out into the lobby—or rather the lobby looked in on us. The room was dubbed the "Fish Bowl," and we were the entertainment for all who entered the building.

The agents were graded on the volume of calls answered and customer satisfaction ratings. I took hundreds of calls each day, typing so fast that sometimes my knuckles cracked without warning. I took pride in my new role and delivered swift, perky service.

Several months later, it was time for a performance

review. I anticipated kudos and instead received a cold reprimand from a drill sergeant disguised in designer clothes and flowery perfume. "Nobody could possibly take that many calls in a day," she said. "You must be doing something wrong."

Later that day, after raising my hand to request an unscheduled trip to the potty, I considered my predicament. This was Corporate America. It was a real job, and I was making a real monthly salary. I had benefits and paid vacation time and wore pumps to work. I was performing well, yet somehow it wasn't good enough. I considered the alternatives and quickly realized that if I wanted to keep living the American Dream, I had to suck it up.

My devotion to Corporate America grew in direct proportion to the increases in salary and benefits. The next company I worked for presented me with stock options. I had no idea what they were, but they sounded fantastic! One of the best perks was in the break room: a refrigerator crammed full of bottles of Snapple. Stock options and free Snapple . . . I thought this place was amazing.

The company was thriving and lavished us with logo-covered merchandise. I amassed a collection of coffee mugs, T-shirts, denim shirts, Frisbees, pens, paper clip dishes, CD holders, candy jars, jackets and even a fancy watch. The quarterly meetings were more like celebrations, complete with kegs of beer and platters of shrimp cocktail.

Eventually the flow of free merchandise slowed to a halt. I wondered if there was some sort of delay in shipping and receiving. When the budget cuts were announced, I knew it was inevitable that the free Snapple would disappear, too. I wondered how the entire office would handle the sugar crash as I watched the workers wheel out the prized refrigerator and replace it with a coin-operated soda machine.

Jump forward a few years to a new company, one that gave me stock options that split just a week after I started. By then I knew a thing or two about stocks, and this was a very good sign. They presented me with my own office, complete with a door and void of a window. I set up shop in my big white closet and fell in love with my new prestige and benefits package. It was a great time in the computer industry; the company was growing faster than the desks could be installed to accommodate all the new employees. I was in the heart of the Silicon Valley, and it felt like winning the lottery!

Employee loyalty ran surprisingly deep. The logo-covered merchandise seemed bigger and better here. Some people even wore leather jackets with the company name emblazoned on the lapel. The break rooms were stocked with free bagels, sodas and snacks, and the company meetings were followed with live entertainment, beer, wine and food. Twenty-five-year-old millionaires were born when the stock took off like a bottle rocket, and those of us who arrived on the scene just a little late watched them with envy as they parked their Porsches.

When the dot-com boom busted, the evening news was flooded with stories of corporate demise. I watched my friends lose their jobs faster than Donald Trump could say, "You're fired!" Some companies didn't even have the decency to let their employees go with dignity. One news broadcast panned a rainy parking lot full of Silicon Valley workers who arrived to find a handwritten note on the locked front door of a large office building simply stating, "Out of Business."

I began to question the virtues of the corporate world. Sure, I still had a job. In fact, by then I had a house and a fancy car, thanks to those overinflated stock options. I had a comfortable bank account, a hefty benefits package and a tidy 401(k). But I was also working twelve-hour days, and just before my thirtieth birthday I was diagnosed with an ulcer. That's when the fog rolled in.

There I was, a loyal worker who wore the company T-shirts to the gym and never took more bagels than I could actually eat. Though I was being rewarded financially for my efforts, I began to wonder how long it would last. How long would it be before another big layoff or corporate merger sent hundreds of us to the unemployment office in our fancy cars? I considered the words of one boss who smirked like a child with too much power and said, "Everyone is replaceable." It was an epiphany. I was no different from anyone else. We were all as disposable as diapers.

I could go to another company, but for what? The impending doom lay in wait no matter where I went. No job was safe. Corporate America, it turned out, was full of high rollers who took out the little guys like they're shooting characters in a video game. Nobody cared that these loyal workers had families to support and mortgages to pay. The massacre didn't even stop in December; pink slips were handed out, and people were sent home to enjoy the holidays without so much as a free turkey as a parting gift.

After more than a year of planning during my precious free time, I quit my job and opened Book Lovers Bookstore in Sacramento, California. My relatives gasped in horror. "But you're giving up all that money and security," my father scolded. "No, Dad," I explained, "I'm finally putting my fate in my own hands." I thought entrepreneurship had an element of prestige, but most people looked at me as if I had snakes in my hair.

True, entrepreneurship is risky. But so is driving on the highway at rush hour, falling in love or eating anything cooked in oil. The perception is that Corporate America is the safety zone, that if you have a job there, you will be able to pay your mortgage and live the American Dream. Sure, the paychecks are cranked out twice each month from some mystical place called "Payroll," but that only matters if you're still on the payroll.

Big companies seem to let employees go whenever the quarterly numbers aren't up to par, yet corporate waste is infamous. As a small business owner, I would never blow money on beach balls with my company logo or regularly splurge on lavish parties to celebrate the fact that it is Friday. I watch my bottom line and do my best to show appreciation for the people who work for me.

Entrepreneurial life is good. My ulcer doesn't bother me anymore, and my office has windows—lots of them. Do I miss Corporate America? I did enjoy those free snacks, and for a while I missed the steady paycheck. But when they called and asked me to return, I knew that there weren't enough stock options on the NASDAQ to lure me back. Why would I do that? I have plenty of Snapple on hand, and the only pink slip I ever have to worry about comes in the form of a phone message. Now that, my friend, is the American Dream.

Stephanie Chandler

EPILOGUE: *When Stephanie Chandler decided to quit her software sales job and open a bookstore, her family and friends were concerned. "I love it when someone tells me I can't do something. It just fuels my fire and makes me want to prove them wrong," shared a smiling Chandler. Determined to follow her entrepreneurial spirit, she wrote a lengthy business plan and used her personal savings to open Book Lovers Bookstore in Sacramento, California, in November 2003.*

Prior to starting her now very successful business, Chandler was frustrated by the fact she still had unanswered questions. "I didn't know how to locate vendors or trade associations. I didn't know how to negotiate a lease. I had to figure it all out on my own," Chandler explained. She was also surprised by the number of people who said to her, "I wish I had the courage to do what you did."

*As a result of these comments, Chandler's passion became helping other fledgling small-business owners become successful entrepreneurs. She launched a Web site dedicated to providing free business resources—*www.BusinessInfoGuide.com*—and has written two books:* The Business Startup Checklist and Planning Guide: Seize Your Entrepreneurial Dreams! *(Aventine Press) and* From Entrepreneur to Infopreneur: Make Money with Books, E-books and Information Products *(Wiley).*

A popular speaker, freelancer, radio show guest and author, Chandler's Web site has been selected by Writer's Digest Magazine *as one of the top ten sites in the nation for writers. To learn more about Chandler, please visit* www.stephaniechandler.com *or* www.BusinessInfoGuide.com.

Dahlynn McKowen

Keep It Simple

Whatever you can do, or dream you can, begin it. Boldness has genius, power, and magic in it.

Goethe

I used to keep saying, "Keep it simple, stupid." But then I realized it was stupid to keep calling myself stupid. So I started saying, "Keep it simple, smarty."

I'm not all that intelligent. A lot of people are much smarter than I am, and they lose me in their thought processes. I never could follow what all those Western philosophers were arguing about.

I'm lazy, too, when I'm honest with myself. I've never done mornings if at all possible, even as a child. If I have a choice between a day when I have to get up with an alarm clock and shower and shave and get to a meeting somewhere or a day when I can sleep as long as possible and then do whatever I want, I'll take that second choice every time.

I'm also completely disorganized. My desk is chaos, my filing system nearly dysfunctional. My desk often reaches what I call "critical mess," and things are buried and forgotten that I really should have handled weeks, even months, before.

What else? Oh yes, my memory is terrible. Don't expect me to remember your name, or our last conversation. I call it a "highly selective" memory. I remember certain things vividly; a lot of other things just somehow neglect to get filed in my brain somewhere.

Yet I started what is now a successful business—a publishing company—the day I turned thirty. I had no capital of any kind, no business experience, no family support and very little knowledge of publishing, and yet I've managed to build a wonderfully successful company, New World Library, which has published some great books and audios (and a few videos) by Eckhart Tolle, Shakti Gawain, Deepak Chopra, Dan Millman and many others. How did this possibly happen? I'll try to keep it really simple.

* * *

The day I turned thirty is the single day that changed my life. I woke up in a state of shock and realized I wasn't a kid anymore. I spent much of the day pacing back and forth in my little slum apartment, thinking about my life—something I had done very rarely in the past.

I realized even back then that I had one great strength, something I was born with. (Now I realize everyone is born with a unique gift of some kind.) The thing I knew in my heart and soul that has served me so well over the years is something a lot of people take years and years to learn, and something some people never learn: I knew how important it was to do what I loved. I knew that if I went for my dreams, it would all work out somehow. I could never understand why so many of my friends didn't seem to understand that, and would settle for jobs—and for lives—they didn't really enjoy.

I had done what I loved through my twenties. I had been an actor and a musician, I'd done a "back-to-the-land" experiment and stayed at a Zen center, but when I looked back I realized I had built nothing for the present or the future. I had no direction whatsoever. I hadn't been setting the course, or even steering the ship of my life. I had no goals! No wonder I had gone nowhere. When I turned thirty, I was unemployed, I had no savings whatsoever, and I was scrounging (a word we used often) to come up with sixty-five dollars a month rent. In other words, I was a poverty case (two other words we used often).

I asked myself a question I had rarely asked before—a simple question, an important question: *What do I want to do with the rest of my life?*

I thought about it for a while, pacing up and down. Then I remembered a little game I had played once in my early twenties during my back-to-the-land experiment. We were sitting around a fire one night, and one couple said, "Let's play a little game we play at church camp. Let's imagine five years have passed, and everything has gone as well as we can imagine. What would our lives look like?"

I have no idea what I even said when I first played the game—so obviously it had no impact on my life. But I remembered that game the day I turned thirty, and it changed my life.

On that day, I set my course in life in a way I never had before. The actual mechanics of it were quite simple. I wrote down my ideal scene on a single sheet of paper, then I listed all of the goals I could think of on another sheet of paper, then I rewrote each of those goals as an *affirmation.* Over time, over a few months, plans started to emerge for each major goal—and the next steps to take became obvious.

Of course, as soon as I dared think of my ideal scene and write my first goal, I was overwhelmed with doubts and fears. Dealing with those doubts and fears was probably the most important work I did. It took me about five years of constant course correction to reach the first of my goals—a profitable business supporting myself and others easily and effortlessly—and about ten years to fully realize my ideal scene, which included a beautiful home in northern California, in one of the most beautiful places I had ever seen on earth.

The Three Essentials

Over the years, I've come to understand that success in business is really very simple. It is not rocket science or brain surgery; it requires only the simplest of math skills. It is much simpler than being a parent, for example, because business follows certain essential rules that have been unchanged for centuries, while when you're a parent, the rules keep changing, and endless creativity is required.

There are simply three things you need to have together to create success:

1. Your product or service. The key here is to make it the best you can—and, ideally, do what you love to do. Don't settle for less.
2. Marketing and sales. It is essential to find some way to market your product or service. The key here is to have a *multipronged strategy.* Keep aware there are a huge number of different ways to sell your product or service. Never put your eggs in one basket. Try something—*anything*—and if that doesn't work, try something else. Try something that has proved effective in the past, and then try something that has never been done. Keep trying, and one way or another you'll

stumble onto something that works. As the actor Bert Lahr said, "Keep on the merry-go-round long enough, and you're bound to catch the brass ring, sooner or later."

3. Financial controls. You have to have the same kind of controls in business that you have in your daily life. In your personal life, you have to spend less than you earn, or you head into debt. In a business, keep your expenses as low as possible, and get to the point as soon as you can where your income exceeds your expenses.

Keep watching those expenses. Break out all your expenses into different categories, and compare them with industry averages. Don't get way out of line in any category.

With good financial controls, you can have a successful, profitable business with a relatively modest income; with bad financial controls, you can blow it on any level, even when you're making millions (or, like Enron, billions).

The Final Word

It gets simpler and simpler for me as the years pass. I understand things more deeply; I know them in my heart and soul and in every cell of my body, somehow, rather than just in my head. And the more I understand, the more my life continues to get better and better. I'll try to sum up what I know in a final sentence. Over the years, I came to understand this—in spite of all my weakness and shortcomings:

We have everything we need
to create the success of our dreams:
a miraculous body, a phenomenal brain,

and a vast and powerful subconscious mind.
Now it's just a matter of focusing them
in the right direction.

We have everything we need, even if we're lazy, unemployed, not too smart, organized, overwhelmed or *whatever.* We have a mind that is capable of making a plan and a body capable of taking the steps necessary to achieve that plan. Along the way, guiding us, showing us what to do at every moment, is a vast and powerful subconscious mind.

All we have to do is ask for guidance, and we find it. You've heard it before, many times: *ask and you shall receive.* Within you are all the tools you need to create the life of your dreams. I know this is true. If I can do it, you can, too.

So, go for it! You'll never regret it.

Marc Allen

EPILOGUE: *Nearly thirty years ago, in the kitchen of a small apartment in Oakland, California, Marc Allen and Shakti Gawain started a publishing firm known as Whatever Publishing to release a few books and booklets they had written. A shoestring operation with very little in capital, total sales were $800 the first year.*

Today, that small publishing company—which changed its name to New World Library in the 1980s—has grown to become one of the most successful independent publishers in the country in the areas of personal growth, alternative health and prosperity. Based in Novato, California, New World Library features authors such as Eckhart Tolle (The Power of Now), *Deepak Chopra* (The Seven Spiritual Laws of Success) *and, of course, Shakti Gawain* (Creative Visualization). *The company releases over fifty books, audio and video projects annually and has an active backlist of over three hundred titles (*www.newworldlibrary.com*).*

An author himself, Allen is also an amazing pianist and musician, having created and recorded several instrumental albums including Breathe, Petals *and* Awakening. *Samples can be heard on his Web site:* www.watercoursemedia.com.

As cofounder, president and publisher of New World Library, Allen's belief in himself and his dreams grew into great financial success, but more important, great personal success. He obviously loves doing what he loves, including taking every Monday off and only working afternoons the rest of the week, after *sleeping in!*

Dahlynn McKowen

Cold Stone Revolution

Have you ever noticed that business magazines love to write stories about successful businesspeople? The ups, the downs, the quirks and the quandaries, and, of course, the extraordinary achievements.

Now that Cold Stone Creamery has grown from a small Arizona company to an international one, I've even had a few stories written about me, too, as have many other members of our "Creamery Team." It's almost surreal to see the headlines and words in print. After all, to me success has become less about the achievements of the individual or even the team, and more about the success you inspire in someone else. But I didn't always think that way.

Before I came to Cold Stone Creamery, I worked in sales and marketing for Procter & Gamble. Any young business graduate couldn't have asked for a better training ground. It was the ideal place to learn the right way to do just about anything in business. But beginning in sales, the emphasis seemed to be on personal achievement. Sure, we wanted our division to achieve its objectives, but first and foremost, *my* success landed squarely on *my* ability to meet *my* sales quota. Success was all about *me* making it happen. Interestingly, when I came to Cold Stone, some of that thinking had to change.

We may as well start at the beginning. Cold Stone Creamery was founded when Don and Susan Sutherland—two ice cream lovers and entrepreneurs in their own right—put everything they had into opening up the first Cold Stone Creamery in Tempe, Arizona. If you doubt their humble beginnings, here's a fact: They came up with the name Cold Stone Creamery while sitting on playground swings in a community park in Mesa, Arizona. There they made a deal: they were going to stay on those swings until they came up with a name for their soon-to-be-open ice cream store. It took all of thirty minutes.

As you might expect, establishing a successful ice cream business took considerably longer. There were many lean days, weeks and months, but together, the Sutherlands turned the first Cold Stone Creamery into a sensation. Their success and their joy for what they were doing inspired other would-be entrepreneurs who were asking them, "Can I own a Cold Stone?" When I joined the small company several years later, my job was to grow the popular local ice cream store into a franchise. We wanted to spread the love of the best ice cream around the world, which at the time we defined as Arizona and Colorado.

The early days of Cold Stone kept me exceptionally busy, and the first franchisees we brought on board taught me more than I could ever convey. You see, at Procter & Gamble my job was to simply serve my customers, keep them happy and make my quota. In the franchise business, I learned franchisees were more than customers; they were "philosophical" business partners who had invested in us, and us in them. Suddenly, I realized, my job wasn't just to keep them happy. It was much more than that.

As we awarded more and more franchises, we really got

to know these early pioneers, the people who, in some cases, risked everything they had on the ice cream they loved and even a stronger desire to have a business of their own. Many told stories of coming to Arizona and stopping by chance at a Cold Stone for ice cream, then immediately calling to find out about owning a store. These people weren't just names on a list, they were ice cream enthusiasts who inspired us with their passion. We cared about their success as much as we cared about our own.

By the time we had about ten stores open, a man named Dan Farr came into our offices unannounced and boldly said, "I want to open up a Cold Stone Creamery in Alaska." I smiled and told him Alaska really wasn't a priority for us right now. And almost with a laugh, I said, "We were thinking of going to California first." Dan wouldn't take "no" for an answer, and by the end of our meeting he had talked me, a young entrepreneur in charge of franchise development, into opening a store in Anchorage.

I came to find out that the late Dan Farr was one of Alaska's true business pioneers, and today I feel honored even to have known him. When Alaska became a success, it was then that we knew that Cold Stone Creamery could be a national phenomenon. Aside from being a great store owner, Dan and his unbridled belief in us opened our eyes to how big the world could really be.

About three years later, in August 1999, with an even greater view of our potential to change ice cream forever, our leadership team (all four of us) went on a strategic planning retreat to figure out where we should take this rapidly growing company. We returned with a vision statement that we were afraid to tell anyone about for fear they might think we were crazy. With just seventy-four stores open, we staked our claim that: "The world will know Cold Stone Creamery as the Ultimate Ice Cream Experience by having one thousand profitable stores open by December 31, 2004."

This was a milestone in our company. But as monumental as that vision was, equally important was a single line in our mission statement that we penned at the very same time. Simply put:

The success of the franchisee
and the ultimate happiness of the consumer
will go hand-in-hand
as our number-one priority.

And what a logical priority this was! After all, our success so far was hardly a solo act. From Don and Susan who struggled together and succeeded together to the early franchisees like Dan Farr who believed in us more than we believed in ourselves, we have been inspired by and have contributed to each others' success.

Today, we have achieved our 1,000-store goal and are now setting our sights on being the number-one best-selling ice cream brand in America. And if history serves as a guide, it will take making each other, not ourselves, successful to do it. Our leadership will continue to support the Creamery Team. The Creamery Team will continue to support the area developers in our markets. The area developers will continue to support our franchisees. And the franchisee will continue to support the crew members who deliver the Ultimate Ice Cream Experience® around the world. Today, that world is truly the world, not just Arizona and Colorado!

Mutual success—the success that you inspire in others and that others inspire in you—is the true success story at Cold Stone Creamery. Our success isn't about an individual, and it isn't really just about a team. It's about putting the success of others before your own. It's about asking, "What are we doing today to make our franchisees successful?" These words, which we proudly display in shining metallic letters at the door of our headquarters office, remind every Creamery Team member who enters what their daily purpose is, how we all got to where we are and what it's going to take for us to realize our future.

Doug Ducey

EPILOGUE: *Cold Stone Creamery has been taking the country scoop-by-scoop, and is one of the nation's fastest-growing franchises. But what makes this ice cream company so special? Why, the ice cream and entertainment, of course!*

Cold Stone's ice cream is freshly made, smooth and creamy. Once a customer selects an ice cream flavor, generous amounts of the treat are placed on a large frozen stone. This is when the magic begins; per the customer's exact specifications (toppings and mixtures, that is), the entire order is then chopped and blended while the customer watches. And don't forget the singing, laughter and all-around rambunctiously fun entertainment provided by the Cold Stone Creamery crew members while they serve their customers. This is one happy place to work!

According to Doug Ducey, CEO and chairman of Cold Stone Creamery, the company's mission is to put smiles on people's faces by delivering the Ultimate Ice Cream Experience®, and the company is doing just that. And what is Ducey's favorite ice cream blend, you ask? Sweet Cream ice cream with black cherries and graham cracker pie crust. Yum!

To learn more about Cold Stone Creamery, visit one of their many locations or www.coldstonecreamery.com.

Dahlynn McKowen

Nitty-Gritty Reasons

I was a young father struggling to make ends meet and find what I really wanted to do with my life the day the life-changing knock on my front door came. It was a timid little knock, and when I opened the door, I looked down at a little girl with big, brown eyes staring up at me.

"Would you like to buy some Girl Scout cookies, Mister?"

She made a masterful presentation—there were several flavors, a special deal, and best of all, they were only two dollars a box. How could anyone refuse? With a big smile, she ever so politely asked me to buy a box of cookies. Her presentation, combined with her smile and pleading eyes, instinctively made me want to say yes. Except for one problem: I didn't have two dollars!

Now, if you're a husband and a father, about twenty-five years old and working as hard as you know how, but you don't have two dollars, it's probably fair to say that you have a problem. And I had a big problem. Pride kept me from telling the little girl with the big brown eyes the truth. So I did the next thing I thought of. I lied to her.

"Thanks, but I've already bought Girl Scout cookies this year," I said. "And I've still got plenty stacked in the house."

My answer got me off the hook, except for the

disappointment showing in the little girl's eyes as she thanked me, turned and walked away.

I closed the door and stood alone, thinking about what I had just done. It was difficult for me to tell which was worse: telling a lie or the embarrassment of not having two dollars. I will never forget how pitiful I felt that day.

I don't want to live like this, I said to myself. *I've had it with being broke. I've had it with lying, making excuses and not having two dollars in my pocket. I've had it!*

It was one of those moments that determine the course of a life for years to come. That day, I discovered that, with strong enough emotional reasons, I could do incredible things. That single, embarrassing moment with the little Girl Scout standing at my door is what I call a "nitty-gritty reason," something that had the power to change my life.

My Girl Scout story does have a happy ending. Several years later, I was living in Beverly Hills, California. One day, I had just come out of a bank, happy with the deposits I had just made, when I saw two young girls selling candy in front of a nearby grocery store. One of the little girls caught my eye. "Mister, would you like to buy some candy?" she asked.

"Well, maybe I would," I said, returning her smile. "What kind of candy do you have?"

"It's Almond Roca, and it's really good," she assured me.

"Almond Roca? That's my *favorite!* How much is it?"

"It's only two dollars."

Two dollars! It couldn't be! Immediately, I thought of the other little girl who had tried to sell me her two-dollar cookies. I was excited. "How many boxes of candy do you have?"

"I've got five."

Looking at her friend, I asked, "And how many boxes do *you* have?"

"I've got four."

"That's nine boxes. I tell you what: I'll take them all."

At this, both girls' mouths fell open as they exclaimed in unison, "Really?"

"Sure," I said. "I've got some friends I can share them with."

They scurried to stack all the boxes together. I reached into my pocket, counted out eighteen dollars and handed them the money. As I was about to leave, the boxes tucked under my arm, one of the girls looked up and said, "Mister, you're really something!"

I had only spent eighteen dollars, but that little girl thought I was really something. What a feeling!

As you might guess, the issue for me wasn't the money or the words of admiration and gratitude the little girl spoke to me. The real issue was the changes I made years earlier because of another little girl, and the pain and frustration I felt because of the lack in my life. Today, I make sure I always carry extra pocket money, just in case I meet another little Girl Scout, or any other similar event that will fan the fire of desire within me—and remind me of a nitty-gritty reason that pushed me to begin a journey to a new life.

Jim Rohn

[EDITORS' NOTE: *During the past four decades, Jim Rohn has shared his success philosophies and principles with more than 6,000 audiences and 4 million people worldwide. As the author of over twenty-five books and audio and video programs, and a past recipient of the Masters of Influence Award from the National Speakers Association, he has trained hundreds of executives from America's top corporations. Rohn has been described as everything from a master motivator to one of the most profound thinkers and mind-expanding individuals of our time. Visit* www.jimrohn.com *to learn more.*]

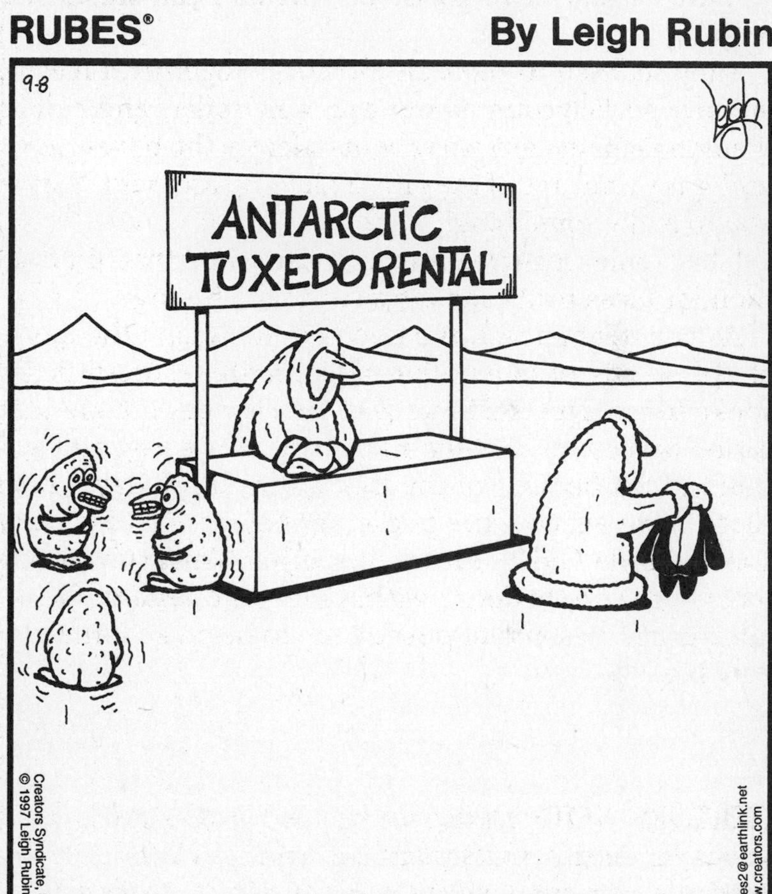
RUBES®
By Leigh Rubin
9-8
ANTARCTIC TUXEDO RENTAL
Creators Syndicate, Inc.
© 1997 Leigh Rubin!
rubes2@earthlink.net
www.creators.com

The Sweetness of It All

I've been asked so many times if being a woman in the business world is difficult. My answer is a definite, "No!" I feel it has been an advantage for me. Women don't fit that typical stereotype of a businessman's man, as those of us women who are successful do stand out in a crowd. We're more sensitive when it comes to our businesses and livelihoods, and plus, we can juggle ten things at a time, even in an organized fashion!

Now in my case, I'm a mother of three growing boys (four, if you count my husband), which keeps me active all the time, between family and school/after-school commitments. Trying to establish my business and juggle my family was hard at times, but as soon as I learned that I must always put my family first, a lot of the difficulties went away. I learned to put my two "lives" into perspective; I have only one chance to be a mother and to raise and watch my children grow up, but I can work anytime.

But wait, I'm jumping ahead of myself. You don't even know my story.

I was destined to work with strawberries. When I was very young, my dad planted a strawberry patch for me, and that's when my love affair with this delectable fruit began.

My job was to go out and pick the berries—one for the bucket, two for me. I loved them! From my pickings, my mom would make yummy strawberry pies, the ones with strawberry gel and thick homemade graham cracker crust. She had to make two so I wouldn't be grumpy at the dinner table watching the size of the pieces she was cutting.

Jump forward about fifteen years, when I was working as a mortgage broker for my brother's company. I did well, made a lot of money and received many accolades including "Rookie of the Year" my first year on the job. Needless to say, I grew up really fast; the business was stressful, and I worked many long hours to earn that award.

Much of my success as a mortgage broker was due to treating my customers well. With the help of my sister-in-law who was a caterer, every year for the holidays we made homemade goodie baskets for my customers and realtors. But they weren't just any ordinary holiday baskets; they were filled with homemade chocolate-dipped strawberries. A creative person by nature, I enjoyed dipping and designing the different types of chocolate-dipped strawberries and creating the gift baskets. It became therapeutic to me and helped with my stress, and also became a great way for me to market my business.

My career eventually led me to the stock business, and I didn't enjoy it as much as the mortgage industry. But I did enjoy dipping strawberries, so I continued on, creating many different types of recipes and dipping patterns. One day, I took some of my sweet creations to a grand opening office party. My spread was even more beautiful than what the caterers had prepared! A gal in our office—a mentor and very important person in my life—said to me, "You're working for me, and you can do this?" Her question made me contemplate going into business for myself.

Things happened fast from that point, and in 1989 I opened Shari's Berries. The rest is history.

I have learned many things from starting a business from scratch—a recipe, if you will—which I attribute to my company's success:

- Always take great care of your employees. Your employees will never treat your customers any better then you treat them. Never ask an employee to do anything you wouldn't do yourself (and believe me, I've done it all).
- Every year, Shari's Berries sends out a present to its top 100 customers with a note telling them how much their business is appreciated.
- Take what you love to do and figure out how to make money and a living. Life is too short to spend so much time at a job you don't enjoy. I'm blessed to have the opportunity to make money, and a livelihood, doing something I truly enjoy.
- The customer is ALWAYS right. Nothing is more important than backing your product with the highest form of customer service. Remember the old rule: *A happy customer will tell three people. An unhappy customer will tell ten people.* My goal is to have only positive things said about my company, and I bend over backward to satisfy each and every customer.
- Support your community. A community loves to patronize a company that helps its own.
- My pastor once shared with me that he has never heard anyone on his or her deathbed say that they wish they had spent more time at the office. A job makes money for us to support our family, so it shouldn't ever hurt our family in any way.
- Count your pennies; the dollars will take care of themselves. This is something that my grandmother taught me a long time ago. Never stop overseeing your money. Oprah still signs every check!

Regardless of whether you're a female or male business owner, I'm sure you have your own offerings to add to my list. This is my advice to you: If I could do it, so can you, and build upon your list daily to become that successful entrepreneur. This will be your recipe for success!

Shari Fitzpatrick

EPILOGUE: *Shari Fitzpatrick is the founder and president of the wildly successful Shari's Berries, Inc., the sweet fruit sensation that can be found throughout the nation via many stores and also at her award-winning online site* www.berries.com.

Shari's Berries features over 200 kinds of exquisite hand-dipped fruit delights, her signature gift being Strawberry Roses. The roses are hand-dipped strawberries, set on hand-made stems with silk rose leaves. The chocolate roses are then arranged with baby's breath and fern to look like a box of elegant long-stem roses. The strawberry rose bouquets are so unique that Fitzpatrick was granted a patent, making the product a truly one-of-a-kind gift.

Fitzpatrick credits her success as an entrepreneur to three simple priorities: God first, family second and work third. According to Fitzpatrick, this special formula has proven sweet for her and her family.

To learn more about Shari's Berries, visit www.berries.com *or e-mail her at* shari@sacberries.com.

Dahlynn McKowen

8

THE BOTTOM LINE

Lead the life that will make you kindly and friendly to everyone about you, and you will be surprised what a happy life you will lead.

Charles M. Schwab

Finding the Soul of Success

In 1970 my wife, Kate, and I started our company—Tom's of Maine—with a $5,000 loan and the idea that environmentalism and consumerism didn't have to be at odds. We wanted to use natural products—those without abrasives, dyes and artificial ingredients that might be harmful to humans and the environment—and we had a feeling there were other people who shared our desire. We set out to build a company on the belief that people and nature deserve respect.

Our initial successes were with natural soap and shampoo. Then, in 1974, we developed the first-ever natural toothpaste. It was a huge hit—eclipsing sales of our other products overnight—and over the next decade we attracted millions of consumers to Tom's of Maine natural personal care products. Our instincts had been right: our "different" kind of company could work.

By the mid-1980s, however, what had started as a new kind of business was looking more like a typical big business. Tom's of Maine had expanded to $5 million in sales. I had hired MBAs and packaged-goods professionals to help break into the mass market, and our products could be found not only in health food stores, but also in supermarkets and drugstore chains. We were growing an average of 25 percent per year. I was flying all over the country serving accounts. On the outside, everything looked great. But on the inside, I was miserable.

Though I called myself an entrepreneur, I hadn't created a new product in five years; in our first ten years in business, Kate and I had created a dozen different products. The management team I'd put in place was focusing the company's energy elsewhere—on tasks like financial planning, management reorganization and market development. In addition, we battled regularly over my commitment to natural ingredients, to our customers and employees and to the environment. They wanted to add artificial sweetener to our toothpastes to make them taste better. They felt employees should punch a time clock. They thought our packaging needed flashy "benefit statements" instead of our simple personal note to consumers. These young MBAs had helped me get what I wanted—a successful, growing company—but I had a feeling there was more to business than being big. Something was missing. Something felt wrong.

In the fall of 1986, I surprised myself when I confided to my friend Reverend Eckel and his wife, Connie, "I'm tired of making money." I confessed how confused I felt about what I should be doing with the rest of my life. I was considering selling the company and retiring at age forty-three. Perhaps I'd like to study more about theology. "I'm not really understanding my mission in life," I shared.

Connie interrupted to ask, "How do you know that Tom's of Maine isn't your ministry?"

Her question made me think: *Perhaps my business was my mission in life.*

After visiting the Harvard Divinity School for a Theological Day, I decided to apply. I became the first sitting CEO to earn a master's degree at Harvard Divinity

School, splitting my workweek between the campus and my company. As I began attending lectures, one overriding thought held my focus: *Could I stick to my respect for humanity and nature and still further the growth of my company, or did I have to sell my soul for success?*

One of my first answers came in my introductory ethics class. My professor, Richard Niebuhr, presented utilitarianism as the dominant ethical norm, where a course of action is calculated on the basis of what gives the most good to the most people. The term "utilitarianism" was new to me, but I recognized it as the value system that drove the business world, where "good" was equated to profits. But Professor Niebuhr went on to say that this was just one type of value system, and he introduced several others. I saw that Kate's and my instinctive way of conducting our lives and our business seemed to follow "formalism"—that inner sense of obligation and human connection that people feel for their friends and neighbors. Our first customers had been family and friends. We respected our customers, and we were not in business to maximize profits by cheating them or skimping on quality. I was beginning to see a philosophical foundation for running a business with our hearts as well as our heads.

My next "aha" moments came when Professor Niebuhr introduced the writings of the twentieth-century philosopher Martin Buber and the eighteenth-century philosopher Jonathan Edwards. In each case, my immediate thought as I read their works was, *Why hadn't I been taught this before?*

Buber wrote about an "I-Thou" versus "I-It" relationship with the world. The "I-It" relationship was the typical business approach: treating the world as an object for us to use. In contrast, the "I-Thou" relationship was about loving and honoring the world for its own sake. Buber believed that both relationships ought to be integrated in our lives. To be fully human, we should approach the world from the mind and the spirit. We can respect what we also use.

Edwards's philosophy was that our sense of identity comes not only from being individuals, but also from a sense of relation to others. Following this logic, I should view my company not only as a private entity but also in relation to other entities: employees, financial partners, customers and suppliers, as well as the community and environment.

I began to see a new approach to a business plan. Tom's of Maine was part of a web of social relationships that called for responsible action. That's exactly how Kate and I had run the company that first decade, with a commitment to using natural ingredients and serving our customers and employees.

Studying theology turned out to be the best business decision I'd ever made. I rediscovered not only what kind of entrepreneur I was and wanted to be, but also the language with which to describe it. I reconfirmed that the intuitions we had started our company with had been on the mark. Before, I hadn't the intellectual confidence to question the standard ways of doing business. I now knew that *my* way of doing business, as different as it was from the traditional approach, had a firm grounding in Western religious and moral thought. I could manage Tom's of Maine for profit *and* the common good.

But how was I to get my management—actually, the whole company—on board with my way of thinking? How could I convince them to trust the kinds of intuitions and values that had accounted for our original success? I decided to bring a bit of theology school to Tom's of Maine. I gave copies of Buber's book *I and Thou* to our managers and members of our board, and then asked Professor

Niebuhr to visit for an open dialog with the board of directors. I hoped to show them that some of the business practices they thought primitive or unprofessional—things like personal messages on our product boxes, no time clock for employees to punch and answering all our consumer mail—were worth keeping.

The strategy was a success. Many executives and board members felt exhilarated by the dialogue. We decided to have more sessions, and over time we developed a statement of beliefs and a mission statement to define the future of Tom's of Maine. We identified core values such as being socially and environmentally responsible as well as financially successful, and core beliefs such as a person's responsibility to his or her community and the inherent worth of people and nature.

Then we made the mission the master we would all work to fulfill. We made our values the starting point for all new initiatives and growth strategies. Not everyone on our staff could adopt and adjust to the new values; those who couldn't ended up leaving. For those who remained, we had a long haul institutionalizing the new culture, training employees and integrating the new way of thinking into the daily practice of business.

By setting our operating standards within our values, business choices became very clear. There was no longer a clash between management and me. Our decisions were driven not by the market, but by what we believed in. For instance, even if our new baking soda toothpaste tasted a little odd, we couldn't add artificial sweeteners. We had to trust that our customers wanted an all-natural product and would appreciate the cleaning power of baking soda. (They did, and the toothpaste was an instant success.) If we wanted our toothpaste to be approved by the American Dental Association, we'd have to find a way to satisfy the ADA's fluoride testing criteria without compromising our policy of no animal testing. It cost us ten times as much to test on human subjects, but Tom's of Maine became the first natural toothpaste to earn the ADA's seal and the first company to receive FDA approval on fluoride toothpaste without animal testing.

As we applied this new value system over the years, something exciting became apparent: better values lead to better value. Tom's of Maine wasn't profitable "in spite of" being socially and environmentally responsible. Rather, our values actually brought the company tremendous success.

Tom's of Maine has become the largest manufacturer of natural personal-care products, offering more than seventy products available in 35,000 stores nationwide. Our toothpaste is the seventh top-selling brand, and our company continues to experience double-digit growth. We are known for our great natural products *and* for our corporate values.

Back when we started, Kate and I sensed there were other people like us who would appreciate natural products. Today, we know 13 percent of the country considers natural products important to them. These people aren't defined by age, sex or income but by values similar to ours. It turns out values-based business isn't just the nice thing to do; it's also the smart thing to do.

Tom Chappell
As told to Julie Long

EPILOGUE: *Sticking to his instincts and putting values at the core of his actions has brought Tom Chappell success far beyond the balance sheet.*

Much as he created the natural products industry, as cofounder and CEO, Tom has created a new model of commerce. Tom's of Maine uses all manner of ecologically sound manufacturing practices, donates 10 percent of pretax profits to nonprofit organizations, encourages employees to spend 5 percent of their paid company time volunteering in their community, and institutes Common Good Partnerships like Dental Health for All and Rivers Awareness Program.

To help other businesses find success through social responsibility, Tom has authored two books, The Soul of a Business: Managing for Profit and the Common Good *(Bantam Books, 1993) and* Managing Upside Down: The Seven Intentions of Values-Centered Leadership *(William Morrow and Company, Inc., 1999). He also founded the Saltwater Institute* (www.saltwater.org)*, an educational foundation that teaches values-centered leadership.*

Tom's of Maine and the Chappells have earned numerous awards and recognitions over the years. Most recently, Tom and Kate received the Salvation Army's "Others" Award for "an extraordinary spirit of service to others," and were the first recipients of "Taking Action for Animals Corporate Ethic Award for Animal Advocacy" presented in 2005 by a collaborative of leading animal rights organizations.

To learn more about Tom's of Maine and the Chappells, please visit www.tomsofmaine.com.

Julie Long

off the mark.com by Mark Parisi
WELL, AFTER FORTY DAYS AND FORTY NIGHTS, IT APPEARS I'M READY TO GO INTO THE FERTILIZER BUSINESS...
ATLANTIC FEATURE © 1996 MARK PARISI
MARK PARISI

Strive for Excellence

Everyone who's ever taken a shower has an idea. It's the person who gets out of the shower, dries off and does something about it who makes a difference.

Nolan Bushnell

I guess I'm a true entrepreneur. I've never had a real job.

Growing up in the suburbs of Claysville, Pennsylvania, (population 500) and being the baby of six boys, I spent lots of time alone amusing myself and thinking up ways to earn money. I worked during the summers in both high school and college, but on my own terms, hawking advertising matchbooks, encyclopedias and even cars; I sold my first used car at age fifteen, before I had a driver's license.

My dad, Sam Antion, was a heavy influence on my entrepreneurial spirit. He came to Ellis Island on a cattle boat in the early 1900s, and at the ripe age of ten he was head of his household. He shined shoes at the local barber shop to earn enough money to take care of his mother, sister and baby brother, and to also buy electrical engineering mail-order courses from the American School. Just three years after coming to America, my dad established his own electrical contracting firm and installed the first electric lightbulb in Carnegie, Pennsylvania. Not bad for a thirteen-year-old.

Dad always made me strive for excellence. Wait, let me rephrase that: Dad *lived* excellence, and that's all I knew my entire life.

An electrician by trade, Dad would always route the flat wires in a nice symmetrical and evenly spaced pattern when he was wiring; he never cut across the shortest distance to save wire, thus making his costs a little cheaper. As a child, I remember watching him and asking why he just didn't run the wires directly between the two points. He said, "Years from now, when someone looks at this job, they'll know that a professional did it. Also, if they ever have any trouble, they'll be able to track down the problem much easier because I did a nice, neat job."

I can't remember Dad ever being out of work even one day. When everyone else was laid off, he was always in demand. His examples of persistence, determination and excellence served me well throughout my entire life.

By using the principles I learned from my father, I became my own boss, just as he did. Before I graduated from college, I owned five apartment buildings and a hotel. Mind you, this was in the 1970s, and all six of these real estate purchases were no-money-down deals, long before the mainstream ever heard of such a thing. I also owned other various successful businesses, including a nightclub, where I survived two gun fights, knife fights and numerous broken noses and arms. I guess being successful in that business meant I walked away alive! But one of my favorite businesses was as owner of a practical joke entertainment company; I received worldwide publicity and notoriety for pulling 4,000 custom-designed practical jokes, and had a ball doing it.

As you can probably guess, my motto during all these business ventures was: *Do anything to avoid working for someone else!*

Then I found out I could talk . . . for money!

The performing skills I perfected as a result of my practical joke company, believe it or not, inadvertently led me to the world of professional speaking. I learned that people were making good money—more important, great money—to talk. That's it, just stand up on a stage and gab away about all sorts of things, mainly business-related topics. And I could be my own boss.

I knew I was great at entertaining, but did I have the skill to make a speech in a business setting? Absolutely not. So, my strive-for-excellence attitude that my dad taught me kicked in. I started studying everything I could about speaking. I bought and read every book I could about speaking. I joined the National Speakers Association chapter in Washington, D.C., and offered to be the chapter's audiotape librarian so that I could listen to hundreds of hours of training materials from some of the best speakers on the planet. I put all my newfound knowledge into play, and over the next couple of years I started to become a pretty darn good speaker.

Due to all of my hard work in becoming a great speaker, I find myself today having to turn down way more speeches than I accept. I've raised the bar for myself, only speaking at the most prestigious seminars and big money events . . . no more engagements at Holiday Inn basements (no offense to Holiday Inn).

And there's a big lesson here: when you get really good at something, people will notice and ask you how you did it. That's when you put your expertise in print: I wrote *Wake 'em Up Business Presentations* (Anchor, 1997) and the *Wake 'em Up Video Professional Speaking System* (Anchor, 1999), which includes a book, video and audio training course. I sell these books as back-of-the-room offerings after my talks.

Then along came the Internet. . . .

I just want to take this opportunity to make sure that everyone reading this knows that *I* invented the Internet, not Al Gore. . . . Anyway, as I became more popular on the speaking circuit, I created back-of-the-room products (books, videos, CDs) to sell after my talks, which augmented my speaking fees. The on-site sales were so successful that I decided to sell these products online also. But sales via the Internet were really slow, so again I decided to become excellent, this time learning how to sell on the Internet.

I studied every course I could find. I took consultations and tried every piece of software designed for Internet marketing. I basically became an Internet fanatic. And guess what happened? Just like before, people started to notice. They begged me to work up an Internet marketing seminar. So I did, but with my comic background I just could not bring myself to call it a "bootcamp" like many other speakers did; since my seminar was all about making money by sitting at home on your rear end, I called it "ButtCamp." Yes, I know it's a crazy name, but it's a serious seminar, and I've done them all over the United States, Canada, Thailand, Singapore, Malaysia, Australia, New Zealand and the United Kingdom. Oh, I forgot—in the United Kingdom, my series is called "Bum Camp."

Since the creation of the marketing series, I've helped thousands of other small-business people use the Web to sell their products and services. I'm considered one of the top Internet marketing speakers in the world, primarily because I don't snow you with technical knowledge (hey, I don't know any). From the thousands I have helped, I can proudly say that many have become "e-millionaires," and others are making an extra $5,000 to $20,000 a month using the ButtCamp seminar.

I also own the Great Internet Marketing Retreat Center, located in my estate home in Virginia Beach, Virginia, where my students come to live in the lap of luxury while studying Internet marketing with me. My book, *The Ultimate Guide to Electronic Marketing for Small Business* (Wiley, 2005), topped all the online business bestseller lists and was number two overall, only behind that little wizard boy Harry Potter.

What I learned from my dad has done wonders for my career. Undoubtedly, Sam is up there adjusting the circuitry on the pearly gates so they open and close perfectly. So the next time you want to open up a world of opportunity for yourself, think of him and strive for excellence.

Tom Antion

EPILOGUE: *Tom Antion and Associates Communication Company provides entertaining and informative keynote speeches, educational seminars, retreats and mentoring on Internet marketing for small businesses.*

A professional entertainer and speaker since 1988, Antion has given over 2,500 paid presentations. Antion was also chief spokesperson for CBS-owned Switchboard.com, one of the most heavily visited Web sites in the world, in their online small-business outreach program MainStreets Online.

To learn more about Tom Antion—as well as his speaking schedule, consulting services and products—please visit www.antion.com.

Dahlynn McKowen

Persistence of Belief

Starting a company taught me, if nothing else, that the less money you have, the more patience you need. My family and I learned with practically no advertising or marketing funds that it takes a long time to establish a brand and gain popularity. It was undoubtedly the persistence of my own belief in Dippin' Dots® ice cream that allowed me to direct my entrepreneurial endeavor from the start to where it is today.

I grew up on a farm near the small town of Grand Chain, which rests along the Ohio River at the southern tip of Illinois. Being a farm boy taught me that farming is actually an entrepreneurial activity, because it involves tremendous patience, a strong work ethic and personal risk.

I can remember my dad teaching me how to drive our "H" Farmall tractor when I was only seven years old. My job was to haul corn from the old barn to the new barn where we fed the livestock. A few years later, I made and sold brooms with a friend, crafted from my family's broom corn and broom-making equipment. We also raised chickens, and I sold eggs at my school for fifty cents a dozen. During the summer months my friends and I baled and hauled hay and straw for extra money.

In school, my interests centered around science. Based on the advice of my college chemistry teacher, I pursued a career in pre-med. After moving from Shawnee Community College to Southern Illinois University in 1979, I thought I was ready to pursue medicine. Right as school started, a friend talked me into another agribusiness. We combined our efforts to raise pigs, but timing was everything, and ours wasn't good. Pork prices fell dramatically, and so did my grades. I clearly remember missing eight classes in one week just to manage our farm.

My life was due a major turning point. As my pig farm business crumbled, I sat depressed in my home (a mobile home on rented property, where my rent was two fat hogs every six months), searching for a career direction. I picked up the *Yellow Pages* and under the heading of Physicians I saw a list of hundreds of names. I asked myself, *Was becoming a doctor really for me? Was it what I really wanted to do?* Because it was nearly impossible to catch up with the rigor of my pre-med classes, my answer was "no." From that point on I devoted my studies to microbiology and its agricultural implementations.

After graduation, I taught at a local prison. The subject was ethanol production, which appeared to be a booming business for agricultural communities in the early 1980s. By this time I was a family man and was, of course, looking for opportunities for advancement. I accepted a job at Alltech, Inc., a Lexington, Kentucky-based biotechnology lab specializing in the enhancement of cattle feed. The focus of my lab work in college had centered around a building block of protein called lysine. Lysine is made from bacterial cultures and subsequently converted into a dried powder. This powder is then mixed into feed to satisfy an animal's requirement for protein.

At Alltech we were growing bacterial cultures for another reason. The "good" bacteria were grown in large cultures, frozen, freeze-dried into a powder, then given to farm animals to ward off "bad" bacteria in a natural way as opposed to using antibiotics. Because it is very important to preserve the freshness and structural integrity of the bacteria, the cultures had to be frozen rapidly. Through a cryogenic freezing process, I eventually was able to freeze the bacterial cultures almost instantly, in pelletized form. Little did I know how those pellets would change my life.

One afternoon, my family and I were making homemade ice cream when it occurred to me that using my same freezing system from the lab might also preserve ice cream's freshness and flavor. So I experimented. Initially I was interested in maintaining a better flavor, but remarkably, the process turned the ice cream into tiny spheres that held their shape. After my friends and family took the first taste tests with good results, I became enthusiastic about once again starting my own business.

Eventually, my family and I started what we would later name Dippin' Dots®. In March 1988, we proudly opened our very first store in Lexington. During our first year in business, we learned how to run the operation the right way by doing everything the wrong way. For example, our store was on the wrong side of town, so we broke even at best, but could not draw a salary to live on. We basically survived on credit cards. Customers were few and far between, and our only advertising was through word-of-mouth and random feature stories in the local media.

The next year, doors began to open. The now-defunct Opryland Theme Park in Nashville, Tennessee, agreed to let us set up a store in the park. Our location was next to a roller coaster! Needless to say, people didn't particularly want to fill their stomachs before or after being twirled through the air!

For the first two years we struggled. Then one day I

received a letter from Opryland saying essentially, "We like you and your product, but come remove your equipment." There it was, printed in black and white. Our endeavor had failed.

Yet we persisted. After renegotiating with Opryland, they gave us a second chance, away from the roller coasters and near the petting zoo. Business remained slow but we made the best of being in the park. We were also allowed to sell outside the booth, so away I would go on my specially built bicycle cart, pushing a freezer, ringing a bell and convincing visitors they just *had* to try this new ice cream!

Our biggest break came in 1992 when we opened up a shop at the Kennedy Space Center. There we became known as the "Ice Cream of the Future®" and gained much more exposure. Following this success, locations sprang up in other amusement parks, malls and stadiums, and we slowly developed a loyal following.

Fast forward to today. Dippin' Dots has locations nationwide and around the globe. Our product line has expanded and, through franchising, people actually pay us for the rights to sell our ice cream! Now, sometimes, when we're faced with the pressure of a big decision, someone will jokingly say, "Relax, it's just ice cream." Maybe so, but to us, it's a whole lot more.

We persisted. We believed.

Curt Jones
with John Paul Penrod

EPILOGUE: *Curt Jones, founder and chairman of Dippin' Dots, has continued to invest his creative energy into his newest entrepreneurial enterprise—Amylase Entertainment.*

Amylase (pronounced "Am-i-lace") is a music publishing and artist management company based in Nashville, Tennessee, that has just recently broken into the film business. Quite unconventionally, Amylase publishes and pitches feature-film screenplays written by staff writers. While this creative process is reminiscent of old Hollywood, it more closely mimics the Nashville music industry model of pitching songs created by songwriters.

The name Amylase was derived from Jones's keen knowledge of microbiology. According to Jones, amylase is a biological enzyme that functions as a catalyst. A catalyst helps change other substances without changing itself in the process. Curt has managed to stay grounded and true to his roots during the successful growth years at Dippin' Dots and hopes for the same with his new company.

To learn more about Curt Jones and Dippin' Dots, please visit www.dippindots.com, *or contact Amylase Entertainment on Music Row in Nashville or at* www.amylase.com.

Dahlynn McKowen

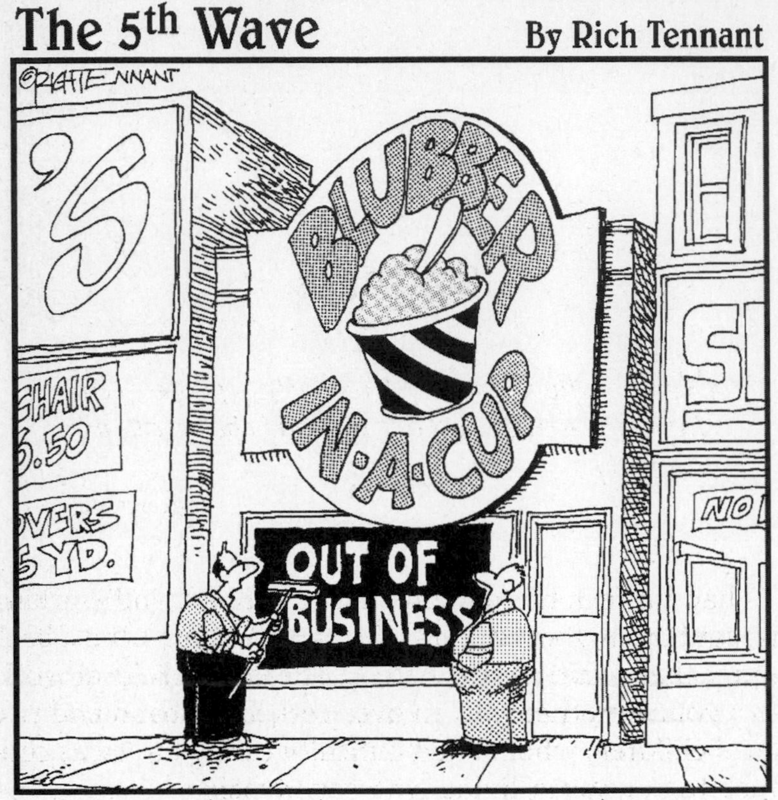

"It's hard to figure. The concept was a big hit in Nome."

Bee-Alive

Never believe that a few caring people can't change the world. For, indeed, that's all who ever have.

Margaret Mead

I had hit rock bottom. Living in the Bronx and working in Manhattan, I was depressed and bedridden from a back injury that occurred while lifting a heavy package at work. As a young mother with an overworked husband and two small children, whom I had difficulty caring for, I was confined to our house, living with severe pain.

Doctors were no longer able to help me after an unsuccessful back surgery. I was living on painkillers with no hope in sight. In the Bible it says that "God is able to do abundantly more than we could ever dare to dream or imagine." At that time, I was totally unable to envision myself well or successful. Yet God had other plans for my life.

The only saving grace that existed in my life was the monthly disability check I received for my children and myself. I willingly handed these checks over to my husband as my contribution to our budget. Then came that dreaded day when the U.S. government stopped sending my checks! It felt like a knife had been jammed into my heart. I sank to the floor and cried, "God, how could you do this? That money was everything, absolutely everything to me." I felt as though all my self-worth was summed up in those monthly checks.

Another factor about my lack of self-worth had to do with my appearance. One of my newest accessories was a hideous back brace, thus causing my wardrobe to shrink to only three pairs of old polyester pants, the only things that fit me comfortably. New clothes were out of the question for me; I was too disabled to even dream of going shopping, and besides, our family budget was way too tight. My hair was out of style, I seldom left the house, and life for me was just too difficult.

Eventually, I found myself getting gradually better and my life took a dramatic turn. I no longer needed painkillers or those clumsy braces for my back and feet. I began to attend every Bible study I heard about, and my life had taken a course toward normalcy.

Years later, as a busy young mom, I felt tired and run down. A friend told me about a food substance called "Royal Jelly," a product derived from the beehive—it was so amazing!

A very exciting feeling began to emerge within me. I was so passionate about this marvelous substance and how it made me feel that I wanted to share it with others. Just the thought of helping people feel their best naturally and, in particular, helping women feel good about themselves energized me. Then I had a realization: *How could a very ordinary housewife and mother with no college education or business experience, and little money of her own, ever get started? I can't even balance my own checkbook!* Then I reflected to a scripture verse that says, "Do not despise the day of small beginnings."

So there I was at my kitchen table pondering the big question: Where do I begin? I knew I needed money, so I went to the bank to borrow $4,000. The loan officer quickly dismissed me and my plan from his office. I thank God for my devoted husband who believed in me and took the money from our account. Thus, Bee-Alive officially began in November 1984.

At the beginning, I bought a small amount of product from a company in England and created a lapel button that read, "Royal Jelly Works." This was my first marketing endeavor. As I wore the button through the town, many people laughed at me and, in private, I often would cry. But I persevered and after repeatedly explaining that Royal Jelly was not jam or jelly, but the exclusive food of the queen bee, some people started listening. Soon my children and six dear friends joined my new little company, and they all wore buttons. Slowly, we began to get orders. Then, something amazing happened, customers were feeling more energetic and began to reorder. Within a year, my vision was taking form, and the basement of my house became the "little hive." We had only one computer and a few telephones and desks. All we needed now were more workers. So I started hiring women like myself, many of whom were delighted customers themselves. Business was buzzing!

Our marketing plan went beyond the buttons to airing one-minute commercials on radio stations across the country. Then we produced our own radio shows and television infomercials. Many celebrities who enjoyed our products endorsed them in print and on-air advertisements. Having outgrown the basement, we moved to a brand-new building—the "big hive"—in Valley Cottage, New York. We also opened our own warehouse and distribution center to safeguard the quality of our products—and to insure direct delviery to our customers. In 1997 we began selling Royal Jelly on a major home shopping network. As demand and interest grew, we expanded our product line to include unique formulations of skin-care products. Now we had a line of products that were helping people inside and out. What a thrill!

Today, over twenty years from its small beginning, Bee-Alive is a national health and beauty company and the foremost Royal Jelly company in the world. I believe that the bottom line for its success is that Royal Jelly is an outstanding product and that God has faithfully guided every step we've taken—and we are smart enough to listen. Our fresh, non-freeze-dried Royal Jelly is helping people and improving their lives. As a direct marketing company, we sell directly to our customers. Our enthusiastic and caring telephone consultants speak with each of them personally, getting to know them and listening to their needs—something I think is very special in this marketplace. The many letters I receive weekly from contented customers remind me of the bond we have with so many people.

Who would have thought a girl from the Bronx with three pairs of polyester pants would become the founder and president of a company that helps people enrich their own lives every day? Wearing silk pants these days and living a blessed lifestyle, I am amazed at how God helps ordinary people do extraordinary things.

Madeline Balletta

[EDITORS' NOTE: *Bee-Alive offers a variety of Royal Jelly products, herbal and vitamin supplements, and skin-care facial products. To learn more about Madeline Balletta and Bee-Alive, visit their Web site at* www.beealive.com.]

Counting My Blessings

I cofounded John Paul Mitchell Systems, a professional hair care company, with Paul Mitchell. We started the company with just $700, which was a lot of money for me at that time. I had usually lived hand-to-mouth, waiting for each paycheck to cover my lengthy list of bills.

Finally, in 1981, almost two years after forming our company (and coming close to financial bankruptcy too many times to count), we were officially running in the black. Personally, for the first time in my adult life, I had all my bills paid; my mortgage, credit cards and utilities were current. To top it off, I still had more than $2,000 left over at the end of the month! That had never happened to me before, and I was ready to celebrate.

I chose to have lunch in a Mexican restaurant in Marina del Rey. It was the first time I ordered off the left side of the menu; I decided what kind of food I wanted instead of running my finger down the right side of the menu to find the price I could afford.

During lunch, I saw a group of a dozen kids and two moms come into the restaurant. They sat down at a table directly in front of me. I noticed one of the moms talking with the waiter, looking at the menu and running her finger down the menu's right side. I could tell she was trying to figure out what they could get for the $3.95 special. The kids didn't seem too worried about what was for lunch; they weren't wearing the "I've-been-here-a-hundred-times" bored expressions and appeared very excited about being there. I guessed that being at a restaurant wasn't an everyday occasion for them. One little boy, who was wearing a ragged T-shirt and jeans, reminded me of myself when I was his age. You wouldn't have seen me in a restaurant when I was little. We didn't have the money. My parents were immigrants, and we lived with our mom in Echo Park in East Los Angeles. My mom worked hard to support us. She couldn't afford childcare for my brother and me, so with too much unsupervised free time, I joined a street gang.

Things didn't change or become easier for me once I became an adult. I worked and held many jobs, but the money never seemed to be enough. Eking out a salary big enough to handle rent and food was my foremost goal, and the threat of living on the streets was not just a distant fear. "Homeless" was often a real part of my vocabulary—a cold and lonely word. It had mercilessly pounded my thoughts as more than once I tossed and turned at night, trying to find a comfortable sleeping position in the back seat of my car. But I had dreams, and being down and out wasn't the result I was going to settle for. I kept working and kept looking.

And here I was enjoying lunch with the knowledge that I had money to spare. *To spare.* I got up from my table and followed the group's waiter toward the back of the restaurant, explaining my situation and telling him that I wanted the kids and their moms to be able to order absolutely anything they wanted. Most important, I told him, "Please don't tell them who did this."

After a few moments, the waiter went back to the table

and shared the news. One of the women immediately stood up and started looking around the restaurant. She looked to her immediate left, straight at me. Wearing casual clothes, I didn't keep her attention but for a second. She quickly looked to the next person, then the next. When no one acknowledged her, she announced in a loud voice, "Whoever you are, thank you and God bless you. You have no idea what you have done for me and these children."

I was blessed; I felt on top of the world! Being able to give in such a way was something new for me. It was then that I decided that for me not to share my success would be to fail, and failure wasn't acceptable. That day, I decided it didn't matter how much success I had, whether I had two or two thousand extra dollars or even two extra hours. I began to look for ways to help others. I had discovered how much joy true success could bring. For me, success unshared is failure.

John Paul DeJoria

[EDITORS' NOTE: *John Paul DeJoria cofounded John Paul Mitchell Systems with the late Paul Mitchell in 1980 to manufacture Paul Mitchell Professional Salon Products. As CEO, DeJoria has seen the company's salon retail sales increase to $700 million.*

DeJoria contributes to many organizations including the Sovereign Diné Nation Weaving Collective, the AIDS Relief Fund for Beauty Professionals, Rescue Missions and the Rainforest Foundation, the Sea Shepherd Foundation and Waterkeepers. He received the Horatio Alger Award in 2004, as well as the Spirit of Life Award from the City of Hope National Medical Center.]

The Very Best

My grandfather's earliest memories were of cold winter nights in David City, Nebraska, where he was born in 1891. Sometimes frost was so thick on the window of his unheated bedroom that a penny would freeze to the glass if he held it there long enough.

Food was scarce in their home; at times their family couldn't even afford to buy a dime's worth of butter for their cornbread. As my grandfather later recalled, his good appetite gave him extra drive to succeed. He wanted to eat regularly and had seen stretches when he couldn't. Poverty, he said, provided him an advantage over people whose lives were more comfortable.

He and his two older brothers began working at early ages to help support the family. My grandfather was wonderfully resourceful. He made lemonade and sold it at the ballpark. When trains stopped in town, he was at the station peddling sandwiches. At age nine, he persuaded an agent with the California Perfume Company to let him sell cosmetics door-to-door.

His brothers eventually made enough money to buy a bookstore in Norfolk, Nebraska, and the whole family moved there. Norfolk was a tough town at the time, with saloons, gambling and gunfights. But there also was a market for the store's books, magazines, cigars and candy.

One evening, a traveling cigar salesman dropped by the store. His enthusiasm for Kansas City's "can-do" spirit convinced my grandfather the city would be an ideal place to start a business. At age eighteen, he was eager to make his mark, so he packed up his belongings, and on a cold January day in 1910 arrived at the Kansas City train station. He had little money—not even enough to take a horse-drawn cab to his lodging at the YMCA—but he had some grand plans.

Inside one of his bags were two shoeboxes full of picture postcards, and inside his head was a mail-order plan for distributing them. He stored his inventory under his bed, printed some invoices and started sending packets of a hundred cards to dealers throughout the Midwest. A few of the dealers kept the cards without paying. Some returned the unsolicited merchandise with an angry note. But about a third sent a check. Within a couple of months, he had cleared $200 and opened a checking account.

Despite this initial success, he was sure illustrated postcards were a passing fancy. He saw more of a market for the higher-quality valentines and Christmas cards mailed in envelopes. In 1912, after one of his brothers had joined him, greeting cards were added to the line.

Then disaster struck. An early-morning phone call brought news that the company's entire inventory, for which they were heavily in debt, had been destroyed by fire. A message on one of the company's cards seemed especially appropriate: "When you get to the end of your rope, tie a knot in it and hang on." They hung on. With determination and luck, they were able to replace their inventory, float a loan and buy a small engraving firm. Before long, they had become manufacturers and were joined by their other brother.

The business begun in a shoebox has since grown into a multibillion-dollar company—Hallmark Cards, Inc.—and my grandfather, J. C. Hall, is regarded as the architect of an industry. Despite his great success, many honors and friendships with world leaders like Dwight Eisenhower and Winston Churchill, he never lost his plain-spoken common sense, nor his entrepreneurial spirit.

My earliest lessons in business came from visiting stores with him. In each shop, he would pay great attention to details and would point out what he felt was working and what wasn't. His passion for new ideas and better ways of doing things helped Hallmark become a retail trendsetter, as well as the leader of the greeting card industry.

One of the company's earliest innovations was the introduction of decorated gift wrap in 1917. Until then, gifts were wrapped in brown paper or colored tissue. But when the brothers ran out of stock right before Christmas, they quickly substituted some fancy decorated envelope linings from France. The decorated paper proved so popular they began designing and printing their own gift wrap.

Although the company's name had been Hall Brothers almost from the start, my grandfather thought it sounded old-fashioned. He became intrigued with the term "hallmark" because it connoted quality and incorporated the family name. So in 1928, he directed that a "Hallmark card" be printed on the back of each greeting card. His next challenge was to get shoppers to turn over the cards and check the name—something several advertising agencies said they'd never do. He didn't agree and wrote the company's first advertisement himself. It appeared in *The Ladies Home Journal* in 1928.

In 1951, my grandfather turned to the new medium of television to sponsor a program—*The Hallmark Hall of Fame*—that would be a cut above standard TV fare so viewers would associate the Hallmark name with quality.

He said, "I'd rather make 8 million good impressions than 28 million bad ones" and always believed "Good taste is good business." The company's well-known slogan—"When you care enough to send the very best"—spoke volumes about his high standards. Over the years, he personally reviewed every greeting card design and sentiment. Not a one went to press without his "O.K.J.C." imprimatur.

His never-ending search for improvement led to innovations in other areas. In the earliest years, merchants kept greeting cards in drawers and would pull them out for shoppers to view. My grandfather was sure sales would increase if customers could make their selection from open display racks—and he was right. The company introduced self-service displays in the late 1930s, and these became a staple not only for cards but for other products as well.

One of his most unusual ventures was in the area of land development. Troubled by the urban decay surrounding the company headquarters, he began quietly purchasing parcels of nearby land. His visionary thinking led him to enlist the aid of some of the country's leading architects and planners, as well as his friend Walt Disney, who recently had opened Disneyland in California.

The plan was unveiled in January 1967. Hallmark would replace eighty-five acres of blight with a privately financed "city within a city," combining offices, hotels, retail and residential space. In the years since, Crown Center became a national model for multiuse developments, as well as a popular Kansas City landmark, office address and tourist attraction. It is an ongoing reminder of J. C. Hall's enormous impact on the city he called home.

By the time Crown Center was announced, my grandfather had stepped aside as CEO in favor of my dad, Donald J. Hall, who moved Hallmark from its entrepreneurial beginnings into a new phase of growth.

Much has changed over the years, but in many ways my grandfather's vision and values still guide Hallmark Cards. Above all, he believed in hard work, integrity and excellence—or, as he put it, "Producing a first-class product that meets a real need is a much stronger motivation for success than getting rich." I couldn't agree more.

Donald J. Hall Jr.

EPILOGUE: *Donald J. Hall Jr. is president and CEO of Hallmark Cards, Inc., a position he has held since 2002. His brother David E. Hall is president of the company's Personal Expression Group.*

Worldwide, Hallmark has more than 18,000 full-time employees. About 4,500 Hallmarkers work at the Kansas City headquarters, and 9,900 are associated full-time with the personal expression business. This includes some 800 artists, designers, stylists, writers, editors and photographers—one of the largest in-house creative staffs in the country.

Hallmark products are found in more than 43,000 retail outlets in the United States. About 5,600 are specialty stores—more than 4,000 of which are certified Hallmark Gold Crown® stores; another 30,000 are mass-merchandise retailers, including discount, food and drug stores. Hallmark publishes cards in more than thirty languages and distributes personal expression products in more than 100 countries.

Responsible corporate citizenship is an important part of Hallmark's values. The company's foundation supports human service, education, health and arts organizations in the communities in which Hallmark operates.

To learn more about Hallmark, visit www.hallmark.com.

Dahlynn McKowen

More Chicken Soup?

Many of the stories you have read in this book were submitted by readers like you who had read earlier *Chicken Soup for the Soul* books. We publish many *Chicken Soup for the Soul* books every year. We invite you to contribute a story to one of these future volumes.

Stories may be up to 1,200 words and must uplift or inspire. You may submit an original piece, something you have read or your favorite quotation on your refrigerator door.

To obtain a copy of our submission guidelines and a listing of upcoming *Chicken Soup* books, please write, fax or check our Web site.

Please send your submissions to:

Web site: *www.chickensoup.com*

Chicken Soup for the Soul
P.O. Box 30880, Santa Barbara, CA 93130
fax: 805-563-2945

We will be sure that both you and the author are credited for your submission.

For information about speaking engagements, other books, audiotapes, workshops and training programs, please contact any of our authors directly.

Supporting Others

The coauthors of *Chicken Soup for the Entrepreneur's Soul* have selected Heifer International, based in Little Rock, Arkansas, to receive a portion of the book's proceeds.

Heifer International is a nonprofit organization that has provided struggling families all over the world a way to become self-reliant for food and income since 1944. The organization was founded by Dan West, a relief worker whose vision was to help starving refugees by giving them cows rather than the temporary relief of powdered milk. Through Heifer International's gifts of livestock and training, an impoverished family can obtain milk, eggs, wool and other income-producing benefits to feed, clothe and educate their children. Part of the organization's plan is to recognize that animals reproduce, and every family receiving livestock makes a promise to "pass on the gift" of one or more of their animal's offspring to others in need.

Heifer International currently supports projects in more than fifty countries, including the United States. To learn more, please visit their Web site.

Heifer International
1 World Avenue
Little Rock, AR 72201
phone: 800-696-1918
Web site: *www.heifer.org*

Who Is Jack Canfield?

Jack Canfield is the cocreator and editor of the *Chicken Soup for the Soul* series, which *Time* magazine has called "the publishing phenomenon of the decade." The series now has 105 titles with over 100 million copies in print in forty-one languages. Jack is also the co-author of eight other bestselling books including *The Success Principles™: How to Get from Where You Are to Where You Want to Be, Dare to Win, The Aladdin Factor, You've Got to Read This Book, The Power of Focus: How to Hit Your Business, Personal and Financial Targets with Absolute Certainty.*

Jack has recently developed a telephone coaching program and an on-line coaching program based on his most recent book, *The Success Principles.* He also offers a seven-day Breakthrough to Success seminar every summer, which attracts 400 people from fifteen countries around the world.

Jack is the CEO of Chicken Soup for the Soul Enterprises and the Canfield Training Group in Santa Barbara, California, and founder of the Foundation for Self-Esteem in Culver City, California. He has conducted intensive personal and professional development seminars on the principles of success for over 900,000 people in twenty-one countries around the world. He has spoken to hundreds of thousands of others at numerous conferences and conventions and has been seen by millions of viewers on national television shows such as *The Today Show, Fox and Friends, Inside Edition, Hard Copy,* CNN's *Talk Back Live, 20/20, Eye to Eye,* and the *NBC Nightly News* and the *CBS Evening News.*

Jack is the recipient of many awards and honors, including three honorary doctorates and a Guinness World Records Certificate for having seven *Chicken Soup for the Soul* books appearing on the *New York Times* bestseller list on May 24, 1998.

To write to Jack or for inquiries about Jack as a speaker, his coaching programs or his seminars, use the following contact information:

Jack Canfield
The Canfield Companies
P.O. Box 30880
Santa Barbara, CA 93130
phone: 805-563-2935; fax: 805-563-2945
e-mail: *info@jackcanfield.com*
Web site: *www.jackcanfield.com*

Who Is Mark Victor Hansen?

In the area of human potential, no one is more respected than Mark Victor Hansen. For more than thirty years, Mark has focused solely on helping people from all walks of life reshape their personal vision of what's possible. His powerful messages of possibility, opportunity and action have created powerful change in thousands of organizations and millions of individuals worldwide.

He is a sought-after keynote speaker, bestselling author and marketing maven. Mark's credentials include a lifetime of entrepreneurial success and an extensive academic background. He is a prolific writer with many bestselling books, such as *The One Minute Millionaire, The Power of Focus, The Aladdin Factor* and *Dare to Win,* in addition to the *Chicken Soup for the Soul* series. Mark has made a profound influence through his library of audios, videos and articles in the areas of big thinking, sales achievement, wealth building, publishing success, and personal and professional development.

Mark is the founder of the MEGA Seminar Series. MEGA Book Marketing University and Building Your MEGA Speaking Empire are annual conferences where Mark coaches and teaches new and aspiring authors, speakers and experts on building lucrative publishing and speaking careers. Other MEGA events include MEGA Marketing Magic and My MEGA Life.

He has appeared on *Oprah, CNN* and the *Today Show,* he has been quoted in *Time, U.S. News & World Report, USA Today, New York Times* and *Entrepreneur* and has had countless radio interviews, assuring our planet's people that "You can easily create the life you deserve."

As a philanthropist and humanitarian, Mark works tirelessly for organizations such as Habitat for Humanity, American Red Cross, March of Dimes, Childhelp USA and many others. He is the recipient of numerous awards that honor his entrepreneurial spirit, philanthropic heart and business acumen. He is a lifetime member of the Horatio Alger Association of Distinguished Americans, an organization that honored Mark with the prestigious Horatio Alger Award for his extraordinary life achievements.

Mark Victor Hansen is an enthusiastic crusader of what's possible and is driven to make the world a better place.

Mark Victor Hansen & Associates, Inc.
P.O. Box 7665
Newport Beach, CA 92658
phone: 949-764-2640
fax: 949-722-6912
Web site: *www.markvictorhansen.com*

Who Is Dahlynn McKowen?

Dahlynn McKowen is one of *Chicken Soup for the Soul's* most trusted coauthors. She, along with her husband, Ken, coauthored *Chicken Soup for the Fisherman's Soul* (May 2004). The McKowens are currently creating a twelve-book travel series for Chicken Soup for the Soul Enterprises and Health Communications, Inc., a first for both companies. The couple are also involved in the development of many more Chicken Soup titles, including *Chicken Soup for the Red Hat Society Soul* and *Chicken Soup for the Menopausal Soul*, both slated for release in 2007.

The McKowens stay active with their company "Publishing Syndicate," a small business that provides writing, ghostwriting and editing services for novels, nonfiction books, screenplays, speeches and news releases. They also offer a free monthly writing tips e-newsletter and have created an e-booklet series entitled "The Wow Principles." This series, which is sold via their Web site, focuses on the aspects of writing for publication and profit. The McKowens also author other books each year, the most recent being *The Best of California's Missions, Mansions and Museums* for Wilderness Press (Berkeley).

Dahlynn is an established freelance writer with many book projects under way and under consideration. Since selling her first feature article in 1987, Dahlynn has produced over 2,000 works, including business features, B&B reviews, restaurant reviews and travel articles. Dahlynn has been a guest newspaper columnist, a writer for the California Office of Tourism and a contract writer for various tourism and business marketing projects. She has ghostwritten stories for a former U.S. president, more than two dozen Fortune 100 and 500 corporate founders and CEOs, as well as a few California governors.

For fun, Dahlynn loves playing board games with her young son, Shawn, giggling about boys with her teenage daughter, Lahre, discovering new travel destinations with hubby, Ken, and watching *Antiques Roadshow*. Reading is also one of Dahlynn's many passions, as well as volunteering at her son's school.

Dahlynn McKowen
Publishing Syndicate
P.O. Box 607
Orangevale, CA 95662
Web site: *www.PublishingSyndicate.com*

Who Is John P. Gardner Jr.?

After twenty years of study and 3,000 interviews with the world's most productive entrepreneurs and military, political and business leaders, John Gardner discovered the habits they employed that led to their success. He studies history and has found leaders and entrepreneurs have employed these same habits for 2,000 years. They are copyable and duplicatable by the young and the old, educated and uneducated, regardless of race or religion. A compelling speaker and writer, John reveals these thought-provoking insights through stories that leave his audiences with the belief that they too can achieve their dreams and that what others may deem impossible is truly attainable.

John is the author of *Bound in the Bible,* coauthor of *Living at the Summit—A Novel Approach to an Exceptional Life,* and one of the Expert Members of Alexander Haig's *World Business Review* Advisory Board. In addition, John is a nationally recognized expert in the field of identity theft and a leader in the rising market of prepaid legal coverage.

He began his career as a third-generation attorney after completing both his undergraduate and Juris Doctor degrees in only five and one-half years. During the twenty-three years that he practiced actively, his law firm grew tenfold in thirty-six months to become one of the largest legal practices in South Carolina—including six locations. The firm won the American Bar Association's award for the most dignified legal marketing in the nation.

While he practiced, he also served for eight years as a member of the South Carolina House of Representatives and for four years as a member of the South Carolina Department of Highways and Public Transportation Commission. He also actively served in Kairos, a prison ministry, and is a Gideon.

For further information about John, please contact:

John Gardner
The Gardner Alliances, Inc.
204 Country Club Road
Darlington, SC 29532
e-mail: *jgardner@entrepreneurialsoul.com*

Who Is Elizabeth Gardner?

Elizabeth Gardner is a talented writer, professional speaker and business strategist.

She has inspired both individuals and audiences of thousands with her message of personal and professional potential. Over the past ten years, she has delivered workshops and training programs on strategic thought and planning. She is a dangerously creative visionary. Her early career as an interior designer won her awards, and then she moved to marketing and within months won the American Bar Association's award for the most dignified legal marketing in America for one of her clients.

Elizabeth then began speaking and training all over the country on balancing family life with a career, effective team management and communication skills. She conceived of and then sold to a Media General television station and ultimately to newspapers the idea of *Designing a Life That Works.* This television segment (and related newspaper column) on life balance and the habits of the highly productive ran live each week for over five years. She is also the coauthor of *Bound in the Bible* and *Living at the Summit.*

Elizabeth is committed to serving as a role model for other women and her family in terms of life balance, following your dreams and setting the appropriate priorities. She resides in Darlington, South Carolina, along with her husband, John, and four children, Burt, Wade, Bryant and Peden.

She may be contacted at:

Elizabeth Gardner
The Gardner Alliances, Inc.
204 Country Club Road
Darlington, SC 29532
e-mail: *egardner@entrepreneurialsoul.com*

Who Is Tom Hill?

After twenty-six years in public education and at fifty years of age, Dr. Tom Hill left the University of Missouri, where he was a professor and administrator, to pursue an entrepreneurial career in real estate franchise sales. With the help of two wonderful partners, Howard McPherson and Dennis Curtin, he developed three RE/MAX regions. He sold his company in 1999 and now spends his time and energy giving back what he learned in becoming what he is today.

Tom is a husband, father, grandfather, airplane pilot, marathon runner, mountain climber, skydiver, author and speaker. His books include *Living at the Summit* and the companion workbook, *Life Plan for Living at the Summit,* which he coauthored with Becky McDannold.

One of Tom's passions is to make a major and positive difference in as many lives as possible. He accomplishes this through his speaking and writing and through his two companies, Eagoal, LLC and Eagle Goal Coach. He would love to hear from you!

Tom Hill
121 Civic Center Drive, Suite 303
Lake Saint Louis, MO 63367
phone: 636-561-6262
e-mail: *thill@eagoal.com*
Web site: *www.eagoal.com* or *www.eagleinstitute.com*

Who Is Kyle Wilson?

Kyle Wilson is president of TSTN (The Success Trainer Network) as well as president and founder of YourSuccessStore.com, Jim Rohn International and Chris Widener International. Kyle has promoted hundreds of seminar events over the past eighteen years and has worked with many of the world's top speakers and authors, including Jim Rohn, Zig Ziglar, Brian Tracy, Mark Victor Hansen, Og Mandino, Les Brown, Denis Waitley and Harvey MacKay. Kyle is founder/editor of six personal development publications, including *Your Achievement Ezine, Messages from the Masters, Quotes from the Masters, The Jim Rohn Weekly Ezine, The Denis Waitley Ezine* and *The Chris Widener Weekly Ezine.* Kyle is also a weekly contributor as well as the co-architect of the Jim Rohn One-Year Success Plan, and has also produced/published well over 100 hours of personal development DVD and CD programs.

Kyle, along with his wife, Heidi, and two children, Rebekah and Daniel, lives in Southlake, Texas (Dallas/Fort Worth area).

Kyle can be contacted at *kyle@yoursuccessstore.com.*

Contributors

Several of the stories in this book were taken from previously published sources, such as books, magazines and newspapers. These sources are acknowledged in the permissions section. If you would like to contact any of the contributors for information about their writing or would like to invite them to speak in your community, look for their contact information included in their biographies.

The remainder of the stories were submitted by readers of our previous *Chicken Soup for the Soul* books who responded to our requests for stories. We have also included information about them.

Marc Allen is a publisher, entrepreneur, author, musician and philanthropist. He is founder and president of New World Library, a leading independent publisher. He is the author of *The Type-Z Guide to Success, The Millionaire Course, Visionary Business,* and other books and audio recordings. He is also cofounder of Watercourse Media, a record company. His music albums include *Breathe, Petals, Solo Fight* and his latest, *Awakening.* He lives with his family in Northern California.

David Anderson is an author, motivating keynote speaker and an unabashed entrepreneur living the American Dream. Dave earned his master's degree from Harvard University without an undergraduate degree. He has authored *Famous Dave's Lifeskills for Success* and *Famous Dave's Backroads and Sidestreets,* the latter a collection of award-winning recipes. Visit *www.davidwanderson.com.*

Tom Antion's bio can be found at the end of the story *Strive for Excellence.*

Amilya Antonetti's bio can be found at the end of the story *A Promise to Keep.*

John Assaraf's bio can be found at the end of the story *Uncertain Certainty.*

Madeline Balletta is founder and president of Bee-Alive. She and her husband, Anthony, are the proud parents of two children and grandparents of two precious grandsons. Madeline resides in Sanibel, Florida, where she enjoys antiquing and spending time with her loving Maltese puppy, Bogie.

Banjo Bandolas' stories have appeared in numerous national publications. His style of storytelling reflects his Southern roots. Previous anthologies include *Dead on Demand, Chicken Soup for the Fisherman's Soul, Ghosts from the Coast* and *Chicken Soup for the Soul Healthy Living* series. He is the advertising sales director for Real Beer Media.

Daryl Bernstein is the author of *The Venture Adventure: Strategies for Thriving in the Jungle of Entrepreneurship* and *Better Than a Lemonade Stand! Small Business Ideas for Kids.* He shares his energy and insight through speaking engagements and consulting. Visit *www.darylbernstein.com* for more information.

Stephanie Chandler is the author of *The Business Startup Checklist and Planning Guide: Seize Your Entrepreneurial Dreams!* She is also the founder of Business Info Guide (*www.BusinessInfoGuide.com*)—a directory of resources for entrepreneurs—and the owner of Book Lovers Bookstore (*www.BookLoversCafe.com*) in Sacramento, California.

Tom Chappell's bio can be found at the end of the story *Finding the Soul of Success.*

Doris Christopher is the founder and chairman of The Pampered Chef. A Berkshire Hathaway company, The Pampered Chef is the premier direct seller of high-quality kitchen tools sold through in-home cooking demonstrations called Cooking Shows. She has been featured in numerous publications, including *Fortune, Working Woman* and *The Wall Street Journal.*

Rachel de Azevedo Coleman is the president of Two Little Hands Productions. She and her husband, Aaron, are the parents of Leah (who is deaf) and Lucy (who has cerebral palsy). When she's not writing music and performing on-camera for Signing Time! Rachel enjoys playing outdoors with her family. E-mail her at *rcoleman@signingtime.com.*

Sue Ellen Cooper is a homemaker, mother and freelance artist, and is the author of two bestselling books. She is married with two grown children and a grandchild. When she is not serving as "Exalted Queen Mother," she enjoys making art, walking her dog and spending time with family.

Janis Dale and her husband, Eldon, met as teenagers. She pursued a career in law enforcement while he served in Vietnam as a Marine. They then started their family and first concession business. Forty eventful years later, the Dale family operates the largest cinnamon roll fair concession in California—Country Fair Cinnamon Rolls.

Paula Deen's bio can be found at the end of the story *The Bag Lady Triumphant.*

John Paul DeJoria's bio can be found at the end of the story *Counting My Blessings.*

Fred DeLuca's bio can be found at the end of the story *The Taste of Success.*

Stefan Doering's bio can be found at the end of the story *Thirty-Five-Minute Miles.*

Doug Ducey, CEO and chairman of Cold Stone Creamery, wants Cold Stone to be the ultimate ice cream experience and the bestselling ice cream brand in America. An Arizona State graduate, Doug's career spans twenty-plus years with companies including Procter & Gamble and Anheuser-Busch. Doug inspires people by challenging them to perform and deliver results. Visit *www.coldstonecreamery.com.*

Terri Duncan received her bachelor of arts, with honors, and master of education degrees from Augusta State University. She is currently pursuing a specialist degree in the field of educational leadership. She is an avid writer as well. Her greatest accomplishments, however, are in her roles as wife and mother.

Stephen Fairchild is 24,472 good days old. He can be found on any given day of the week speaking before international groups, exploring caverns worldwide, scuba diving, doing geologic research, growing his cavern business or flying his own plane in an evening sunset.

Shari Fitzpatrick, along with her husband, three sons and two Boston terriers, lives in the beautiful mountain wine country of the great Sierra Nevada. She enjoys wine tasting at her local wineries, traveling, interior decorating, landscaping, photography and cooking, especially creating new chocolate gourmet gift ideas. E-mail her at *Shari@sacberries.com.*

Carol Gardner's bio can be found at the end of the story *From Underdog to Top Dog.*

Adam Ginsberg's bio can be found at the end of the story *Mother Knows Best.*

Drew and **Myra Goodman** are the founders of Earthbound Farm and currently serve as president and executive vice president, respectively. In 1984, the then-recent college graduates started Earthbound Farm on 214 acres in Carmel Valley, California. The company is now the largest grower of organic produce in the world.

David Green's bio can be found at the end of the story *Life's a Hobby.*

Renee Griffith, CEO and founder of Zephyr-TEC, launched her company in 1991 after becoming disabled with de Quervain's disease. Renee used speech recognition sofware to start the company, and Zephyr-TEC quickly became, and remains, the industry leader in speech recognition training and support. E-mail: *rgriffith@zephyr-tec.com.*

Donald J. Hall Jr.'s bio can be found at the end of the story *The Very Best.*

Patrick Hardin is a freelance cartoonist. His work appears in a variety of publications around the world. He may be reached at 810-234-7452.

Shelly Hartmann's bio can be found at the end of the story *Blueberry Thrills.*

Jonny Hawkins is an entrepreneurial cartoonist who has been his own boss full-time for the last sixteen years. Thousands of his cartoons appear in over 300 publications, his ten published books and his annual calendars (Medical Cartoon-a-Day, Fishing Cartoon-a-Day and Cartoons for Teachers). He dedicated the cartoons in this volume to his entrepreneurial father, Ron Hawkins, who instilled in him his maverick spirit. He can be reached at *jonnyhawkins2nz.@yahoo.com.*

Kathy Heasley is founder and principal of IMS, Inc., a full-service communications company in the "moments" business. A Penn State graduate, Kathy's passion is helping people excel by connecting the heart with the mind and bringing it to life within the organization. She's a published author, award-winning video producer and entrepreneur. Visit *www.imsbreakthrough.com.*

Gary Heavin has a degree in health and nutrition counseling and is the author of two *New York Times* bestselling books on exercise and nutrition. He was honored with IHRSA's first-ever Visionary of the Year award and was named a 2004 Ernst & Young Entrepreneur of the Year.

Trent Hemphill and **Joel Hemphill Jr.**'s bios can be found at the end of the story *The Wheels on the Bus Go 'Round and 'Round.*

Curt Jones received both his undergraduate (1981) and graduate (1986) degrees in microbiology from Southern Illinois University. Currently, he oversees his newest entrepreneurial venture, Amylase Entertainment, in Nashville. He lives with his wife and daughter in Brentwood, Tennessee.

Fred Joyal's bio can be found at the end of the story *Two Guys, Three Buckets.*

Don Katz has been in the hospitality business since the age of sixteen. Before opening Symposium Wine Bar, Don held both cooking and management positions. He describes himself as "The Blind Wine Guy." When not tasting wine he enjoys reading, dancing, exercising and playing the drums. He can be e-mailed at *don@symposiumwinebar.com.*

Paul J. Krupin operated IMEDIFAX, a custom publicity service. A retired federal government scientist and once-upon-a-time attorney, Paul is a longtime PR guru and has developed sure-fire, proven strategies for getting publicity. Read his book *Trash-Proof News Releases.* Contact Paul at 800-457-8746 or visit *www.DirectContactPR.com.*

Gail Kulhavy started out trying to write a newsletter and ended up with a monthly column, articles in *RV Journal* magazine and as the author of the *Living in Oklahoma Guide* for the last five years. She was born in Arkansas, grew up in California and has been an Oklahoman for eight years. Gail lives to read and loves to write!

Cookie Lee's bio can be found at the end of the story *To Be There for My Kids.*

Austin Ligon's bio can be found at the end of the story *Project X.*

Julie Long is a freelance writer, published author and writing coach. She is coauthor of *BABY: An Owner's Manual,* and her story *The Worm* is included in *Chicken Soup for the Fisherman's Soul.* In 2004, Julie cofounded FatPlum.com to provide coaching and workshops for writers. Reach her at *Julie@julielongwrites.com.*

Chris MacAskill grew up on the streets of East Oakland, missing part of elementary school when he lived with his homeless mother. He has a master's degree from Stanford University and was the founder and CEO of Fatbrain.com, which went public and was later acquired by Barnes & Noble. He is currently cofounder and president of SmugMug.com, a top photo-sharing Internet site.

Jim McCann is founder and CEO of 1-800-FLOWERS.COM®, one of the world's most recognized floral and gift companies. Jim is also a published author, award-winning public speaker and a respected member of the board of directors of Willis Group Holdings Limited, GTECH Holdings Corporation and Boyd's Collections, Ltd.

Ken McKowen is an established author, freelance writer, photographer, editor and speaker. He and his wife, Dahlynn, are coauthors of *Chicken Soup for the Fisherman's Soul* and are working on additional *Chicken Soup* titles. Their business—Publishing Syndicate—provides writing, editing and related publishing services. To learn more, visit *www.PublishingSyndicate.com.*

Judi Sheppard Missett's bio can be found at the end of the story *The Dancer in All of Us.*

Ian and **Shep Murray**'s bio can be found at the end of the story *For the Love of It.*

Assunta Ng was born in China and came to America to study. She received her B.A. and M.A. degrees from the University of Washington. She is the publisher of two weekly newspapers, and a writer and speaker. Assunta's mission is to empower young women and minorites to be leaders. She is married and has two sons. Her e-mail is *assunta@nwasianweekly.com.*

Mark Parisi's "off the mark" comic panel has been syndicated since 1987 and is distributed by United Media. Mark's humor also graces greeting cards, T-shirts, calendars, magazines, newsletters and books. Please visit his Web site at: *www.offthemark.com*. His wife, Lynn, is his business partner and their daughter, Jenny, is an inspired contributor along with their three cats.

John Paul Penrod received his bachelor of arts degree with honors from Vanderbilt University in 2005. He majored in film studies, which emphasizes writing, film theory and critical analysis. Currently, John Paul writes screenplays and other articles for Amylase Entertainment, based in Nashville, Tennessee.

Gina Romanello is coauthor of *Chicken Soup for the Bride's Soul* and marketing liaison for the six *Chicken Soup for the Kid's Soul* titles. She lives in Southern California, where she enjoys running, skating, biking, hiking, traveling and spending time with her friends and family. E-mail: *Gina@Lifewriters.com* or visit *www.bridesoul.com.*

David Roth lives and works in Chicago. In addition to running Cereality, he loves all things epicurean: David is an avid cook, enjoys hosting dinner parties for his friends and family, is always on the lookout for great dining experiences and is a big fan of decadent hotels.

Herman G. Rowland Sr.'s bio can be found at the end of the story *The Candy Man Can.*

Leigh Rubin is a sit-down comedian: in his own way, he delights in making other people laugh. Originally self-syndicated, Rubes is now distributed by Creators Syndicate to more than 400 newspapers worldwide.

Harley Schwadron, a freelance cartoonist, lives and works in Ann Arbor, Michigan. His cartoons appear in *Readers Digest, Barron's, Wall Street Journal, Woman's World* and other publications. He has worked as a newspaper reporter and college PR editor, but enjoys drawing cartoons the best. He can be reached at P.O. Box 1347, Ann Arbor, MI 48106.

Lahre Shiflet is in high school and is an outgoing, fun, cool teen to hang out with. She loves shopping at the mall with her friends (when she has time) and is always checking out the cute teenage boys. She's always ready for an adventure and loves herself very much!

Harland Stonecipher's bio can be found at the end of the story *Closer Than a Brother.*

Jeff Taylor's bio can be found at the end of the story *Monster Ideas.*

Peter Vegso is cofounder of Health Communications, Inc. (HCI), publisher of the *Chicken Soup for the Soul* series along with many other bestselling books. HCI has been recognized twice by *Publishers' Weekly* as the #1 Self-Help Publisher. Visit *www.hcibooks.com.*

J. Mignonne Wright is publisher and editor-in-chief of *Chicken Soup for the Soul Magazine,* a bi-monthly national consumer publication. Created at the request of fans of the bestselling book series, it launched to rave reviews in July 2005.

Sandra Yancey's bio can be found at the end of the story *Let's Talk Business, Woman-to-Woman.*

Bob Young's bio can be found at the end of the story *The Idiot Entrepreneur Theory.*

Permissions *(continued from page iv)*

The Accidental Entrepreneur. Reprinted by permission of James McCann. ©2005 James McCann.

Turning Tragedy into Triumph. Reprinted by permission of Gary Heavin. ©2003 Gary Heavin.

Uncertain Certainty. Reprinted by permission of John Assaraf. ©2005 John Assaraf.

A Recipe for Success. Reprinted by permission of Doris Christopher. ©2005 Doris Christopher.

Better Than a Lemonade Stand. Reprinted by permission of Daryl Bernstein. ©2004 Daryl Bernstein.

Life's a Hobby. Reprinted by permission of Gail Kulhavy. ©2005 Gail Kulhavy.

Reasoning for the Seasonings. Reprinted by permission of Mo Siegel. ©2006 Mo Siegel.

Let's Talk Business, Woman-to-Woman. Reprinted by permission of Sandra Yancey. ©2005 Sandra Yancey.

Fields of Dreams. Reprinted by permission of Myra Goodman. ©2005 Myra Goodman.

The Shackmeisters. Reprinted by permission of Tommy Polk. ©2005 Tommy Polk.

Ripples. Reprinted by permission of Paul J. Krupin. ©2005 Paul J. Krupin.

It Started with a Sparkle. Reprinted by permission of Terri Duncan. ©2005 Terri Duncan.

Monster Ideas. Reprinted by permission of Jeff Taylor. ©2006 Jeff Taylor.

Look Mom, No Hands! Reprinted by permission of Renee Griffith. ©2005 Renee Griffith.

Mother Knows Best. Reprinted by permission of Ken McKowen. ©2005 Ken McKowen.

The Cave Collector. Reprinted by permission of Stephen Fairchild. ©2006 Stephen Fairchild.

Two Guys, Three Buckets. Reprinted by permission of Fred Joyal. ©2005 Fred Joyal.

The Taste of Success. Reprinted by permission of Fred DeLuca. ©2005 Fred DeLuca.

Beer Goggles. Reprinted by permission of Banjo Bandolas. ©2006 Banjo Bandolas.

Built from Scratch. Reprinted by permission of Homer TLC, Inc. ©2005 Homer TLC, Inc.

From Underdog to Top Dog. Reprinted by permission of Julie Long. ©2005 Julie Long.

Closer Than a Brother. Reprinted by permission of Harland Stonecipher. ©2005 Harland Stonecipher.

See Reality. Reprinted by permission of David Roth. ©2006 David Roth.

Following Our Hearts. Reprinted by permission of Chris MacAskill. ©2006 Chris MacAskill.

The Bag Lady Triumphant. Reprinted by permission of Terri Duncan. ©2005 Terri Duncan.

For the Love of It. Reprinted by permission of Shep Murray and Ian Murray. ©2005 Shep Murray and Ian Murray.

A Sign of the Times. Reprinted by permission of Rachel de Azevedo Coleman. ©2005 Rachel de Azevedo Coleman.

The Wheels on the Bus Go 'Round and 'Round. Reprinted by permission of Terri Duncan. ©2005 Terri Duncan.

The Fair Entrepreneur. Reprinted by permission of Janis Dale. ©2005 Janis Dale.

Thank You, Mr. Wayne. Reprinted by permission of Gina Romanello. ©2005 Gina Romanello.

Pride and Prejudice. Reprinted by permission of Assunta Ng. ©2004 Assunta Ng.

Thirty-Five-Minute Miles. Reprinted by permission Stefan Doering. ©2004 Stefan Doering.

The Candy Man Can. Reprinted by permission of Herman G. Rowland Sr. ©2006 Herman G. Rowland Sr.

A Promise to Keep. Reprinted by permission of Amilya Antonetti. ©2000 Amilya Antonetti.

The Nose Knows. Reprinted by permission of Don Katz. ©2005 Don Katz.

Blueberry Thrills. Reprinted by permission of Terri Duncan. ©2005 Terri Duncan.

No Dream Is Too Big. Reprinted by permissions of J. Mignonne Wright. ©2005 J. Mignonne Wright.

The Idiot Entrepreneur Theory. Reprinted by permission of Bob Young. ©2005 Bob Young.

Moment by Moment. Reprinted by permission of Kathy Heasley. ©2005 Kathy Heasley.

The Dancer in All of Us. Reprinted by permission of Judi Sheppard Missett. ©2005 Judi Sheppard Missett.

American Dreamin'. Reprinted by permission of Stephanie Chandler. ©2005 Stephanie Chandler.

Keep It Simple. Reprinted by permission of Mark Allen. ©2006 Mark Allen.

Cold Stone Revolution. Reprinted by permission of Doug Ducey. ©2006 Doug Ducey.

Nitty-Gritty Reasons. Reprinted by permission of Jim Rohn. ©1985 Jim Rohn.

The Sweetness of It All. Reprinted by permission of Shari Fitzpatrick. ©2005 Shari Fitzpatrick.

Finding the Soul of Success. Reprinted by permission of Julie Long. ©2005 Julie Long.

Strive for Excellence. Reprinted by permission of Tom Antion. ©2005 Tom Antion.

Persistence of Belief. Reprinted by permission of John Paul Penrod and Curtis Jones. ©2005 John Paul Penrod and Curtis Jones.

Bee-Alive. Reprinted by permission of Madeline Balletta. ©2005 Madeline Balletta.

Counting My Blessings. Reprinted by permission of John Paul DeJoria. ©2005 John Paul DeJoria.

The Very Best. Reprinted by permission of Donald J. Hall Jr. ©2005 Donald J. Hall Jr.

Also Available

Chicken Soup African American Soul
Chicken Soup African American Woman's Soul
Chicken Soup Breast Cancer Survivor's Soul
Chicken Soup Bride's Soul
Chicken Soup Caregiver's Soul
Chicken Soup Cat Lover's Soul
Chicken Soup Christian Family Soul
Chicken Soup College Soul
Chicken Soup Couple's Soul
Chicken Soup Dieter's Soul
Chicken Soup Dog Lover's Soul
Chicken Soup Entrepreneur's Soul
Chicken Soup Expectant Mother's Soul
Chicken Soup Father's Soul
Chicken Soup Fisherman's Soul
Chicken Soup Girlfriend's Soul
Chicken Soup Golden Soul
Chicken Soup Golfer's Soul, Vol. I, II
Chicken Soup Horse Lover's Soul, Vol. I, II
Chicken Soup Inspire a Woman's Soul
Chicken Soup Kid's Soul, Vol. I, II
Chicken Soup Mother's Soul, Vol. I, II
Chicken Soup Parent's Soul
Chicken Soup Pet Lover's Soul
Chicken Soup Preteen Soul, Vol. I, II
Chicken Soup Scrapbooker's Soul
Chicken Soup Sister's Soul, Vol. I, II
Chicken Soup Shopper's Soul
Chicken Soup Soul, Vol. I-VI
Chicken Soup at Work
Chicken Soup Sports Fan's Soul
Chicken Soup Teenage Soul, Vol. I-IV
Chicken Soup Woman's Soul, Vol. I, II
